# CRASH:

# WHEN UFOs FALL FROM THE SKY

## A HISTORY OF FAMOUS INCIDENTS, CONSPIRACIES, AND COVER-UPS

# KEVIN D. RANDLE, PhD

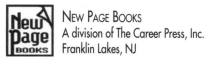
NEW PAGE BOOKS
A division of The Career Press, Inc.
Franklin Lakes, NJ

CRASH: WHEN UFOs FALL FROM THE SKY
EDITED BY JODI BRANDON
TYPESET BY EILEEN MUNSON
Cover design by Lucia Rossman / DigiDog Design
Printed in the U.S.A. by Courier

To order this title, please call toll-free 1-800-CAREER-1 (NJ and Canada: 201-848-0310) to order using VISA or MasterCard, or for further information on books from Career Press.

The Career Press, Inc., 3 Tice Road, PO Box 687,
Franklin Lakes, NJ 07417
www.careerpress.com
www.newpagebooks.com

**Library of Congress Cataloging-in-Publication Data**
Randle, Kevin D., 1949–
    Crash--when UFOs fall from the sky : a history of famous incidents, conspiracies, and
    cover-ups / by Kevin D. Randle.
        p. cm.
    Includes index.
    ISBN 978-1-60163-100-8
    ISBN 978-1-60163-736-9
        1. Unidentified flying objects--Sightings and encounters--History. 2. Conspiracies.
    3. Government information. I. Title.

TL789.R3235 2010
001.942--dc22
                                                                                    2009051608

# CONTENTS

# PROLOGUE

There are those who would tell us that the first UFO crash came more than 12,000 years ago in China. Others would suggest that the first crash, in the New World, came nearly 4,000 years ago in what is now called the Grand Canyon. Still, others would date the first of the UFO crashes from the Middle Ages, and others still from the late 19th century.

In what we call the modern world, the first report of a UFO crash was made during the first week in July 1947, and, although most people would suggest that was the Roswell case, Roswell wouldn't be called a UFO crash until much later. Instead, the July 7th case near Bozeman, Montana would be the first widely reported flying saucer crash.

It was the late Len Stringfield who opened the door to the study of UFO crashes, which is not to say he was the first proponent of them. That honor, such as it is, belongs to Frank Scully, who, in 1949, was a columnist for *Weekly Variety*, a Hollywood trade paper. In October of that year, Scully reported (with his tongue in cheek, given the style of the article), that a flying saucer had crashed, and both it and the bodies of the alien flight crew had been recovered by the U.S. government.

In 1950, Scully would publish a book, *Behind the Flying Saucers,* in which he would tell the tale of a government project of 1,700 scientists led by Dr. Gee. He would tell of three crashes, including one near Aztec, New Mexico. The book was a best-seller and it, inadvertently, set the tone for interest in UFO crashes for the next several decades.

J.P. Cahn, a reporter in San Francisco, was given the assignment by *True,* a men's magazine that featured war stories, exposés, and other features of interest to men, to learn what he could about the UFO crash. His assignment was to either prove it true or prove it a hoax. I'm not sure if the magazine cared one way or the other, as long as the facts could be verified and they got a good story out of it.

Cahn was able to unmask the mysterious Dr. Gee as Leo GeBauer, met with one of the other sources, Silas Newton, on many occasions, and was able to obtain some of the metal samples that Newton claimed came from the flying saucer. When the story was printed, exposing the hoax, research into tales of crashed flying saucers ended then and there.

Certainly in the years that followed, there were hints of something like that. On May 22, 1955, Dorothy Kilgallen, a columnist with a national audience, in an International News Service column, reported that she had been told by a high-ranking official of the British government that British scientists and airmen had examined "one of the mysterious flying ships...[and that] flying saucers originate on other planets."

Although there was speculation that the source had been Lord Mountbatten, that was never confirmed. There was not a follow-up report and, because of that, the whole thing was dismissed as a hoax— or, an outgrowth of the stories that Scully had published.

Frank Edwards, in his 1965 book, *Flying Saucers—Serious Business,* reported on the Roswell crash, mentioning the location, but from that point on, he got nearly everything else wrong. He didn't have a name to go with the story, and I suspect he was working off the photographs that had appeared in the newspapers in 1947. He had the information to begin an investigation, but didn't bother with it. He might have suspected there wasn't much to it, but he could get in a couple of shots at the Air Force, and that might have been the reason to include the story.

The subject of UFO crashes didn't reach the mainstream of UFO literature again until 1975, when a retired college professor, Robert Spencer Carr, claimed that he had interviewed five people who told him about a UFO crash. Carr assumed, it seems, that they were speaking of the Aztec, New Mexico crash that Cahn had exposed more than 20 years earlier. Carr refused to divulge the names of his witnesses, and that made his story suspect.

Mike McClelland, in an exposé published in *Official UFO,* proved, once again, that the idea of a UFO crash in Aztec was a hoax. McClelland spoke to longtime Aztec residents, recounted part of the Scully-Newton-GeBauer tale, and said that he had found nothing to suggest the story was grounded in reality. To him, it was a hoax.

Carr's response? He said that he wasn't sure that the crash had taken place in Aztec. It could have been some other town. There was nothing in this latest tale that could be verified, and that is where it ended.

Three years later, that all changed. First, Len Stringfield, a respected researcher who lived in Ohio, began to quietly gather reports of UFO crashes. He prepared to publish his research at a Mutual UFO Network (MUFON) Symposium in 1978. The document told a number of what could only be called anecdotes about UFO crashes. Most were single witness, undocumented, and uncorroborated.

It was about this same time that Jesse Marcel, Sr. appeared on the scene. As the story goes, Stan Friedman, in New Orleans to lecture on flying saucers, was told by a television station manager that he, the manager, knew someone that Friedman might want to interview. This was Jesse Marcel, who told of picking up pieces of a flying saucer while he was an intelligence officer stationed in New Mexico.

Friedman talked to Marcel, and then to Stringfield, telling him what he had learned and putting Stringfield in touch with Marcel. Stringfield included the tale in his MUFON paper when he presented it, but it was not in the written version. It wasn't until Stringfield published his first *Crash Retrieval Status Report* that the Marcel story appeared in print, but it didn't receive much attention. It was just one of many included in that document, and there were many more that seemed to be more interesting.

There was one other thing that Stringfield knew, and he told me this in the early 1990s: He said that he knew Carr and he had asked Carr for the names of his witnesses, which Carr supplied him. To Stringfield's surprise, he already knew them and had interviewed them. Carr's mistake, it would seem, was not in telling the story, but assuming that it had anything to do with the Aztec UFO crash report.

Stringfield continued his research into reports of UFO crashes, adding many other cases to his collection. I put together a long list of crashes for *A History of UFO Crashes,* and others have added to that list for years. Some of those lists now top 200 entries, which seems excessive. If that many flying saucers, meaning craft from other worlds, had crashed here, then we would have the evidence in the hands of many private individuals, and it could not have been hidden away by the various governments for so many decades. These lists contain way too many such tales.

But once the door was opened, first with Marcel's story and then with Stringfield's acceptance of other stories, the reluctance to investigate UFO crashes ended. Other similar events soon got a great deal of publicity inside the UFO field.

No, it wasn't quite that neat. Stan Gordon, a UFO researcher living in Pennsylvania, had been investigating a UFO crash there since it was first reported late in 1965. With the blinders finally off, UFO researchers looked at Gordon's work and saw how good it was, and Kecksburg became another of those stories that seemed to have a great deal of documentation and eyewitness testimony to support it.

Following up on other leads in the 1990s, I found a case in the Air Force Project Blue Book files from April 1962 in which an object was seen to explode in the sky northeast of Las Vegas, Nevada. This one had radar confirmation and, contrary to an Air Force claim that there was no visual sighting, I found quite a few who had seen the craft as it detonated far to the east of Las Vegas.

There was another exception to this idea that UFOs don't crash, and this was a report from Ubatuba, Brazil in 1957. The object there was seen to explode in the sky with bits of debris raining onto a beach and into the ocean. Some of that debris, small amounts of it anyway, found its way into the hands of UFO researchers and later on the Air Force for analysis.

What is interesting about all this is that, back in the late 1960s, the Air Force had contracted with the University of Colorado to make a "scientific" study of the phenomena. Although it was at first believed to be a legitimate study, it was quickly learned that neither the Air Force nor Dr. Edward U. Condon, the scientist in charge of the study, planned on an unbiased report. Documents surfaced proving that the conclusions of the study were written before the first research began.

None of this would be important to us if it wasn't for an event in October 1967. Near Shag Harbour, Nova Scotia, Canada, a number of people, including police officers, saw something fall into the water. It churned up the bottom of the bay, and it seemed that some sort of luminous yellow foam bubbled to the surface. This appeared to be a UFO crash that happened on the watch of the Condon Committee UFO study.

Their response? They made a telephone call or two, learned that some teenagers had reported the object to the police, but nothing from the other witnesses, including police officers. No one in Colorado thought much of the report, and they investigated no further. Here was a chance to do some real, on-site investigation of a case that had, literally, fallen into their laps, and they didn't pursue it.

Chris Styles and Don Ledger did. They found official Canadian government documents that validated their beliefs. No, they found nothing to prove that what had fallen was extraterrestrial, but they did find proof that something strange had crashed, and they found that some of the information had been buried by authorities. In other words, they found the event real, and they found evidence of the conspiracy to keep the information out of the hands of the public. If nothing else, scientists should take a look at the evidence from this case before dismissing, out of hand, most of what UFO researchers have been saying for decades.

But, by the end of the 1980s and the beginning of the 1990s, the climate for UFO crashes had changed, thanks in large part to the work done by Len Stringfield. UFO researchers, who would have never even considered the tale of a crash, were now devoting a major effort in learning more about some of these stories with Roswell, of course, moving to the top of the list. Here was a UFO story in which the names were available, and others could corroborate the story. Not only had Jesse Marcel been identified, but so had Walter Haut and then a huge group of officers and soldiers who had been assigned to Roswell. Even the Chief of Staff of the Eighth Air Force, the parent organization for the military based in Roswell, had been found, and he confirmed the story. Something truly strange had fallen, and the Eighth Air Force had trotted out a balloon to cover it up. Or, as Thomas DuBose, Chief of Staff, would say on videotape, they were to get the reporters off General Ramey's back about all this.

Though nearly everything began to revolve around Roswell, other extraordinary cases were found as well—cases that had documentation and witnesses and other supporting evidence. The floodgates had been opened and the information began to pour out. Unfortunately, as happens all too often in the UFO field, much of that information was inaccurate, misunderstood, or simply invented. It became the duty of the UFO researcher to determine what was good and what was bad.

We have now reached the point, more than 50 years after the Newton–GeBauer hoax, where UFO investigators will look seriously at stories of UFO crashes. Unfortunately, it seems the door has swung open too wide and everything that happens is called a crash. A landed UFO in Brazil becomes the Brazilian Roswell. The events at Bentwaters in 1980 become the British Roswell. A bolide, an extremely bright meteor, becomes another crash, falling into the mountains of Colorado.

That's why some lists of UFO crashes top 200, and many are racing toward 300. That works out to nearly six every year since the Roswell crash in 1947, and excludes most of those prior to the beginning of the 20th century.

We need to reduce those lists, and that can be done with careful research. That is the purpose here: Examine the tales of UFO crashes, present the best information available today, and provide some answers. Most of the UFO crash tales are mistakes, misidentifications, or the reports of single witnesses. But once we push through that mass, we still have a solid core of reports that are not easily explained or rejected. We have something that demands research because, if we can find that one, solid case—and one is all we need—then we have unlocked the biggest mystery of the last 1,000 years.

So now we begin the journey with a case from France in 840 AD and we'll end it in 2009. In between, we'll see lots of reports, and I'm sure that many of you will see answers for some of the cases as you read the details. In others, the solutions are a little more difficult to spot, but they are there. All you need to do is look carefully.

When we've finished, we should have a better understanding of flying saucers, we should have developed something of a critical eye for these sorts of reports...and, if we're lucky, we'll be amazed at the residue.

1947
Pre-Roswell

July 1947

October
1947—1948

1949—1952

1953—1964

1965

1966—1978

1979—1999

2000—2009

# Chapter 1

## A Chronology of UFO Crashes

### 840 AD

#### LYONS, FRANCE

There are those who include the following account in with their lists of UFO crashes. W.R. Drake, in his *Spacemen in the Middle Ages,* reported, "Agobard, Archbishop of Lyons, wrote in *De Grandine et Tonitrua* how, in 840 AD he found the mob in Lyons lynching three men and a woman accused of landing from a cloudship from the aerial region of Magonia. The Archbishop halted the execution and freed the victims."

Brad Steiger, in his book *The Fellowship,* also claimed contact between aliens and humans was made in 840 AD using the same account of the Archbishop as his source. He suggested that the French referred to the aliens as sky people because they descended from the upper reaches of the atmosphere in spacecraft. The locals called the spacecraft "ships from the clouds."

The description of the aliens offered by Steiger was of creatures with large heads, pointed ears, and bulging eyes, which isn't all that different from some of the descriptions of the gray aliens said to be responsible for modern abductions. Steiger also wrote, as have others, that these aliens told the French that their home was a place called Magonia. These creatures interacted with the local peasants and tradesmen, making them sound more like sailors or merchants than alien creatures from some kind of a spacecraft.

For some reason, according to Steiger, a dispute erupted between the French and the four aliens, who were then seized and bound with chains. Steiger said that after being held for several days, the prisoners were paraded before a mob, which suddenly went berserk and stoned them to death. Notice the subtle change from hanging to stoning.

The Archbishop, according to still another variation of the story that was offered in still another UFO book, was an eyewitness to the alien's execution. This all was revealed by Hayden Hewes, a fellow from Oklahoma and who, with Steiger, co-authored the *UFO Missionaries Extraordinary,* which was published in 1976. Yes, the same Brad Steiger who had a slightly different interpretation in a different book. This, of course, is in conflict with other accounts, including that of Jacques Vallee, a scientist and UFO researcher, who said that the mob was attempting to lynch the men and woman, but apparently stopped by an impassioned plea by the Archbishop.

Text, written in Latin in the *De Grandine et Tonitrua,* and available in various libraries today, actually reads (as translated into English):

We have seen and heard many men plunged in such great stupidity, sunk in such depths of folly, as to believe that there is a certain region, which they call Magonia, whence ships sail in the clouds, in order to carry back to that region those fruits of the earth which are destroyed by hail and tempests; sailors paying rewards to the storm wizards, and themselves receiving corn and other produce.

Out of the number of those whose blind folly was deep enough to allow them to believe these things possible, I saw several exhibitions in a certain concourse of people, four persons in bonds—three men and a woman who said they had fallen from these same ships; after keeping them for some days in captivity they had brought them before the assembled multitude, as we have said in our presence to be stoned. But truth prevailed.

So, we're now left with a tale of four people who came from ships that travel in the clouds, as opposed to "cloudships" and who, according to the original text, were about to be stoned. The Archbishop, apparently, was able to stop the execution with the truth. There is no description in the original that matches modern-day aliens, and only a reference to a ship that sails in clouds suggests the reason for making this some sort of UFO report. The description could refer to many things, and none of them require an alien spacecraft.

Somewhat less controversial is the story of demon ships in the skies above Ireland, which here means that there aren't many different interpretations of the sighting. According to the information contained in *Flying Saucers on the Attack*:

> There happened in the borough of Cloera, one Sunday, while the people were at Mass, a marvel.... It befell that an anchor was dropped from the sky with a rope attached to it and one of the flukes caught in the arch above the church door. The people rushed out of the church and saw in the sky a ship with men on board, floating before the anchor-cable, and they saw a man leap overboard...as to release it....

Each of these sightings, including reports of beings or creatures from them, could not only refer to a classical UFO, but could also mean sightings of natural phenomena inhabited by humans rather than alien creatures. There is simply not enough information for us to draw any kind of specific conclusion or to suggest this is a flying saucer sighting and, actually, no reason to believe it so.

## March 3, 1557

### FRANCE

According to the old sources, a "thunderbolt pierced the bridal chamber of Francois Montmorency and Diane de France, running into every corner of the tent before it exploded harmlessly." That sounds suspiciously like ball lightning, a natural phenomenon that has only recently been accepted by modern science and something that would have easily startled someone living in the 16th century. I mention it here only because the report does appear on some lists of UFO crashes, but more importantly, is similar to other stories that come from the 19th and 20th centuries. It is for comparisons with those that I have included it.

## September 1862

### INDIAN OCEAN

An old Danish sailor told John Leander of El Campo, Texas, who in turn wrote to the *Houston Daily Post,* that, as a mate on a Danish brig *Christine,* he, the Danish sailor, had been caught in a storm in the Indian Ocean. The ship had broken up, but he and a handful of others managed to reach a small rocky island that had no plant or animal life. While the storm raged around them, they saw a strange aircraft as large as a battleship with four huge wings slam into a cliff.

The men investigated and discovered many strange "implements and articles of furniture" as well as some food contained in "metal boxes covered with strange characters." To their horror, they found the bodies of more than a dozen men dressed in strange clothes. The men were huge, possibly measuring as much as 12 feet tall and had skin that was described as a dark bronze. They wore beards and had long hair that was said to be "as soft and silky as the hair on an infant."

The sight drove one of the men insane and he jumped from the cliff. The others left the scene, but returned two days later. After disposing of the bodies in the ocean, they built a raft from the material of the craft. Three days after they set sail, they were rescued by a Russian ship. Unfortunately, three more of the sailors died from their injuries and from the "awful mental strain."

The source of the story, a man identified only as Oleson, claimed that he had some proof. He owned a finger ring of "immense size" that was made of "metals unknown to any jeweler who has seen it." (The article from the *Houston Daily Post* from May 2, 1897, also appeared in the *International UFO Reporter* in July/August 1993.)

## June 6, 1884

### DUNDY COUNTY, NEBRASKA

Some of the crashes lists place this near Holdrege, Nebraska, but that is where the newspaper the *Nebraska Nugget* was published on a weekly basis. The story came from an anonymous source in Benkelman, which is in Dundy County in extreme southwestern Nebraska.

According to the story, four cowboys heard a whirring noise overhead and looked up to see a cylindrical object drop from the sky and crash into the ground. At the crash site, they found bits of machinery and gears glowing with heat. It was so hot that it was impossible to approach, and the grass around the smashed object was scorched.

The *Nebraska Nugget* reported the story first, but then it was picked up by other newspapers. The *Nebraska State Journal,* on June 8, 1884, reported:

BENKELMAN, June 7.—A most remarkable phenomenon occurred about 1 o'clock yesterday afternoon at a point thirty-five miles northwest of this place. John W. Ellis, a well known ranchman, was going out to his herd in company with three of his herders and several other cowboys engaged in the annual roundup. While riding along a draw they heard a terrific rushing, roaring sound overhead, and looking up, saw what appeared to be a blazing meteor of immense size falling at an angle to the earth. A moment later it struck the ground out of sight over the bank. Scrambling up the steep hill they saw the object bounding along half a mile away and disappear in another draw.

Galloping towards it with all their speed, they were astounded to see several fragments of cog-wheels and other pieces of machinery lying on the ground, scattered in the path made by the aerial visitor, glowing with heat so intense as to scorch the grass for a long distance around each fragment and make it impossible for one to approach it. Coming to the edge of the deep ravine into which the strange object had fallen, they undertook to see what it was. But the heat was so great that the air about it was fairly ablaze and it emitted a light so dazzling that the eye could not rest on it for more than a moment.

An idea of the heat may be gained from the fact that one of the party, a cowboy named Alf Williamson, stood with his head incautiously exposed over the bank, and in less than half a minute he fell senseless. His face was desperately blistered and his hair singed to a crisp. His condition is said to be dangerous. The distance to the aerolite, or whatever it is, was nearly 200 feet. The burned man was taken to Mr. Ellis' house, cared for as well as circumstances would allow and a doctor sent for. His brother, who lives in Denver has just been telegraphed for.

Finding it impossible to approach the mysterious visitor, the party turned back on its trail. Where it first touched the earth the ground was sandy and bare of grass. The sand was fused to an unknown depth over a space about twenty feet wide by eighty feet long, and the melted stuff was still bubbling and hissing. Between this and the final resting place there were several like spots where it had come in contact with the ground, but none so well marked.

Finding it impossible to do any investigating, Mr. Ellis returned to his house and sent out messengers to neighboring ranches. When night came the light from the wonderful object beamed almost like the sun, and the visitors who went out to see it were entirely powerless to bear the glow.

This morning another visit was made to the spot. In the party was E. W. Rawlins, brand inspector for this district, who came into Benkleman tonight, and from whom a full verification of particulars is obtained. The smaller portions of the scattered machinery had cooled so that they could be approached, but not handled. One piece that looked like the blade of a propeller screw of a metal of an appearance like brass, about sixteen inches wide, three inches thick and three and a half feet long, was picked up by a spade. It would not weigh more than five pounds, but appeared as strong and compact as any known metal. A fragment of a wheel with a milled rim, apparently having had a diameter of seven or eight feet, was also picked up. It seemed to be of the same material and had the same remarkable lightness.

The aerolite, or whatever it is, seems to be about fifty or sixty feet long, cylindrical, and about ten or twelve feet in diameter. Great excitement exists in the vicinity and the round-up is suspended while the cowboys wait for the wonderful find to cool off so they can examine it.

Mr. Ellis is here and will take the first train to the land office with the intention of securing the land on which the strange thing lies, so that his claim to it cannot be disputed.

A party left here for the scene an hour ago and will travel all night. The country in the vicinity is rather wild and rough, and the roads hardly more than trails. Will telegraph all particulars as fast as obtained.

That wasn't the last heard about this. In another article published by the *Nebraska State Journal,* on June 19, 1884, they offered something of an explanation for the crash. This article said:

BENKELMAN, June 9, 1884—Your correspondent has just returned from the spot where the aerial visitor fell last Friday. It is gone, dissolved into the air. A tremendous rain storm fell yesterday afternoon beginning around 2 o'clock. As it approached, in regular blizzard style, most of those assembled to watch the mysterious visitor fled to shelter. A dozen or more, among them your correspondent, waited to see the effect of rain upon the glowing mass of metal. The storm came down from the north, on its crest a sheet of flying spray and a torrent of rain. It was impossible to see more than a rod through the driving, blinding mass. It lasted for half an hour, and when it slackened so that the aerolite should have been visible it was no longer there. The draw was running three feet deep in water and supposing it had floated off the strange vessel. The party crossed over at the risk of their lives.

They were astounded to see that the queer object had melted, dissolved by the water like a spoonful of salt. Scarcely a vestige of it remained. Small, jelly-like pools stood here and there on the ground, but under the eyes of the observers these grew thinner and thinner till they were but muddy water joining the rills that led to the current a few feet away. The air was filled with a faint, sweetish smell.

The whole affair is bewildering to the highest degree, and will no doubt forever be a mystery.

Alf Williamson, the injured cowboy, left yesterday for Denver, accompanied by his brother. It is feared he will never recover his eyesight, but otherwise he does not appear to be seriously injured.

There has been a continued stream of investigators here for the past two days, among them a number of members of the press. The Denver Tribune representative was among the witnesses to the evanishment [sic] of the wonderful visitor. There are a thousand theories afloat as to how it came and what it was, but they are now unfortunately incapable of solution.

Jerome Clark reported in the *International UFO Reporter* for July/August 1993 that, "In later years folklorist Roger Welsch, journalist Russ Toler, and I would separately interview older Dundy County residents, including members of the local historical society, none of whom had ever heard of any such event despite extensive knowledge of the county's frontier period."

## June 13, 1891

### Dublin, Texas

According to information discovered by Mark Murphy and Noe Torres and reported on their Website (*www.ufodigest.com/ news/0408north-texas.htm*), it was late on a Saturday afternoon when residents of Dublin, Texas, were startled by a bright, oblong-shaped object about 300 feet above them. They reported a loud sound, like a bomb going off, and they saw the object disintegrate, hurling metal and debris over the town, near the Wasson & Miller flour mill and cotton gin.

On June 20, 1891, the *Dublin Progress,* the local newspaper, published an article about the event on page four. They reported:

### A Meteor Explodes in the City
#### An Eye Witness Describes the Scene to a Progress Reporter— Scared.

Quite a little excitement was created last Saturday night by the bursting of what is supposed by those who were present to have been a meteor, near Wasson & Miller's gin. Quite a number witnessed the explosion and nearly everyone in that portion of the city heard the report eminating [sic] therefrom, which is said to have sounded somewhat like the report of a bomb-shell. Our informant (who, though a little nervous at times, is a gentleman who usually tells the truth, but did not give us this statement with a view to its publication) says he observed the meteor when it was more than three hundred feet in the air, before bursting, and that it bore a striking resemblance to a bale of cotton suspended in the air after having been saturated in kerosene oil and ignited, except that it created a much brighter light, almost dazzling those who percieved [sic] it. The gentleman in question seems to have been so badly frightened that it was utterly impossible to obtain an accurate account of the dimensions and general appearance of this rare phenomenon, but we are convinced from his statements that his position at the time must have been very embarrassing and that very little time was spent in scientific investigations. However, on the following morning he returned to the scene so hastily left the previous night, to find the weeds, grass, bushes and vegetation of every description for many yards around the scene of the explosion burned to a crisp, also discovering a number of peculiar stones and pieces of metal, all of a leaden color, presenting much the appearance of the lava thrown out by volcanic eruptions. He also picked up some small fragments of manuscript and a scrap, supposed to be part of a newspaper, but the language in both was entirely foreign to him, and, in fact, no one has yet been found who has ever seen such a language before, hence no information could be gained from their examination. At this juncture your reporter requested that he be shown these wonderful fragments of such a miraculous whole, but the narrator had worked himself up to such a pitch of excitement that it was impossible to get him to grasp the significance of our request, and were compelled to leave him a victim to his own bewildered fancy and to ruminate the seemingly miraculous story he had just related. Thus was a repotorial [sic] zealot denied the boon of seeing fragments of the most remarkable substance ever known to explode near Wasson & Miller's gin.

P.S. Since the above was put in type we learn that our reporter was given the above information by a contributor to the *Dublin Telephone,* but the information came too late too late to prevent its insertion in this paper.

The description of the object sounds like a bolide—that is, an extremely bright meteor. They are so bright that they can easily be seen in the daytime, and they are often accompanied by sonic booms, which the people of Dublin in 1891 wouldn't have known. The only problem is the description of it hovering above the mill. That could have been an optical illusion if the meteor had left a smoke trail, something else bolides do. In this case, I suspect that the description in the article— that a meteor exploded over the city—is the proper solution here.

## December 3, 1896

### STANFORD HEIGHTS, CALIFORNIA

According to Jerome Clark, this was a practical joke that was played by the director of an amusement park. The story was that, late in the evening, there was crashing sound, followed by cries for help. Local dairy farmers rushed to the scene of what appeared to be a damaged airship with two injured pilots. One of the farmers noted that there were marks on the airship that seemed to indicate that it had been dragged over the ground and that the construction was flimsy. He concluded that the whole thing was a fake. Not long after that, J.D. de Gear, who had been posing as one of the pilots, confessed the hoax to the *San Francisco Chronicle* on December 4, 1896, saying that the airship "had been hauled to the crest of a hill on a wagon, dumped over, and dragged down into a gulch where it was found."

## Early April 1897

### BETHANY, MISSOURI

An unidentified man wrote to a Missouri newspaper to report that he'd seen the airship strike a flagpole and crash. The bodies of the two pilots were so badly mangled that they couldn't be identified, but letters they carried suggested they were from San Francisco, or maybe Omaha.

## April 9, 1897

### RHODES, IOWA

According to the Marshalltown [Iowa] *Evening Times-Republican* of April 13th, a bright light was seen to come down over the town at 11:00 p.m., growing brighter as it got closer. It fell into a reservoir near the railroad tracks: "The light was so large and had created so much heat that the horrible hissing which occurred when the monster plunged into the lake could be heard for miles, and the water of the reservoir was so hot that the naked hand could not be held in it."

## April 9, 1897

### LANARK, ILLINOIS

Johann Fliegeltoub reported that an airship spun out of control during a morning blizzard and crashed on his farm, killing the two occupants and injuring a third. Fliegeltoub pulled the injured pilot from the wreckage. He was dressed in the fashion of the Greeks in the time of Christ. The pilot shouted at him hysterically and then fell unconscious. Once he had the injured man in his house, he advertised what he had found, charging people a dollar a look. A newspaper correspondent, after steadying his nerves with "morphine and cocaine," according to story in the *Sterling* [Illinois] *Evening Gazette,* entered the room and talked to the man who regained consciousness. They spoke in Volapuk, which is an artificial language. The pilot said that he came from Mars. Eventually, the pilot regained his strength, repaired his craft, and, after collecting the bodies of his companions, took off.

In what might be the best information contained in the story, the reporter said that he returned to his hotel and "sat up all night smoking opium and eating hasheesh [sic] to get in condition to write this dispatch."

In other words, he was stoned when he wrote it and it all could have been a drug-induced dream if not fiction created without the help of the drugs. His full report was carried in the *Sterling* [Illinois] *Evening Gazette*.

## April 11, 1897

### PAVILION, MICHIGAN
An airship was reported to have exploded over the city, raining small fragments onto a rooftop. A propeller blade, fused, made of some light metal, was also found.

## April 14, 1897

### DECATUR, ILLINOIS
A farmer, while milking a cow, heard a loud crash, as most of the barn roof was torn away. The cow kicked him in the head, but before he lost consciousness, he saw an airship pull itself from the wreckage and limp off, whatever that means.

## Mid-April 1897

### HUMBOLDT, TENNESSEE
Sam McLeary claimed that he spotted the sole occupant of an airship that crashed into the woods near Forked Deer River. It was encased in a block of ice, probably, according to the newspaper, in the "pitiless cold" of the upper atmosphere. His story was told in the April 18, 1897, issue of the *Nashville American*.

## April 15, 1897

### WATERLOO, IOWA

The *Waterloo Courier* reported that an unusual craft "came to rest on the fair ground" and one of the pilots went to the police station to ask that they guard his ship. Arriving at the fairgrounds, the police found a large, twin-cigar-shaped object. All during the day, people came to see the ship, the first tangible object to be found that didn't disappear into the night or vanish like the morning mist. That made the story a little more plausible than those being told in so many other locations, including the original sightings in California.

A heavily accented "professor," who claimed to come from San Francisco, told of the dangerous flight across country that ended in tragedy when the leader of the expedition fell into the Cedar River. Attempts to rescue the man failed, and they landed nearby to attempt to retrieve the body.

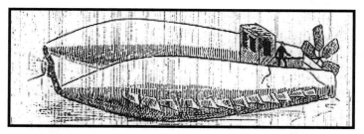

*1.1 Waterloo airship. Courtesy of the Cedar Rapids Gazette.*

By late afternoon, interest was waning, and then ended abruptly. The professor was recognized as a local man, E.A. Feather. He dropped his accent, and the ship, such as it was, was finally dismantled and removed from the fair grounds, but not before hundreds had seen it and more than one newspaper article had been written about it.

## April 15, 1897

### HIGHLAND STATION, KANSAS

The occupant of an airship that crashed because of a chemical explosion was dragged from the wreckage, moaning. When he regained consciousness, he said that his name was Pedro Sanchez and that he was from Cuba.

## April 15, 1897

### NEAR JEFFERSON, IOWA

The *Jefferson Bee* reported that an airship had crashed in a farmer's field on the north edge of town. Most of the town's residents gathered around the huge, smoking hole. The next day, a man was lowered into the hole on a rope, along with a Volapak dictionary, which is the second time that this artificial language has been mentioned in connection with an airship crash. Once in the hole, the man claimed he entered the airship that seemed neat and clean, despite the violent crash.

## April 17, 1897

### AURORA, TEXAS

The Aurora crash story, as it was told just days later, suggests the airship appeared about dawn on April 17, 1897, came in low, buzzed the town square, and then continued north, toward the farm owned at the time by Judge Proctor. There it hit a windmill and exploded into a shower of debris, damaging the judge's flower garden and house, not to mention his windmill. The townspeople rushed to the scene and found the badly disfigured body of the alien pilot. T.J. Weems, a Signal Corps officer (think intelligence officer here in 1897), thought the pilot was probably from Mars.

Being good Christians, and apparently because no one had anything else to do, they buried the pilot after a short memorial service that afternoon. They also gathered several documents covered with a strange writing found in the wreckage, and picked up tons of material, including silver and aluminum, that came from the wrecked airship. Not surprisingly, all that evidence has long since disappeared.

And that's it. No follow-up stories as tourists flocked to Aurora to see the wreckage or visit the grave. No mysterious scientists arriving to inspect the metal or wreckage and add their voices to the speculation. No Army response, though one of their own was on hand to report what he had seen and apparently confirm the authenticity of the report. And finally, most importantly, no one ever produced those documents or bits and pieces of the wreckage, though there had been tons of it, at least according to the newspaper report.

The story died at that point in 1897, and then was resurrected in the 1960s by UFO researchers who stumbled onto the airship tales, which had been dormant for about six decades. Suddenly the story of the tragedy reappeared and Aurora, Texas, was now on the map with those scientists, researchers, and tourists finally making the trek to the northern part of the state.

A large number of people, including Hayden Hewes of the now-defunct International UFO Bureau (and one-time partner of Brad Steiger), Jim Marrs, who had most recently suggested the story was real, and even Walt Andrus, the former International Director of the Mutual UFO Network (MUFON), at various times journeyed to Aurora in search of the truth. They all reported they found a strange grave marker in the Aurora cemetery, they found strange metal with metal detectors, and they gathered reports from longtime Aurora residents who remembered the story, remembered seeing the airship, or remembered parents talking about the crash. And, as to be expected today, there was also discussion of government attempts to suppress the data. To them, that made the story of the crash real.

The problem here is that I beat most of these people to Aurora by several years to conduct my own investigation in 1970. I talked to some of those same longtime residents, who told me in the early 1970s that nothing had happened there. I talked to the historians at the Wise County Historical Society (Aurora is in Wise County), who told me that it hadn't happened, though they wish it had (now probably thinking of Roswell and the tourist dollars pouring into that New Mexico town). I learned that T.J. Weems, the famed Signal Corps officer, was, in fact, the local blacksmith by the name of Jeff Weems. I learned that Judge Proctor didn't have a windmill, or rather that was what was said then by the Wise County Historical Society. Now they suggest that he had two windmills, and evidence of one of them has been found, or rather evidence that a windmill did stand on the property prior to the 1930s. I wandered the graveyard, which isn't all that large (something just more than 800 graves) and found no marker with strange symbols carved on it, though there are those who suggest a crude headstone with a rough airship on it had been there at the time. I suspect that the strange marker that was seen and photographed by those who came after I did was planted there by someone between the time I searched the cemetery and those others that got there in the mid-1970s. I found nothing to support the tale and went away believing, based on my own research and interviews of several of the longtime residents conducted on the scene, this to be another of the airship hoaxes.

Metal collected by all those others who followed me, when analyzed here in the United States, turned out to be nothing strange or unusual. Some of it was later analyzed in a Canadian lab, and their results mirrored those of American labs. So much for the idea that the government, in the guise of the CIA, the Air Force, or the mythical MJ-12, conspired to suppress evidence of the Aurora UFO crash.

Isn't it interesting, though, that none of the metal supposedly gathered by the town's residents has ever surfaced? The metal analyzed was always recovered by researchers with metal detectors. Isn't it interesting that the strange grave marker has since disappeared and there is no real photographic record of it? There should pictures for all the research that has been done, and the single picture that has turned up showed not an airship, but a triangle with circles in the center scratched on the stone. And isn't interesting that there were never any follow-up reports from Aurora? First the big splash with the crash, and then nothing for more than 60 years.

Finally, it should be noted that in a couple of histories of the town written during the turn of the last century, or in the early part of the 20th century, mentioned nothing about this crash. It would seem that an event of this magnitude would have been recorded, because those histories were written within 10 years of the event. There was no real follow-up of the story, either in the newspapers of the time or in the histories of the town and the county. There should be, but there isn't.

## April 22, 1897

### SAN ANGELO, TEXAS

A longtime resident of San Angelo claimed that he had been out looking for the airship, which had been visiting Texas on a regular basis. He spotted it near the town. As he watched, it flew into a flock of birds and exploded. He didn't mention this to anyone until the 1960s and we all had become interested in airship stories.

# July 2, 1907

## BURLINGTON, VERMONT

Ten years after the Great Airship disappeared from the headlines, another incident that has now joined the ranks of the crashed flying saucers was reported. Again, the true explanation for what happened seems to be contained in the article, but this has been added to some lists created by others. Joe Trainor in his *UFO Roundup,* an Internet-based magazine, reprinted the text of the story from the Burlington, Vermont, from page 7 of the *Free Press* for June 3, 1907. The text of that follows:

### SAW BALL OF FIRE

#### Electrical Disturbance that Startled Burlingtonians Yesterday

A forerunner to one of the heavy and frequent thunderstorms that have characterized the early summer in this vicinity startled Burlingtonians yesterday just before noon. Without any preliminary disturbance of the atmosphere, there was a sharp report, the like of which is seldom heard. It was much louder in the business portion of the city than elsewhere, and particularly in the vicinity of Church and College Streets. People rushed to the street or to windows to learn what had happened, and when a horse was seen flat in the street in front of the Standard Coal and Ice Company's office, it was the general impression that the animal had been struck by lightning and killed. This theory was not long entertained, as the horse was soon struggling to regain his feet.

Ex-Governor Woodbury and Bishop Michau were standing on the corner of Church and College Streets in conversation when the report startled them. In talking with a Free Press man later in the day, Governor Woodbury said his first thought was that an explosion had occurred somewhere in the immediate vicinity, and he turned, expecting to see bricks flying thru the air. Bishop Michaud was facing the east and saw a ball of fire rushing through the air, apparently just east of the National Biscuit Company's building. Alvaro Adsit also saw the ball of fire, as did a young man who was looking out of a window in the Strong Theater Building. Another man with a vivid imagination declared that the ball struck the center of College Street near the Standard Coal and Ice Company's office, knocked the horse down by the jar and then bounded up again to some undefined point in the sky.

The unusual disturbance was followed in a few minutes by a downpour of rain, which continued, with brief interruption, for nearly two hours.

The Burlington weatherman, who might be considered way ahead of his time, suggested that this was a case of ball lightning. Usually these displays are small, last seconds, and wink out of existence with a pop rather than a boom. This seemed to be an extreme case.

Again, according to the information Joe Trainor collected and reprinted on his *UFO Roundup*, "Here are the eyewitness accounts," as they appeared in the newspaper:

Bishop John S. Michaud: "I was standing on the corner of Church and College Streets, just in front of the Howard Bank and facing east, engaged in conversation with Ex-Governor (Alexander) Woodbury and Mr. A.A. Buell, when, without the slightest indication or warning we were startled by what sounded like a most unusual and terrific explosion, evidently very near by.

"Raising my eyes and looking eastward along College Street, I observed a torpedo-shaped body some 300 feet away, stationary in appearance and suspended in the air about 50 feet above the tops of the buildings. In size it was about six feet long by eight inches in diameter, the shell cover having a dark appearance, with here and there tongues of fire issuing from spots on the surface resembling red-hot unburnished copper."

"Although stationary when first noticed, this object soon began to move, rather slowly, and disappeared over Dolan Brothers' store (corner of College and Mechanic Streets—J.T.), southward. As it moved, the covering seemed rupturing in places and through these the intensely red flames issued."

"My first impression was that it was some explosive shot from the upper portion of the Hall Furniture Store (corner of College and Center Streets—J.T.). When first seen, it was surrounded by a halo of dim light, some 20 feet in diameter. There was no odor that I am aware of perceptible after the disappearance of the phenomenon, nor was there any damage done so far as was known to me."

"Although the sky was entirely clear overhead, there was an angry-looking cumulo-nimbus cloud approaching from the northwest; otherwise there was absolutely nothing to lead us to expect anything so remarkable."

"And, strange to say, although the downpour of rain following this phenomenon, perhaps twenty minutes later, lasted at least half an hour, there was no indication of any other flash of lightning or sound of thunder."

"Four weeks have passed since the occurrence of this event, but the picture of that scene and the terrific concussion caused by it, are vividly before me, while the crashing sound still rings in my ears. I hope I may never hear or see a similar phenomenon, at least at such "close range.""

Alvaro Adsit: "I was standing in my store (Ferguson and Adsit's Store, on the corner of College and Mechanic Streets across from Dolan Brothers—J.T.) facing the north. My attention was attracted by this 'ball of fire' apparently descending toward a point on the opposite side of the street in front of the Hall Furniture Store, when within 18 or 20 feet of the ground, the ball exploded with a deafening sound. The ball, before the explosion, was apparently 8 or 10 inches in diameter; the halo of light resulting from the explosion was 8 or 10 feet in diameter; the light had a yellowish tinge, somewhat like a candle light; no noise or sound was heard before or after the explosion; no damage was done so far as is known to me."

W.P. Dodds: "I saw the 'ball' just before the explosion. It was moving apparently from the northwest (over the Howard Bank Building—W.P.D.) and gradually descending. I did not see it at the moment of the explosion of afterward; no damage resulted so far as known to me."

## June 30, 1908

### TUNGUSKA, SIBERIA

Early on the morning of June 30, 1908, there was a tremendous explosion over the Tunguska region of Siberia. Seismographs around the world recorded the event, a huge area of forest was devastated, and a cloud of smoke was seen climbing into the sky. That an event took place is not questioned by anyone. Scientific instrumentation recorded it, and expeditions into the region in the decades that followed it proved that something had crashed or exploded there. The mystery is what had hit the Earth.

The earliest scientific expedition into the region was hampered by the huge swampy areas, clouds of biting insects, no roads, and a site that was about as far from civilization as it was possible to be. Because of all this, a good survey of the site wasn't made until many years after the event. The conclusions drawn by that first expedition, made a few years after the explosion, were considered unreliable and explained nothing. Additional research expeditions would wait decades.

In 1961, the USSR Academy of Sciences sponsored two expeditions, one headed by Kyrill Florensky and the other by Alexei V. Zolotov. The two teams came to differing conclusions. Florensky believed the evidence showed that there had been a cometary impact, but Zolotov held that there had been a nuclear explosion. This was based on the pattern of the trees felled during the event and the fact that those directly under the blast were still standing. It was similar to the blast effects observed in relation to atomic testing.

It was clear that the Tunguska event was not from a meteor because there was no crater, or rather that was the thought in 1961. Besides, all the impact craters that had been discovered on Earth contained meteoric material. No impact crater was found, and research produced no evidence of a large amount of meteoric material.

Given that, and the fact that blast effects resembled those created by an aerial burst of an atomic weapon, the theory was developed that Tunguska was the result of a nuclear-powered spacecraft that had exploded. The discovery of higher-than-normal radiation levels by some of the research teams added to the conclusion. Because there was no atomic research, as such, being conducted on Earth at the time of the explosion, the conclusion was drawn that the craft was of alien design.

However, Dr. James A. Van Allen, an astrophysicist and discoverer of the radiation belts that surround the Earth, after reviewing the evidence, held to the cometary impact theory. Van Allen told me that the kinetic energy potential would account for the destruction. If the comet disintegrated in the air, the resulting explosion would create the blast devastation that was recorded. Tests conducted by the Soviets using conventional explosives did recreate the same effects as that of a nuclear detonation. In other words, the blast wasn't necessarily nuclear in nature, just very big.

Van Allen also pointed out that, although the types of radioactivity were consistent with a nuclear explosion, the radiation readings hadn't been taken until later expeditions. By then, high levels of radiation could be found in other areas. Van Allen said that Cesium 138 was found in the snow that fell in Iowa City, far from any atomic testing site. Without comparison readings made before the beginning of aboveground atomic testing, an intelligent conclusion couldn't be drawn.

Scientists at the National Aeronautics and Space Administration and the University of Wisconsin at Eau Claire studied the data and decided that the Tunguska explosion was the result of an asteroid detonating between 9 and 20 miles up. The explosion destroyed the asteroid and created a shock wave that produced the damage. Because the object exploded, there was no impact crater, and the swampy nature of the territory hid the debris created by the explosion.

Van Allen, in his study of the event, told me that meteoric debris had been found. He thought that if it had been a comet, there wouldn't have been a huge rock, but a "dirty snowball" filled with stones. Searches of the area had produced that sort of debris. Van Allen also explained that the latest findings didn't rule out a comet, and the debris located suggested something other than an asteroid.

Given the information available, it seems that the nuclear-powered spacecraft is the least likely explanation. In fact, a cometary impact is the best of the answers available today.

# Spring 1941

### CAPE GIRARDEAU, MISSOURI

Charlette Mann wrote to Ray Fowler, a longtime and well-trusted UFO researcher, who sent the letter on to Len Stringfield. She wrote that her grandfather, a minister, received a telephone call asking him to go to the scene of an aircraft accident. Stringfield, quite naturally, called her to ask for more detail and convinced her to rewrite her letter into a more structured report, which he published in his *UFO*

*Crash/Retrievals: The Inner Sanctum* and which is dated July 1991. He shared his report with many of his fellow UFO researchers.

According to Mann's letter, her grandfather, Reverend William Huffman, was "born in August, 1888 and he grew up in Missouri. He attended college in Bolivar and after graduation, he went to a seminary. He was an ordained Baptist minister... he was a quiet man who was well respected."

This, of course, means that his credentials are just fine. He was a well-educated man for the times (any time, actually) and he was a minister, which suggests he was also an honest man—again, for the times. He died before telling Mann about the case. This information came from her grandmother, known as Floy, and I don't believe I need to point out that it is, therefore, secondhand.

In her May 6, 1991 letter to Stringfield, she provided all the details that she had heard from her grandmother. She wrote:

> It happened in the Spring of 1941. About 9 to 9:30 one evening, granddad got a telephone call from the police department, saying they had received reports that a plane had crashed outside of town and would he go in case someone needed him. Of course he said yes. A car was sent to get him, but my grandmother said it wasn't a police car.
>
> After grandfather returned that night, he explained what he had seen to grandmother, my father, Guy, and Uncle Wayne, but that they were never to speak of it again....
>
> He said they drove out of town 13-15 miles or so, then parked the cars on the side of the road and had to walk 1/4 of a mile or so into a field where he could see fire burning.
>
> Grandfather said it wasn't an airplane or like any craft he'd ever seen. It was broken and scattered all around, but one large piece was still together and it appeared to have a rounded shape with no edges or seams. It had a very shiny metallic finish. You could see inside one section and see what looked like a metal chair with a panel with many dials and gauges—none familiar looking to him. He said that when he got there, men were already sifting through things. There were some police officers, plain clothes people and military men. There were three bodies not human, that had been taken from the wreckage and laid on the ground. Grandfather said

prayers over them so he got a close look but didn't touch them. He didn't know what had killed them because they didn't appear to have any injuries and they weren't burnt. It was hard for him to tell if they had on suits or if it was their skin but they were covered head to foot in what looked like wrinkled aluminum foil. He could see no hair on the bodies and they had no ears. They were small framed like a child about 4 feet tall, but had larger heads and longer arms. They had very large oval shaped eyes, no noses just holes and no lips just small slits for mouths. There were several people with cameras taking pictures of everything. Two of the plain clothes men picked up one of the little men, held it under its arms. A picture was taken. That was the picture I later saw. Then, one of the military officers talked to granddad and told him he was not to talk about or repeat anything that had taken place for security reasons and so as not to alarm people. Granddad returned home, told his family. That was all. About two weeks after it happened, he came home with a picture of the two men holding the little man.

After my grandfather died, my Dad kept the picture and was very interested in UFO info. Then when I was 10 or 11, a close friend of my Dad's asked if he could borrow it to show to his folks so Dad let him have it and never got it back.

Stringfield was concerned about that picture. First, as has happened in all similar stories, the picture has disappeared, so we don't have that bit of physical evidence.

Stringfield was also worried because he had seen, as I have seen, a picture that sounds similar and has been published around the UFO field for years. In it are two military men holding the long arms of what is supposed to be an alien creature, but what is clearly a monkey. It is an obvious and well-known hoax.

Mann, in her May 6, 1991, provided a lengthy description of that photograph. She wrote:

My recollection from what I saw in the picture was a small man about 4 feet tall with a large head and long arms. He was thin and no bone structure was apparent; kind of soft looking. He had no hair on his head or body with large, oval, slightly slanted eyes but not like oriental from left to right, more up and down. He had no ears at all and [no] nose like ours. His mouth was as if you had just cut a small straight line where it should have been. His skin or suit looked like crinkled-up tin foil and it covered all of him.... I believe he had three fingers, all quite long, but I can't be sure on this.

Stringfield got a copy of the picture he remembered from Michael Hesemann and sent it on to Mann. She replied, "It is nothing like what I saw. Your picture showed men in overcoats while in my picture, the man had no coats (sic)... Your picture shows two women; mine none. The alien in yours looks like a tiny doll, much smaller and shorter than mine."

Mann has now granted interviews to many others, and some of the details of her story have expanded. For example, in a 2008 interview she said that when her grandfather arrived, two of the alien creatures were dead, but the third was still alive. She said that it, or he, or possibly even she, died while her grandfather was praying over it. He then moved on to the other two to offer prayers for them.

She also said that the symbols he had seen inside the craft "looked similar to hieroglyphics."

Neither of these details were in the original story, and I'm not sure that makes much difference. Oh, the skeptics will grab on to this and suggest it is proof that she is inventing the tale. I think a more likely situation is that she either remembered more as she thought about it, or it could be a simple case of confabulation, which is not lying, but filling in missing details. That does nothing to negate the core of the story.

And, according to other reports, there is some corroboration. In what might be considered a not-very-persuasive bit of evidence, Clarance R. Schade, who is the brother of the sheriff in the Cape Girardeau area in the 1940s, said that he remembered hearing of a crash, and he seems to remember talk of little people associated with it. Certainly not startling information, but not a quick denial, either.

Ryan Wood, in his *Majic Eyes Only,* reported that Mann's sister provided a sworn affidavit that confirmed the story. In other words, other members of the family are aware of the family history and report they too have seen the photograph.

In February 2008, Tyler, Texas, television reporter Gillian Sheridan interviewed Charlette Mann. According to that report, Mann said:

We got validation by going to the archives in Washington D.C. and to see a top secret declassified document that stated that there was in fact a crash retrieval in 1941 in Cape Girardeau, Missouri, for me, I have not forgotten holding that paper in my hand and realizing that my families (sic) story was real, was solid, and for me was just an answer to a long time question.

Samples of that document appeared on Frank Warren's blog (found at *www.theufochronicles.com*), but they seem to be almost too good to be true. One of the samples said:

Based on all available evidence collected from recovered exhibits currently under study by AMC, AFSWP, NEPA, AEC, ONR, NACA, JRDB, RAND, USAAF, SAG and MIT, are deemed extraterrestrial in nature. This conclusion was reached as a result of comparison of artifacts (small part redacted) discovered in 1941. The technology is outside the scope of US science, even that of German rocket and aircraft development.

The problem with this statement is that it proves that there have been extraterrestrial recoveries, and even uses that term. This is apparently part of a leaked MJ-12 document and is dated September 24, 1947. The MJ-12 documents themselves are wrapped in controversy.

This returns us to the original story. At the moment, the major witness is Charlette Mann. Her sister has corroborated hearing the family talk of the night their grandfather, Rev. William Huffman, was called out to pray over the bodies recovered from the wrecked craft, and the brother of the sheriff also seems to remember something about this.

The problem for me is simply this: If there had been this crash in 1941, then the military would have been aware of the possibility of interplanetary (as opposed to interstellar, because people in the era thought in terms of interplanetary) travel, and they would have been on the lookout for other examples. That means they wouldn't have been caught by surprise with the flying saucers were first reported in June 1947, and would have been better prepared for the Roswell crash. That argues against the extraterrestrial nature of this case.

That said, there is more than enough here that the case deserves more research. There are interesting leads that need to be followed, and there are certainly witnesses that could be located, though time is growing short.

## October 1941

### NORTH CAROLINA

Len Stringfield, in his *UFO Crash/Retrievals: Search for Proof in a Hall of Mirrors,* reported Walter Webb, a veteran UFO investigator, had found a UFO report involving a former Army serviceman named Guy Simeone, who was with the 28th Infantry Division. According to Webb, Simeone was part of a massive war game in North Carolina when he wrote to family members about a secret assignment. Webb said that a witness told him that she had overheard Simeone's mother talking about her son being in a situation where a crashed, round, metallic object was found and that there were little dead bodies from space.

Stringfield reported, "The best guess, said Webb, is that something crashed in North Carolina where his unit was active during the month of October in 1941. Concludes Webb, 'Taking everything into account, I believe the Simeone episode should be considered classified as a tentative unknown.'"

## 1942

### "NORTH OF GEORGIA"

In February 1994, Len Stringfield, in his *UFO Crash/Retrievals: Search for Proof in a Hall of Mirrors,* reported that Mary Nunn (not her real name) told him of a friend, serving in a "key civil capacity" at the time of the event. She, Nunn, was afraid that her source would be punished for talking.

The craft was still at the Army post where it had crashed in a state that is north of Georgia. The craft was round, about 15 feet wide and 10 feet high, and divided into three main sections. There was a control room, another room with four seats, and a bottom bay that had a trap door. The control room had a large window and a number of smaller windows on each side. The craft was silver, and there were markings on both the inside and the outside.

There were four crew members that were recovered alive, but all died about two weeks later, apparently from starvation. They were about 5 feet tall, and weighed about 100 pounds. They had milky white skin and no hair. The eyes were large and black like a bug's, ears were small, and lips were thin slits. They had five long, bony fingers and flat feet. There was a female, which was suggested by small breasts, but there was no hint as to their genitalia. They did have teeth that were white, wide, and short. There was a suggestion that communication was through telepathy.

The problem with this story is that it is, at best, secondhand and might be even further removed from the original source. There is no corroboration for it, and Stringfield had hoped that someone else involved in the retrieval would come forward.

## July 9, 1946

### OCKELBO, SWEDEN
Jerome Clark, in the *International UFO Reporter* (July/August 1993), wrote that a silvery, cigar-shaped craft traveling at a low altitude "tumbled right down against the ground and was gone in a few moments."

## July 9, 1946

### LAKE BARKEN, SWEDEN
The witnesses watched an object with alternating blue and green lights come from the northeast and plunge into the lake about a hundred yards away from them.

## July 9, 1946

### MOCKEJARD, SWEDEN
Jerome Clark reported in his *UFO Encyclopedia, 2nd Edition,* "A shiny, silvery 'star' accompanied by a whistling sound descended toward Mount Landholm. Just as it was about to hit the mountainside, at 175 altitude, its light blinded the witness, who thus did not see the collision, though apparently he could hear it. He detected a strong burning odor for the next quarter-hour."

## July 10, 1946

### BJORKON, SWEDEN
A number of people watched as a "projectile trailing luminous smoke" slammed into a beach, leaving a yard-wide shallow crater containing a slag-like material, some of it reduced to powder, according

to Jerry Clark in the July/August issue of the *International UFO Reporter (IUR)*. A newspaper reporter found a cylinder about 20 or 30 meters in diameter. Military authorities investigated, produced ambiguous results, and finally accused the witnesses of imagining things.

## July 18, 1946

### LAKE MJOSA, NORWAY

Two 8-foot-long missiles with wings set about 3 feet from the front plunged into the lake, creating "notable" turbulence, according to Jerome Clark in his *UFO Encyclopedia*. While in flight, the wings seemed to flap, as if made of cloth, and the object whistled.

## July 19, 1946

### LAKE KOLMJARV, SWEDEN

Witnesses watched a gray, rocket-shaped object with wings crash into the lake, sparking a three-week hunt for it by military authorities. Nothing was found. Nearly 40 years later, a Swedish UFO researcher, Clas Svahn, interviewed some of the civilian witnesses and military investigators. An Air Force officer speculated that the object might have been made of a lightweight material that could disintegrate easily. A civilian witness claimed she heard a 'thunderclap' that might have been the object exploding as reported in the *IUR* for July/August 1993.

## August 16, 1946

### MALMO, SWEDEN

One of the "ghost rockets" exploded, breaking windows and dropping fragments.

## Mid-October 1946

### SOUTHERN SWEDEN

Two people on a lake heard a noise that drew their attention to an object that appeared over the trees. They described it as looking like a small dart with wings and a ball-shaped tip. It exploded as it crashed into the water, not far from the shoreline.

## November 1946

### ARKANSAS

An unidentified Army Air Forces private at Wright Field told UFO investigator Clark McClelland that he had seen a recovered disk-shaped craft stored in a building on the base. He said that he was delivering documents to the building in which the craft was stored when a friend standing guard asked if he wanted to see something strange.

Inside he saw an object about 15 feet in diameter and about 7 feet high. There was a row of windows around the center set about 8 or 10 inches apart, and he said that it reminded him of two soup bowls sealed together.

The guard told him that scientists had been trying to get in and tried to use a diamond drill to break through the glass, but the drill hadn't even scratched the window. They could find no obvious doors or hatches, and there were no insignia or flags or any type of writing or numbers visible. It looked as if it was brushed aluminum but it wasn't.

Both of them looked through the windows, but couldn't see anything inside except for a cylinder that was about 3 feet in diameter. They thought this might be a power unit.

This story, however, like so many others, doesn't have a ring of truth to it. A guard on a secret of this magnitude wouldn't have easy access to the interior, and it's not explained where the scientists were while the two were touring the room.

This also places a craft at Wright Field about 10 months before the Roswell case and, if they had something like that in 1946, the reaction at Wright Field as well as at higher headquarters would have been different than it was when the Roswell case was reported. They would have been better prepared for both the Roswell case and for the appearance of the flying saucers in June 1947.

Pre-1947

1947
Pre-Roswell

July 1947

October
1947–1948

1949–1952

1953–1964

1965

1966–1978

1979–1999

2000–2009

# Chapter 2

**May 31, 1947** ————————————————————

### NOGAL CANYON, NEW MEXICO

Before there was a UFO crash at Roswell, there was a UFO crash in Nogal Canyon, near Socorro, New Mexico, on the western side of the state and a couple of hundred miles from Roswell, according to some researchers. This crash site, not part of the San Agustin UFO crash as cited by Barney Barnett and Gerald Anderson, was described by an Army cameraman who was called from Washington, D.C., to film, first a preliminary autopsy of an alien creature in a tent in the desert, and later the autopsies of other aliens held in a Texas hospital.

The location of this site, then, comes from the statements made by an Army cameraman, based on his experiences in the field in New Mexico as he related the story to others. In that respect, this becomes a single-witness case, but with an added feature: There is a film, or rather a number of short films, that show part of the autopsy of the alien creature in a tent, part of the autopsy of an alien creature in the hospital morgue, and some of the wreckage of the alien ship retrieved that was displayed on tables at an undisclosed location. That means it is a case that has more than just the story told by a single witness. It is backed up by a type of physical evidence that was available to others for testing and analysis.

Ray Santilli, a British record promoter, claimed to have interviewed the man who said that he had taken the footage of the various activities in New Mexico and Texas, and that he had somehow managed to keep several short segments of the film. These were "out-takes," or reels that needed special processing, according to Santilli's source, the cameraman, but that somehow were never returned to Army control. It seemed to be a fairly cavalier way to handle material that should have been highly classified, but that was the cameraman's story and we all know that classified material is sometimes mishandled.

Kent Jeffrey, a former airline pilot who had a real interest in UFOs, tried to learn more about the autopsy and the film, but early on seemed to have very little real luck. According to Jeffrey's information, Santilli had paid about $100,000 for the film. The story circulated by Santilli during that time was that the cameraman had made a duplicate of the original film so that the Army wouldn't know that some of it was missing. That was, of course, a different story than the film being "outtakes."

There were other reports by other researchers as well. The first word was that there were 15 rolls of film of about 10 minutes each. That meant two hours and 30 minutes of film. There was a preliminary autopsy in a tent, more autopsy footage in a hospital operating room, film of the debris field with President Truman walking across it, and pictures of the alien spacecraft as it was lifted onto a flatbed truck. All of these descriptions made it sound as if the film was spectacular and authentic. It would be next to impossible to create footage of Truman walking the debris field, special effects or not, and it would certainly take a great deal of time and money to create a scene of the craft being lifted onto a truck.

Still more information and quite a few rumors were being circulated as more people began to ask questions. In a spring 1995 letter from Philip Mantle, a British researcher of note, sent to various UFO investigators, the cameraman's name was revealed as Jack Barnett. Apparently, according to some sources, Santilli had slipped up and inadvertently mentioned the man's name. Researchers began trying to locate any Barnett who had a connection to motion picture photography, whether through the military, old newsreel services, or Hollywood.

Several Jack Barnetts were found scattered around the United States, but none seemed to be the right man. Either they were too young, or they had no connection to photography or to the military. And Santilli began to hint that the Barnett name wasn't quite right. It was really Barrett, but he allowed the wrong name to circulate as a "cover" for the real man.

The story of Barnett didn't end there. In spring 1999, rumors began to circulate that Barnett had died. To many this meant that now his identity could be revealed because he was beyond the reach of government investigators and regulations. There was speculation that many of the questions would finally be answered. Within days, however, Bob Shell, who was the editor of *Shutterbug* magazine at the time, and who had an interest in UFOs, posted a message to various computer newsgroups that Barnett hadn't died. The shroud that had hidden his identity would remain in place.

In July 1995, more of the cameraman's story began to leak into the public arena. Obviously, the leaks were through Santilli and his organization for purposes of publicity, but they did provide a few new clues for investigators. The cameraman, whether under the name of Barnett or anything else, now claimed to have photographed the first atomic test at Trinity Site in New Mexico, which, coincidently, isn't all that far from Nogal Canyon, and is about halfway between Roswell and Socorro. Here was something that could be independently verified.

It wasn't long before a list of names of those associated with the Manhattan Project, as photographers who would have been at Trinity, was developed and circulated. There was no Jack Barnett on the short list. Santilli's cameraman seemed to indicate he had been in charge, but the name of the man who was in charge was Berlyn Brixner.

John Kirby, a UFO researcher living in Portland, Oregon, wanted to pursue that lead. Using a CD-ROM telephone directory, he easily found a phone number for Brixner. Kirby was apparently the first researcher to call Brixner, a friendly, 84-year-old man in 1995, who wanted to help. He provided Kirby with a list of the men he had worked with as photographers during the Manhattan Project in the late stages of the Second World War. Again, Barnett, or Barrett, failed to appear on the list. Santilli had an answer for that too, of course. According to Santilli, his man had been an Army cameraman who had been on one of the aircraft flying near Trinity Site to photograph the detonation from the air, and had never been directly associated with the Manhattan Project. Because of that, he never had the opportunity to meet Brixner, according to Santilli, so it made sense that Brixner didn't know who he was.

All this was just one more area in which what Santilli had said originally didn't seem to fit in with what could be established historically as fact. There were Army cameraman involved in the Manhattan Project, but the story told by Santilli's cameraman seemed to be at odds with historical fact. This, of course, caused many to conclude that the cameraman didn't exist.

The whole film of the autopsy, eventually sold by Santilli for broadcast by various television networks around the world, including FOX in the United States, lasted just more than 20 minutes. In addition, there were then scenes of the metallic debris collected and displayed on tables in a single room. A lone figure is seen, moving among it and lifting some of it, but he is photographed from the rear so that his identity, like that of those in the autopsy footage, is masked.

The point here, however, is that if the footage is real, then clearly it proves that something alien crashed. The film would be a better "witness" if it could be authenticated because the facts were there for all to see. If the validity of the film could be successfully challenged, then the story by the cameraman would be compromised severely. With that in mind, researchers, investigators, and reporters began to look for the cracks in the case.

Before any of the TV specials and documentaries could be aired, the *Sunday Times* in London published an article with the headline "Film that 'proves' aliens visited earth is a hoax." The article, written by Maurice Chittenden, reported that "experts called in by Channel 4 [a British television network that had bought the British rights to the footage], which is due to screen the film as part of a documentary on August 28 [1995] have declared it bogus. A source close to the documentary said: 'We have had special effects guys look at it and they say it's a fake.'"

Chittenden continued in the article, writing:

Among the flaws found by *The Sunday Times* are: 'Security coding' on one film disappeared when its accuracy was challenged. A 'letter of authentication' from Kodak was signed by a salesman. President Truman, supposedly visible on the film, was not in New Mexico at the time. Symbols seen on particles of wreckage are totally different to those remembered by an eyewitness. 'Doctors'—performing a supposedly unique autopsy on an alien—remove black lenses from his eyes in a matter of seconds, as if they knew what to expect.

These points were, for the most part, the same that had been raised by UFO researchers during their attempts to verify the authenticity of the film. What was most troubling was not that there were problems, but that the revelation of those problems resulted in an alteration of the story. When evidence was presented that suggested the security markings, for example, were more appropriate to Hollywood than to the U.S. military, those markings quickly disappeared. That, in and of itself, suggested the film was a hoax.

Santilli, however, maintained that the film was authentic. To prove it, he was going to allow some of the documentary producers an opportunity to meet with the cameraman. But those meetings never materialized. John Purdie, the producer of the Channel 4 documentary in Great Britain, did receive a phone call from a man who claimed to be the cameraman. They spoke for two minutes, and almost no questions were answered.

Kodak came up again. In its September 1996 issue, *Forteantimes* reported, "The hint of conspiracy is underlined by Ray Santilli.... Asked whether he still plans to accept Kodak's offer to analyze the film, he answers: 'With all due respect to Kodak, I simply do not trust an American corporation with lucrative defence contracts.' Way to go, Ray."

Small pieces of the film began to circulate in spring 1995, as the story began to leak. A short segment of leader, the opaque strip at the beginning of a movie, was provided for analysis. Kodak confirmed that a coding on it, a square and a triangle, suggested the film might be from 1947. The problem was that Kodak recycled the codes, so the film could have been manufactured in 1927 or 1967. Besides, there were no images on the leader, so it could have been a piece of film from anything or anywhere, not necessarily from the autopsy footage, and therefore proved nothing.

Santilli did provide a few people with small sections of film with some kind of image on them. Philip Mantle had three or four frames that contained a brightly lighted doorway, or what might have been a doorway, that might have been part of the autopsy footage. But Mantle told others that he had no footage with the alien or the interior of the autopsy room visible, which would prove that it was part of the film. He just had footage of that brightly lighted door, which might have been part of the original autopsy footage, or might have been just a few frames of another film used because the film was from the right era.

Bob Kiviat, producer of *Alien Autopsy: Fact or Fiction,* broadcast on Fox Television in the United States, was also given a small section of film. Again, nothing that would identify it as having come from the actual autopsy footage could be seen. His original section of film was even shorter than that provided to Mantle.

Kodak insisted that they could provide fairly accurate dating, but they required several feet of film. They suggested that, over the years, film would shrink, and, by measuring the distance between the sprockets, they could estimate the age. Chemical analysis, especially since the basic composition of film had changed after 1947, could provide additional clues. Kodak insisted they receive, at a minimum, one frame with the alien visible on it. That way they would know that their analysis was not being wasted. That didn't happen.

After the British and American specials were aired, there was renewed interest, and Santilli's company began selling raw video tapes of the autopsy footage for about $50 each. Santilli claimed that additional footage not seen in the specials was on the video, but that was of the tent autopsy, which was so dark as to be nearly useless as evidence, more of the debris footage, and little else.

It should be noted here that originally Santilli had said there was more than two hours of film showing the autopsy and related material. All the footage reviewed by various researchers, news reporters, and documentarians added up to little more than 20 minutes.

Almost universally, UFO researchers, television producers and reporters, and anyone else interested in the film were demanding the cameraman come forward. Without him to complete the chain of custody, the film was nearly useless. Couple this with the fact that Santilli, to that point, had refused to provide anything that would be of value in authenticating the film, and the arguments were all over nothing. The film was just an interesting aberration, but it proved nothing.

Santilli, through his various contacts, including former editor of *Shutterbug* magazine Bob Shell, finally offered the cameraman's alleged audiotaped statement. Shell, appearing on Cable Radio Network's September 2, 1995 edition of *UFOs Tonight!* hosted by Don Ecker, said that the transcript being circulated by him and Santilli was an exact transcript of the cameraman's statement. Under close questioning by Ecker, Shell said that he had heard the original tape and read or typed the transcript himself. At any rate, the transcript was an exact copy of what the cameraman had said. This discussion, recorded as a matter of course by Ecker, would become important to understanding more about the case.

During the conversation, Ecker said:

> *Somebody in the United Kingdom sent me allegedly the cameraman's statement, along with some facsimiles that were allegedly the film labels. Now, a number of weeks ago I read this entire statement verbatim on the air. And I think this is somewhat telling in itself. Now, this is purportedly this gentleman's actual statement. And I think it's very safe to say in this statement may be information he originally gave Ray Santilli, this is not the way an American former service man would ever describe himself. Have you—*

Shell interrupted and said, "What you have is probably the first version of that."

"Yeah," said Ecker. "And what I'm saying [is] this was passed off as his actual statement by Santilli, originally. And I think it's very safe to say that just ain't so, okay? It was passed off deceptively."

Shell responded by saying, "Well, yeah, but I think you have to understand what exactly happened. The cameraman made a taped statement. The tape was mailed to Santilli.... Santilli had one of his secretaries transcribe it. The secretary is British."

"Okay."

Shell continued. "So quite a bit of British [terminology] got into the transcript.... I have gone over and retranscribed it and posted it this week on CompuServe's library."

Ecker asked, "From the actual tape?"

"Yes."

"You have a copy of the tape?"

"Yes."

Later, Shell would deny that he had heard the actual tape or that he ever spoken to the cameraman. In other words, Shell, if he repaired the "transcript," did so without having heard the tape himself. It would mean that he was altering the transcript for no reason, other than to remove the incriminating British colloquialisms from it.

Santilli, when questioned about the transcript, said, using the same excuse that Shell had given, that the tape had been transcribed by a British secretary and she had changed the wording. It was a clumsy attempt to explain why common British terms were sprinkled through a statement allegedly made by an American. It also meant that Shell's claim of an exact transcript were false. He had been mistaken when he said otherwise.

The cameraman claimed he remembered very clearly that he had received a call to go to White Sands. On the statement, parenthetically, it says Roswell. But Roswell is not the same as White Sands. The missile range at White Sands was, and is, an Army facility, and it is nearly 150 miles from Roswell. If the cameraman was going to White Sands, why not fly him to the Alamogordo Army Air Field (now Holloman Air Force Base) less than 20 miles away? That part of the statement made no sense, unless it was an attempt to keep Roswell attached to the story for the commercial value of the Roswell name.

The cameraman, apparently casually, made a change in the scenario that is quite significant. Through Santilli, he said, "I was ordered to a crash site just southwest of Socorro."

He was not content to drop that single bomb. He added others, explaining that he had been in St. Louis a few days earlier, where he claimed he had been filming tests of a new ramjet helicopter. He returned to Washington, D.C., where he was given his orders and then flew out of Andrews Army Air Field, on to Wright Field, and then on to the Roswell Army Air Field. From Roswell, he was driven overland to the crash site.

To anyone who has studied a map or the Roswell case, this makes absolutely no sense. Why fly a cameraman from Washington to Dayton, Ohio, and then on to Roswell? Even if they felt the need to land first in Ohio, the trip on to Roswell makes no sense. Why not fly into Kirtland Air Force Base in Albuquerque or directly into Alamogordo? In 1947 there was no interstate highway system, but there was U.S. Highway 85. A trip from either base to Socorro was easy and quick. Even today, a trip from Roswell to Socorro is long and difficult.

The statement by the cameraman did little to increase knowledge about Roswell. Once again, there had been nothing that could be verified properly because there were no names attached to it. Some researchers did try to learn who would have been at both the Trinity Test in 1945 and at the "Little Henry" helicopter ramjet tests in St. Louis. No single name surfaced from both those events. In other words, there were two different groups of cameramen assigned.

In October 1995, Television France One (TF1) had finished their documentary about the autopsy film. They'd had access to material that had been unavailable to others as they put together their specials. For example, Nicolas Maillard of TF1 faxed a letter to the public relations department of McDonnell-Douglas (the corporate entity of the former McDonnell Aircraft Company) that confirmed that McDonnell had used its own employees for the photographic work concerning the Little Henry. Chester Turk shot the motion pictures, and Bill Schmitt took the stills. No military personnel were used, though Santilli's cameraman had claimed to have been there, and his own statement suggested he was in the Army until 1952, or about five years after those tests had been made.

Although Santilli's promises to others, such as John Purdie of Channel 4 in the United Kingdom and Bob Kiviat of FOX in the United States, that they would be able to speak to the cameraman had not happened, he made a similar promise to those at TF1. The call, promised in early September 1995, never came. Santilli did agree to submit a list of questions to the cameraman. TF1 drew up the list, and on September 14th, about three days after the list was submitted, TF1 received a fax from Santilli with the answers.

Two of the answers were of interest to researchers. TF1 asked, "What tests of the ramjet 'Little Henry' did you film in St. Louis in May 1947?" The answer from the cameraman, according to Santilli, was, "The initial tests." This was a claim that was known to be false, given the information provided by McDonnell Aircraft several weeks earlier.

A second question that must have seemed somewhat irrelevant when asked, but that would become important later, was, "Why didn't the Army use color film for such an event [filming the autopsy]?"

The answer was, "I was given instructions to leave immediately to film an aviation crash of a Russian spy plane. I did not have time to order either colour film stock or special camera equipment. I used standard issue film stock and a standard Bell and Howell."

Kent Jeffery, in the *MUFON Journal,* wrote, "Hypothetically, such an answer could explain why the cameraman didn't use color film at the initial crash scene. However, such an answer in no way explains why he didn't use color film for the autopsies—which he claims took place a month later in July in Fort Worth, Texas."

TF1, however, wasn't finished with their work. At the end of September 1995, Nicolas Maillard located Cleveland, Ohio, disc jockey Bill Randle, who was the real source of the early Elvis footage that supposedly started this whole episode. This is the footage that Santilli claimed had been sold to him by the cameraman who had also filmed the alien autopsy. According to Randle, the purchase of the Elvis film took place in his office on July 4, 1992, in the presence of Gary Shoefield.

That wasn't the end of it. According to Bill Randle, the footage Santilli bought was two short segments from two concerts held in Cleveland on July 20, 1955. The afternoon concert was at a Cleveland High School and the second at a Cleveland auditorium. The program featured the Four Lads, Bill Haley, Pat Boone, and the then-unknown Elvis Presley. Randle hired a freelance photographer to film the concerts named Jack Barnett.

This provided the information needed to check out Jack Barnett and suggested that Santilli's first statement about the name was accurate. He was born to Russian parents in 1906 and died in 1967. He had been a newsreel cameraman during the Second World War, had been in on the Italian campaign, but had not been in the Army.

TF1 planned to confront Santilli with this information to gauge his reaction during a live interview on October 23, 1995, on the Jacques Pradel special. According to Kent Jeffrey's "Santilli's Controversial Autopsy Movie" published in the *MUFON Journal* (No. 335), once the interview with Bill Randle was played for Santilli, he said, "Well, firstly, I'm very pleased that you have found Bill Randle...."

Santilli then provided a new scenario for the discovery of the autopsy footage. Kent Jeffrey wrote in the MUFON Journal:

> ...the person from whom he had purchased the Elvis footage was not really a military cameraman after all. He now claimed that he had met the real cameraman after he purchased the rights to the Elvis film from Bill Randle in Cleveland during the summer of 1992 (previously Santilli had given the year as 1993). Everyone, including the host, Jacques Pradel, seemed incredulous....

In the August 28, 1995, Channel 4 documentary, Santilli referred to the collector who had paid for the autopsy footage. He had said, repeatedly, that he, Santilli, did not have access to the film itself because the collector had it in a vault. It would be up to the collector to offer samples of the film for analysis. Santilli could do nothing to help researchers.

Through the efforts of the investigative team of TF1, however, the name of the collector was learned. Volker Spielberg was the man who supposedly owned the film. Coincidentally, Spielberg, like Santilli, is in the video distribution business.

During a live interview on TF1, Santilli, when pressed about providing the original film, said that it was out of his hands. TF1 then showed taped clips of Spielberg's business office, and the reporter said that TF1 had learned that Spielberg was not a film collector as claimed. Contrary to what Santilli had said about not knowing Spielberg personally, when questioned by others, TF1 learned of a confidential meeting in Hamburg, Germany, among Spielberg, Santilli, and one or two others. It was revealed that Santilli and Spielberg were friends and business partners, and had worked together on several different occasions.

Michael Hesemann, who was working with, if not for, Santilli, has told many that the alien autopsy footage is from near Socorro, New Mexico. Hesemann had claimed that he had located the "real" crash site and at that time was the only researcher to have done so. He has also claimed that the real date of this crash is May 31, 1947. Because this is not the Roswell case, Hesemann believed it explained the discrepancies between what researchers have learned about Roswell and the facts that have surfaced around the Santilli autopsy film. None of that made sense to researchers because Santilli continued to try to link Roswell to the autopsy footage.

What should have been the final and crushing blow for the alien autopsy film came in July 1998. Philip Mantle, writing with Tim Matthews, alerted their colleagues in the UFO field that the tent footage was faked. They had found and interviewed one man who claimed to have worked on that segment of the autopsy footage.

According to Mantle, Matthews learned that the tent footage had been created by a firm in Milton Keynes called A.R.K. Music Ltd. Those who put the tent footage together had experience with video and computer equipment. Mantle and Matthews named the names of those men involved.

In December 1998, the situation became even more complicated. Santilli, learning that Bob Kiviat, who had produced the original autopsy special in the United States for FOX, was now producing a second in which he would show the tent footage was a fake. The spin began again.

According to Santilli, the tent footage was not part of the alien autopsy. According to Santilli, he has maintained this position all along and had warned Kiviat in 1995 about the tent footage. Santilli claimed that Kiviat was going to run a disclaimer about the tent footage, but in the end, Santilli claimed he won and the tent footage was pulled from the broadcast. Of course, it is possible it wasn't used because the footage was of such poor quality, dark to the point of being obscured, that it made no sense to broadcast it. The footage I saw had little detail in a very murky background.

The tent footage was part of the material that Santilli had received from the cameraman but, because it was so bad, he had asked a studio in Milton Keynes to do what they could to enhance the image. Sometime after he had received the enhanced image, he returned to the United States to show it to the cameraman. At that point, the cameraman said that he didn't remember photographing the tent footage or the style in which it had been filmed.

When Santilli returned to England, he learned that his friend and the owner of the studio had played a joke on him. They had been unable to retrieve anything from the film so he, the studio owner, had staged it as a joke. Santilli, then, not to compromise the importance of the "real" autopsy film, told all that the tent footage should not be used as part of the autopsy film.

Santilli went on to say some things that are extremely important. He said that Andy and Keith (one of the men who worked at the studio owned by Andy) were good friends of his. They didn't act out of malice, but just to play a joke on their friend. This statement, however, shows that Santilli did know people who could fake the film, and, in fact, had faked some of it.

This is just one more aspect of the story that has collapsed, and the information about that collapse has proved to be accurate. Philip Mantle, to his credit, revealed what he had learned, and Santilli, after a fashion, confirmed it, but said it wasn't relevant. Of course, the fact that some of the autopsy footage, as offered to various people, was faked, is extremely relevant. The spin on it doesn't matter.

The story didn't end there. Many still believed that the autopsy and the wreckage footage were real. Santilli had made a mistake by trying to "improve" the tent footage, but that didn't mean the rest of the story and the rest of the film weren't authentic. Well, at least to the twisted logic of some.

In the United States, UFO researcher and retired teacher Ed Gerhman studied the autopsy film carefully, tried his best to interpret the statements attributed to the cameraman, and believed that in 2002 he had found the real crash site, out beyond where Hesemann had gone. Hesemann hadn't traveled deep enough into the desert.

In September 2004, working with New Mexican Ufologist Wendy Connors, Gerhman returned to the area southwest of Socorro that was at the entrance to Nogal Canyon. Connors said that it took about 45 minutes to reach the location once they left Socorro.

Connors eventually made a public statement, which was reported by Ryan Wood in his *Majic Eyes Only*. According to Connors:

> Upon entering the site I encountered trees that appear to have been burned from the top, the burn marks ending before the ground. General layout of the area appears to closely resemble the drawings made by the cameraman. Most noticeable is the splattering of what appears to be a bluish-green concentration of mineral over the rock faces composing the crater of the site. The materials [sic] appearance is much like hot wax having been splattered over the area. This substance, at certain places, appears to have been melted over the rocks. I took various samples from the site. Since I have yet to have these specimens analyzed independently, I will defer judgement as to what the mineral appearing material may be at this time.

Then Philip Mantle entered the picture again. Having revealed that the tent footage of the autopsy had been "re-created" as a joke, he now learned more disturbing things about the rest of the film. He sent out an Internet alert to various UFO researchers that said:

> The show starts off with Santilli claiming that he saw the real film of aliens and that he purchased it from a former US military cameraman. However, there is now a change in the story. Santilli & his colleague Gary Shoefield claim that it took 2 years to buy the film & that when it finally arrived in London 95% of it had "oxidized" and the remaining 5% was in very poor condition.
>
> They therefore decided to "reconstruct" it based on Santilli's recollection and a few frames that were left. To do this they hired UK sculptor John Humphreys. Humphreys tells of how he used sheep's brain for the brain and lamb's leg for the leg joint.
>
> The cameraman's interview film is also a fake. The man in the film is someone they literally brought in off the street and gave him a prepared script to read from.
>
> Santilli and Shoefield continually try to insist that the AA film as we know it is a restoration, but in fact it was made by John Humphreys.

To try and justify they claim that some of the surviving original frames are seen mixed in with the reconstruction/restoration. Interestingly neither Santilli, Shoefield or Humphreys could point out where and which are these frames when viewing the AA film.

Santilli admitted that the six-fingered panels in the debris film were the result of "artistic license" and he even produced one of the I-beams from the boot of his car. The debris film was also made by John Humphreys.

In fact, Humphreys is the surgeon in the film, and a former employee of Shoefield's [is] behind the window. He's Gareth Watson, a man I met several times in Ray's office.

Nick Pope and myself appear briefly in this show and I dare say Nick will have his own comments to make.

For anyone interested in the AA film I do recommend watching this if you can. I've taken part in another show for Channel Five in the UK the content of which I am not permitted to disclose.

After watching this tonight I can honestly say that I do not believe one word of either Santilli or Shoefield and I have no doubt that the film is nothing more than a complete fake.

There is [not] and never was any original film and there is [not] and never was any US military cameraman. Santilli & Shoefield had little credibility as it was but now they have none.

The alien autopsy film is dead and I hope to put it to rest, once and for all, soon. Watch this space.

That would seem to end all discussion on the Nogal Canyon crash, because the site location was based on the cameraman's testimony, and that had been rendered useless. If there was no cameraman, then there was no Nogal Canyon crash site.

I had always thought that this crash made no sense in a historical way. If there had been a crash in May, in New Mexico, then those at the higher levels in the military and in Washington, D.C. would have known about it, and their reactions, when flying saucers began to be reported all over the country and when the next crash happened near Roswell, would have been different.

For example, the day after the Roswell crash was announced in the newspapers, the Associated Press reported that both the Army and the

Navy moved to suppress the stories of "flying saucers whizzing through the atmosphere." If there was a crash in Nogal Canyon, then they would have begun the effort when the Arnold sighting broke in the media in late June. They wouldn't have waited until the second week in July to begin their campaign of suppression.

Second, there probably wouldn't have been the confusion displayed in Washington with both military and civilian leaders making contradictory statements about flying saucers and suggesting all sorts of explanations, including secret projects. They would have been able to act promptly to stop the stories. Because they didn't, at that time, it means they were just as confused as everyone else. They didn't see any reason to stop them until the Roswell crash.

So, it now seems that the Nogal Canyon crash joins the ranks of other hoaxes, exposed for what it is because the main source of information probably never existed, and the film that supported the tale has been shown to be a hoax. An admitted hoax. We are done with Nogal Canyon.

Well, not quite. On October 17, 2008, Mantle—yes, the same Mantle who told us the alien autopsy was dead, and I would have thought Nogal Canyon with it—reported that he, along with Ed Gehrman, had gone to Nogal Canyon in June and collected more samples.

According to their privately published report, they found rocks

> burnt on one side and trees burnt at the top, but this was only the beginning. At the end of a dry river bed the rock face up and surrounding loose rock was literally covered with a bluish material. This was not part of the rock, instead it was "splattered" all over the rock face and surrounding loose rocks.... The bluish material was later identified as cristobalite.

They sent the samples they collected to Dr. R. Ronald Rau, a physicist with the Brookhaven National Laboratory in New York. According to Mantle's internet posting, "In two technical reports Dr. Rau concluded that the cause of the effects found at the site in Nogal Canyon were the result of a UFO."

He tried to explain his conclusions in a short report that he put into simple terms. He wrote:

> In ref. to report CNM-080108RAU the report basically is saying that there are small traces of radioactivity. The radioactivity traces

was a measurable amount 238 U [which is the most common isotope of uranium found in nature] but is very surprising that it would be on these samples. The other micro-trace picked up was 214Pb [lead] and 214Bi [bismuth] which has very short half-lives but to my account this can be viewed as negligible. What is interesting is 238 U on the rock samples. This can be caused by a condition called Locard's Exchange Principle. This also can be explained in my second report [CNM-080109RAU] as the same phenomena.

2. Basically here is what Locard's Exchange does—"Every Contact Leaves a Trace". So when you have a huge high impact and high temperature yield you can a transfer of materials from the source to destination at the point of impact. For example from so-called ship to the surrounding area in that impact area can be very well the cause.

I would conclude that something very fast high temperature yield caused the surrounding area to exhibit the Locard's Exchange transformation.

Would I tag it a "UFO"......Probably because the unknown source is unknown!

This was, of course, startling news. Here was a reputable scientist who had suggested the material found was from a UFO. Those who made the Internet search would learn that Dr. Rau was indeed a scientist with the Brookhaven National Laboratory. Some of the information in his bio suggested he was old and might be retired, but he did work there and did have a lab there.

But just days after Mantle sent out the information about Rau and his incredible report, there was a new development: Rau denied that he had ever tested any material that suggested it was from a UFO. Mantle, in a statement he circulated on the Internet, wrote:

I am a UFO researcher and author in the UK. Last year I visited a location in the New Mexico desert that a colleague believes is the location of a UFO crash. There are various anomalies there and I brought back some rock samples. Earlier this year I was contacted via email by a Dr Ronnie Milione from New York. During an email conversation I mentioned these rock samples and he informed me that he had a colleague at the Brookhaven National Laboratory who could take a look at them for me. I sent the rock samples to Milione and just a few weeks ago the lab reports were sent to me. These are attached for your attention. If anyone would like a copy please feel free to contact me direct.

Milione's colleague was allegedly a Dr Ronald Rau. I contacted the BNL via email and their media department confirmed there was such a person but he was retired but still held a post there.

The lab reports confirmed a UFO crash site and I published these in the national news media in the UK. The story was subsequently sent around the world. In the meantime Ronnie Milione had supplied me with a telephone number and an email address for Dr Rau. I could not reach him on the phone but had several e-mail's from him. The BNL had supplied me with a different email address but they were not sure if it was correct.

Yesterday, I received an email from a Frank Warren of *The UFO Chronicles* web site (www.theufochornicles.com) who had been contacted by someone from the BNL stating that they had spoken to Dr Rau and he denied all knowledge of any such tests and labs reports. I phoned Ronnie Milione is New York and he gave me a not too convincing story. I then contact Dr Rau via the email address provided by the BNL and he has told me that he has never tested any such rock samples and that's it. His full email is reproduced here:

"Mr. Mantle, all of this is nonsense. I have never dealt with rocks from New Mexico or any other place. I am a High Energy Physicist not a geologist. I am retired from Brookhaven National Laboratory and they know about this fabrication. I do know casually Dr. Milione as he helped me set up a new computer a few months ago.

Please stop this fabrication. Thank you Dr. R. Ronald Rau."

I also checked with a person I respect in the USA who gave me a long list of frauds and falsehoods that Ronnie Milione had previously been involved with. I could not however find anything on the internet that detailed anything suspicious about Ronnie Milione. I had checked this before but drew a complete blank. However, I have no doubt that my colleague in the USA is telling me the truth.

Basically this whole thing has been a fraud perpetrated by Ronnie Milione. He has produced fake lab reports on Brookhaven headed stationary and has used one of their doctor's names fraudulently. As a result I will be consulting my lawyer on Monday to see if I can sue for damages.

I have emailed Dr Rau to apologise and advised him to consult a legal representative. I have also contacted the BNL to advise them of this and have suggested they too seek legal advice. I have offered my assistance to both Dr Rau and the BNL should they choose to take legal action against Ronnie Milione.

If you require any further information please do not hesitate to ask. I can only apologise to the BNL and Dr Rau for any embarrassment caused but the culprit is Ronnie Milione and the BNL. Dr R.Ronald Rau and I are the victims.

I would like to thank Frank Warren for alerting me to this and for my colleague in the USA for supplying me with the low down on Ronnie Milione. For the record I phoned Milione on his land line this morning but guess what, it was coming up and [sic] engaged. I did however leave a message on his mobile answering service telling him just what I thought of him. Any further communication with him will now be with my lawyer. However, if anyone would like his full contact details please let me know and I will gladly supply them.

This, I suspect, will be the end of the Nogal Canyon UFO crash. The site was located based on the alleged testimony of a cameraman who apparently never existed, which was part of a hoax about an alien autopsy. The material found has been identified as a structure that is often associated with the high temperatures of volcanos, and there are the remains of volcanic eruptions all over western New Mexico. Dr. Rau has denied that he ever tested the material, and there is no reason to doubt that the man who made the denial is the real Dr. Rau.

This should close this episode. Yes, I know there will be those who will discover it in the future and we will again be subjected to this tale. They will suggest that the CIA, or the Air Force, or the Men in Black forced the lab and Dr. Rau to change his story. There are those who see conspiracy everywhere, even where none exists. That is the way it is with nearly everything in the UFO field. It never dies, but it does recycle.

# June 21, 1947

## MAURY ISLAND, WASHINGTON

Kenneth Arnold's "flying saucer" sighting of June 24, 1947, when he learned of it, excited Ray Palmer, the editor of science fiction magazine *Amazing Stories*. Palmer had taken a science fiction magazine on the verge of folding and turned it into one with wide circulation in a matter of months. One of the stories—or, more accurately, a series of stories, were the tales of Richard Shaver that Palmer hinted were true and that he credited with the amazing turnaround of the magazine. Shaver, in his rambling style, told of an underworld accessed through deep caves, of a war between the Deros and Teros, two "robot" societies, one good and one bad, and of their influence on the human race. Almost all of that robotic influence was bad in our world and could be traced to the evil robots. By coincidence, the June 1947 issue of *Amazing Stories* was filled with more of Shaver's tales.

Palmer had suggested as he published the stories that these underground entities, good and bad, did leave their caves occasionally, and when the flying saucers first appeared over Washington state in June 1947, Palmer was convinced that this was the proof of the reality of Shaver's tales. In fact, in an editorial published in October 1947, Palmer excitedly wrote, "A part of the now world-famous Shaver Mystery has now been proved!"

When the Arnold story broke in the national press, Palmer saw the opportunity to publicize his case and, by doing that, validate the Shaver mystery. Palmer, as did so many others, wrote to Arnold, asking that he, Arnold, prepare a report for the magazine. Arnold didn't want to do that, but did send Palmer a copy of the report that he had written for the Army Air Forces.

In a few days, Palmer wrote again, this time telling Arnold that he, Palmer, had a letter from a harbor patrol officer telling of a flying saucer sighting three days before Arnold had seen anything. Palmer asked if Arnold would investigate and Palmer would pay him $200, which, in 1947, was quite a bit of money.

The story, as it was told by Palmer and later by the harbor patrolmen, was that Harold Dahl, his teenaged son, and two other harbor patrolmen, sighted six doughnut-shaped objects in the sky near them.

Five of the craft seemed to be circling the sixth, which was in trouble. According to Project Blue Book, as that object passed overhead, no more than 500 feet above them, it started "spewing a white type of very light weight metal," and some kind of "dark type metal which looked similar to lava rock." That injured Dahl's son and killed the dog. When the object stopped dropping the metal, it took off, but not before Dahl took pictures.

In another, slightly different version of the story, the sixth object landed, or crashed, on Maury Island in Puget Sound and disintegrated, leaving behind some strange debris. Dahl collected some of this material and then returned to Tacoma, Washington.

Now things get a little more confusing. According to what Dahl told Arnold, he hadn't said a word to anyone about the damaged object, but the next day, a dark-suited stranger who seemed to know everything about the sighting appeared to warn Dahl not to talk about it. But Dahl ignored this warning and told his "supervisor" Fred Crisman about it. Crisman then went out to the beach and found some of the metallic debris, or so he said. He collected his own samples.

Having interviewed Dahl, or rather talked to him, Arnold and Dahl then headed to Crisman's home to interview him. Crisman showed Arnold the debris that he had recovered, but Arnold was unimpressed. He recognized it as lava and began to suspect the story being told was a hoax.

Even with his suspicions aroused, Arnold wasn't sure what he should do. He called Captain E.J. Smith, a United Airlines pilot who, along with his crew and passengers, had seen several disk-shaped objects during a flight on the July 4, 1947 weekend. Arnold, as a private pilot, had respect for Smith, an airline pilot, and Smith joined Arnold in Tacoma. (For those interested in such things, Arnold had Room 502 in the Winthrop Hotel.)

The next day, Crisman and Dahl visited Arnold at the hotel. Crisman added a new detail: He told Arnold that, when he had gone to the beach, he'd seen one of the doughnut-shaped flying saucers that seemed to be searching the bay for something. Crisman, who hadn't been on the boat when the six objects had been seen, now dominated the conversation, as if he knew everything about it.

Arnold was less than impressed with all this and ordered breakfast in his hotel room. There wasn't much talk as Arnold ate and read some of the newspaper clippings he had brought with him. Later Arnold would tell others that one story caught his attention. Flying saucers over Mountain Home, Idaho, had dropped or expelled cinder or lava ash. Here, suddenly, was another, independent report about a craft, or several craft, dropping the same kind of material that Dahl and then Crisman had talked about.

Sometime in the night, Arnold received a call from Ted Morello, a reporter for the United Press, and who seemed to know everything that had happened in Arnold's room during his discussions with Dahl and Crisman. Fearing the room was bugged, Arnold and Smith began looking for hidden microphones. They found nothing.

The next morning, at the hotel, but downstairs, Dahl and Crisman introduced Arnold to a couple of tough-looking men who were supposed to be the crew who had also seen the object. Arnold didn't question them, but did study some of the debris that Dahl and Crisman had brought with them. Arnold thought it looked more like aluminum such as that used in large military aircraft rather than something from another world.

That wasn't all. Dahl, or Crisman, also suggested that photographs of the objects had been taken. Crisman had the film, he said, which Dahl had given him. Once they saw the film, everyone would know the truth. Pictures wouldn't lie.

Arnold didn't know what to do. There was physical evidence and there were photographs, but the story told by the men seemed to have holes in it. During the Army Air Forces investigation of his sighting, Arnold had been interviewed by an officer from the Fourth Air Force, Lieutenant Frank Brown. Arnold decided to call him and let him take a turn at trying to figure all this out.

Ed Ruppelt, one-time chief of Project Blue Book, the Air Force study of UFOs, put it this way in his book, *The Report on Unidentified Flying Objects*:

> For the Air Force the story started on July 31, 1947, when Lieutenant Frank Brown, an intelligence agent at Hamilton AFB, California, received a long-distance phone call. The caller was a

man whom I'll call Simpson [which, of course was Arnold, Ruppelt changed the name because of privacy considerations] who had met Brown when Brown investigated an earlier UFO sighting.... He [Arnold] had just talked to two Tacoma Harbor patrolmen. One of them had seen six UFOs hover over his patrol boat and spew out chunks of odd metal.

Brown left California with another officer, Captain William Davidson, and they met with Arnold at his hotel in Tacoma. Arnold showed the two officers the fragments; both apparently recognized it as worthless slag, which probably hadn't come from a flying saucer, and lost interest. Neither told Arnold this, apparently not wanting to embarrass him. Ruppelt later wrote: "Simpson [Arnold] and his airline pilot friend [Smith] weren't told about the hoax for one reason. As soon as it was discovered that they had been 'taken,' thoroughly, and were not a party to the hoax, no one wanted to embarrass them."

Davidson and Brown, claiming they had to return their aircraft to California, went back to McChord airfield, where their B-25 was parked. They spoke, briefly, with the intelligence officer there, Major George Sander, telling him that they believed Dahl and Crisman had made up the tale.

Not long after take-off, the engine on the left wing caught fire and though the two passengers, crew chief Woodrow D. Matthews and a "hitchhiker" identified as Sergeant Elmer L. Taff, with them bailed out safely, the wing burned off and smashed into the tail. The aircraft spun out of control and neither of the pilots, Brown nor Davidson, got out. They were killed in the crash.

The story had suddenly turned deadly. The Army Air Forces—or maybe more appropriately, the FBI—investigated and learned that, contrary to published reports, there was no sabotage of the aircraft and no one had shot it down. It was a tragic accident that seemed to focus more attention on the UFO sighting than it warranted.

Ruppelt, in his 1957 book, The Report on Unidentified Flying Objects, wrote:

Both—(the two harbor patrolmen, Dahl and Crisman] admitted that the rock fragments had nothing to do with flying saucers. The whole thing was a hoax. They had sent in the rock fragments to

[Ray Palmer] stating that they could have been part of a flying saucer. He had said the rock came from a flying saucer because that's what [Palmer] wanted him to say.

The Army Air Forces then found a solution to the case and although two men had been killed investigating it, that had nothing to do with the UFO sighting. The men were not prosecuted for inventing the story.

According to Jerome Clark, Arnold apparently never learned the truth about Maury Island. As late as 1977, Arnold was still talking about the case. He also used it in an article he wrote for the first issue of *Fate* and in his book, written with Palmer, called *The Coming of the Saucers.*

But there was another problem, as laid out in the Project Blue Book files about the case and in the FBI document that is a part of the file: The mystery caller, who had been telling reporters everything that went on in Arnold's room, was able to substantiate part of the tale. The first wire stories of the crash didn't mention the names of the officers killed, but the mystery caller knew them anyway. He suggested that the aircraft was shot down by 20 mm cannon, and that was because it carried some of the fragments picked up in the Maury Island area. He suggested that, if he had the correct names of the officers killed, then they could believe that the rest of his information was also correct.

It turned out that the mystery caller had the right names, and the *Tacoma Times* and a few other newspapers, including one in Chicago, carried the story that the B-25 had been shot down. Ted Lantz, one of the reporters, learned that that both men had been intelligence officers. With that story out, the Army Air Forces, among other agencies, had to find the truth.

But the story turns again. The mystery caller turned out to be one of the two harbor patrolmen, so of course he knew what had gone on in Arnold's room, and knew the names of the pilots killed, because he had met them. Of course, with that information verified, the newspapers printed the rest of his information. There had been verification for some of it.

Then, as so often happens, there was another twist: Fred Crisman, it seems, and according to John Keel, among others, had written a letter to the editor of *Amazing Stories,* Ray Palmer, in 1946. He warned Palmer about continuing the story of Deros and Teros because he knew it was all true. He had seen them in the caves of Asia while he had been assigned to the Second Air Commando, an aviation unit designed to use special tactics against the Japanese in the China-Burma-India Theater. He wrote:

Sirs:

I flew my last combat mission on May 26 [1945] when I was shot up over Bassein and ditched my ship in Ramaree roads off Chedubs Island. I was missing five days. I requested leave at Kashmere (sic). I and Capt. (deleted by request) left Srinagar and went to Rudok then through the Khese pass to the northern foothills of the Karakoram. We found what we were looking for. We knew what we were searching for.

For heaven's sake, drop the whole thing! You are playing with dynamite. My companion and I fought our way out of a cave with submachine guns. I have two 9" scars on my left arm that came from wounds given me in the cave when I was 50 feet from a moving object of any kind and in perfect silence. The muscles were nearly ripped out. How? I don't know. My friend has a hole the size of a dime in his right bicep. It was seared inside. How we don't know. But we both believe we know more about the Shaver Mystery than any other pair. You can imagine my fright when I picked up my first copy of *Amazing Stories* and see you splashing words about the subject.

What surprised me here is that Crisman knew about the Second Air Commando, which did serve in CBI Theater, and the place names all have the ring of authenticity. Of course, for a con to work, there must be some elements of truth in it, and these little nuggets put Crisman into the right place at the right time to tell his otherwise outrageous story. Besides, Palmer now had another man telling "eyewitness" stories of the Deros and the Teros.

Palmer kept that mystery alive as long as he could, but the Army was more than annoyed about the deaths of two officers for what seemed to be nothing more than a magazine article and some science fiction stories. The investigation, which included the FBI, resulted in both Crisman and Dahl saying that it had been a hoax that had gotten out of hand. They had never meant it to be taken nearly as seriously as it was.

In fact, Crisman tried to blame Palmer, saying he only told Palmer what Palmer wanted to hear. But it was Crisman who contacted Palmer with his story of debris from a flying saucer and, although it might be suggested that Palmer ignored the shaky nature of the information and evidence, it was Crisman who was there pushing his own agenda. Palmer knew Crisman from his earlier letter, which was published without a name attached. Palmer would later admit that Crisman was the author.

The military investigation—or rather, the documents in the Project Blue Book files, suggest that neither Dahl nor Crisman were harbor patrolmen, but owned a salvage boat that they used to patrol Puget Sound for anything they could find. Ruppelt suggested they had a couple of beat-up old boats they used in their salvage work.

Others who investigated privately later said that the characterization of the boats was unfair. They didn't have a couple of boats; they had a single boat known as the *North Queen,* which was only five years old and had been renovated not long before the sighting.

Palmer, of course, was not going to allow Ruppelt or the Air Force destroy a good story. He claimed that Crisman wanted investigators to believe the story was a hoax. Crisman suggested that the Maury Island case could not be separated from the Shaver mystery, and that flying saucers didn't come from outer space, but from the inner Earth. Maury Island proved that, at least in Crisman's mind, and, if Palmer didn't believe it, he sure wanted to promote it. The Shaver mystery had boosted the sales of his magazine by tens of thousands.

The metallic debris that everyone had been so concerned about was identified as slag and, it was suggested, bore a resemblance to similar material from a smelter near Tacoma. Although some suggested the slag had been radioactive, there is nothing in the FBI report to confirm this.

To show that some things just can't be simple, Crisman pops up on the radar in the late 1960s as New Orleans district attorney Jim Garrison began to investigate Clay Shaw in relation to the Kennedy assassination. Crisman became one of the minor players when it was claimed that he was one of the three hobos seen in the railroad yards not long after the fatal shots had been fired. Crisman was in the photograph of the hobos that has become part of the assassination legend.

So now we have moved from the possible crash of an alien spacecraft, to the possible crash of a craft from the inner Earth, to a story of a disabled craft that dumped metallic debris and maybe disintegrated, to the Kennedy assassination. But in all that, we have seen no evidence of anything extraordinary. There are only the tales told by Dahl and Crisman, and even those are undercut by retractions of the two men. They both told investigators that the story had started as a joke and that it had gotten out of hand.

Dahl's son, Charles, located years after the event, said that it had never happened. Of Crisman, Charles Dahl said he was a smooth-talking conman and that the Maury Island incident was a hoax.

It should be noted that no material with anything unusual about it has ever surfaced, though Crisman had suggested in the 1960s he still had some of it. The photographs were supposedly taken by the military, through no one ever saw them, and in the 1960s, Crisman suggested that he had made duplicate negatives so that the military had not gotten them all, but of course the pictures never surfaced.

Finally Crisman's obituary mentioned his military service and suggested that he had received the Distinguished Service Cross. No record to support this has been found, and it's probably only fair to note that nothing suggests Crisman made the claim. It surfaced after he died.

Pre-1947

1947
Pre-Roswell

July 1947

October
1947–1948

1949–1952

1953–1964

1965

1966–1978

1979–1999

2000–2009

# Chapter 3

## July 1947 ——————————————————

### Roswell, New Mexico

The Roswell crash case has become a confusing mass of information, misinformation, lies, distortions, inaccuracies, mistakes, and witnesses, both real and imagined. It hasn't been helped by the conflicts of the investigators, the commercial success of the yearly celebration, and the addition of charlatans who see it as a way to achieve some sort of fame and maybe make a quick buck. But, in the end, this is the case that could very well be the key to solving the answer of life on other planets and the feasibility of interstellar travel. All we need to do is cut through the nonsense, the hype, the misunderstandings, and the purposeful distortions of so many to get to the truth.

We can say that the case began when Mack Brazel, a New Mexico rancher, found a field filled with strange metallic debris on a July morning in 1947. He didn't know what it was and didn't know exactly what to do with it. Others suggested that he tell the Air Force (the Army Air Force in those days) because it was something that came from the sky and it would be their responsibility to clean it up.

Mack Brazel died before any UFO researchers talked to him, and, if there is a record of what he said to the military, that record is buried deep in an impenetrable archive. He died before he told much about the crash to anyone with the possible exception of his son Bill Jr., though he did discuss the events with some, showed debris from the crash to others, and complained to many, including his son, about being "put in jail."

Brazel did talk to Loretta Proctor and her husband, Floyd. I never had the chance to interview Floyd, who told of seeing Mack in town escorted by military officers, and he said that he had seen some of the debris. Although Bill Moore recounts his interview with Floyd in his 1980 book, *The Roswell Incident,* Floyd died before other researchers had a chance to interview him.

I did talk to other neighbors who mentioned Brazel being away from the ranch and complaining about being held in Roswell. Marian Strickland told me, as recorded on videotape, that Brazel sat in her kitchen and talked about being in jail. He was talking to her husband, but she was nearby, ready to serve them coffee if they wanted it.

His son, Bill Brazel, said that he had read (please note the use of the word *read*) about his father in one of the Albuquerque newspapers and realized that his father would need help on the ranch. He drove

*3.1. Bill Brazel, Roswell. Author's photo.*

down there and found the ranch house deserted, his father away. Mack Brazel arrived a couple of days later and told Bill that he had been in jail. He was quite annoyed about it.

Bill Brazel thought he was at the ranch two or three days before his father returned, and his father had been gone for two or three days before Bill arrived. In other words, Mack was gone from four days to more than a week after he made the find.

And finally, the Provost Marshal at the base, meaning the chief of law enforcement officer, then Major Edwin Easley, told me that Brazel had been held in the guest house—not exactly jail, but certainly about the same thing if your freedom is restricted.

There was a newspaper article printed on July 9, 1947, in the *Roswell Daily Record* about Brazel. Clearly, based on that article, we know that Brazel was, in fact, in Roswell. What all this means here is that the evidence is quite clear: Brazel left the ranch, was in Roswell for a period of time, and eventually returned. The question that follows from there is: What did he find that would impel him to take the long drive into Roswell and for the authorities there to hold him in the guest house for a period of time?

What did Brazel find that would put him in the hands of the military for a week or so? Was it something extraordinary, or was it just a lot of rubbish from a weather balloon and radar target array known as Mogul?

The first people Brazel talked to about this were Floyd and Loretta Proctor. There are some good reasons to believe that he went to their ranch because their son, Dee, was with him when he discovered the debris field. Dee would remain close-mouthed about this for the rest of his life, only speaking to one researcher, and that time by accident.

I interviewed Loretta in 1989 and again in 1990. She told me that Brazel had wanted her and Floyd to drive out and look at the field, but they weren't inclined to do it. She mentioned that gas and tires cost money, and the drive would have been something like 20 miles round trip. It was just not something they cared to do with money so tight in the ranching community.

So I asked if Brazel had described the debris to her and she said, "...he did bring a little sliver of a wood looking stuff up but you couldn't burn it or you couldn't cut it or anything.... I would say that it was a brownish tan but you know that's been quite a long time. It looked like plastic; of course there wasn't any plastic then but that was kind of like what it looked like."

Although she didn't see it, she did talk about some of the other material. She said, "...he was telling us about more of the other material that was so lightweight and that was crinkled up and then would fold out. He said there was more stuff there, like a tape that had some sort of figures on it."

There were others who talked about the strange properties of the debris. One of those was Bill Brazel, who told Don Schmitt and me in

1989 that he had found some bits and pieces of the stuff over the next two years. We met Bill Brazel in Carazozo, New Mexico, and he described what he had found for us and that was recorded on audiotape.

He said:

*...oh, not over a dozen and I'd say eight [little pieces of debris]. Just different little pieces. There were only three items involved. Something on the order of balsa wood and something on the order of heavy-gauge monofilament fishing line and a little piece of...it wasn't really aluminum foil and it wasn't really lead foil but it was on that order. A piece about the size of my fingers with jagged edges.*

Though he called one of the objects monofilament fishing line, it was actually something more technologically advanced than that. Brazel said, "...this was before monofilament fishing line was a popular item and that's the nearest thing I could compare it to. Now there's this plastic...they put a light down that thing and it comes out the other end."

He was, of course, describing what we now know is fiber optics. This was not something being tested or discussed in 1947. It's a much more recent development.

The wood he talked about wasn't really balsa wood, just the nearest thing he could think of. He said the piece he had was about 5 inches long and as light as balsa, but so strong he couldn't cut it with his pocket knife. He had wanted to get a little sliver of it to see if there was any stratification to it, but couldn't even scratch it.

*3.2. Don Schmitt lecturing abount Roswell. Author's photo.*

Then he described the foil-like material. He told Schmitt and me:

*The only reason I noticed the foil was that I picked this stuff up and put it in my chaps pocket. I had it in there, two, three days and when I took it out and put it in the box I happened to notice that it started unfolding and flattened out. Then I got to playing with it. I would fold it or crease it and lay it down and watch it. It was kind of weird.*

Brazel made it clear that this foil was as strong as the rest of the stuff. He couldn't tear it as he could other bits of foil from a more conventional source. He said that he didn't try to cut it with his knife.

If Bill Brazel had these bits and pieces, then why haven't we seen them? According to him, sometime after the events, he let it be known what he had found. He said that four soldiers, airmen by this time, came to his house. One of them was an officer he thought was named Armstrong, but he wasn't sure if that was right. Armstrong let it be known that he was there to "recover" the debris, and it was clear to Bill Brazel that Armstrong and his fellows were not going to leave without it.

So Brazel lost the debris, which could have ended the debate. He surrendered it, you might say willingly, to officials of the government who asked for it. We are left with just his word that he had it and that it had something to do with the UFO crash.

We can point out that Bill Brazel did show the bits to his father, who told him it looked like "some of the contraption I found," which, of course, is still from Bill Brazel, but also does tie it to the debris that Mack had found.

And there is the testimony of Sallye Tadolini, the daughter of Marian Strickland who said that Bill Brazel had shown her some of the debris one day long ago. Here, too, we have an opportunity to point out the duplicity of the Air Force when they created their Roswell report in the mid-1990s. They used part of the affidavit signed by Tadolini, but not all of it.

Quoting from Tadolini's affidavit, the Air Force reported:

What Bill showed us was a piece of what I still think of as fabric. It was something like aluminum foil, something like satin, something like well-tanned leather in its toughness, yet it was not precisely like any one of those materials. While I do not recall this with certainty, I think the fabric measured about four by eight or ten inches. Its edges, which were smooth, were not exactly parallel, and its shape was roughly trapezoidal. It was about the thickness of very fine kidskin glove leather and a dull metallic grayish silver, one side slightly darker than the than the other. I do not remember it having any design or embossing on it.

This is all well and good, and certainly doesn't seem to suggest anything extraordinary. The next paragraph, the one the Air Force didn't reprint, said:

Bill passed it around and we all felt of it. I did a lot of sewing so the feel made a great impression on me. It felt like no fabric I have ever touched before or since. It was very silky or satiny, with the same texture on both sides. Yet when I crumbled it in my hands, the feel was like that you notice when you crumple a leather glove in your hand. When it was released, it sprang back into its original shape, quickly flattening out with no wrinkles. I did this several times as did the others. I remember some of the others stretching it between their hands and "popping" it, but I do not think anyone tried to cut or tear it.

Tommy Tyree, who was the sometimes ranch hand of Mack Brazel said that he had seen a piece of the debris, but he had not retrieved it. He was riding with Mack Brazel when they looked into a sink hole and floating on the water at the bottom was a shiny bit of the debris. It was too far down for them to get to, so Tyree just looked at it.

Frankie Rowe was the daughter of Roswell fire fighter Dan Dwyer. She told me, and has told others since, that she had handled a piece of the debris brought to the firehouse by a New Mexico State Police officer. She said that he was passing it around and that she got to feel it. She mentioned that it returned to its original shape in a fluid motion that she described as like that of quick silver (mercury).

*3.3. Frankie Rowe. Author's photo.*

What we have explored here are some of the facts. Strange debris seen by many, a field filled with it so that it was obvious it came from the sky, and nothing that suggests a craft, other than speculations about what happened. What many have asked about this case, or have suggested, is that we don't know that it came from space because no one had seen it in the sky. At least that was the criticism.

William Woody was a boy in 1947, living on a ranch south of Roswell. Woody, in an affidavit produced for the Fund for UFO Research, said that he had been outside on a hot summer night, working with his father. He said that it was well after sundown when the sky lit up. He said that he saw a very bright object in the southwest, moving to the north:

"The object had the bright white intensity of a blow touch, and had a long, flame-like tail, with the colors of a blow-torch flame fading down into a pale red. Most of the tail was this pale red color. The tail was very long, equal to about 10 diameters of the full moon."

This sounds suspiciously like a meteor, but Woody continued, saying, "We watched the object travel all the way across the sky until it disappeared below the northern horizon. It was moving fast but not as fast as a meteor, and we had it in view for what seemed like 20 to 30 seconds. Its brightness and colors did not change during the whole time...."

Now, if I was following the Air Force rules, or trying to convince everyone that my point of view was correct, I would leave out this next part. Woody, in his affidavit, said, "My father thought it was a big meteorite and was convinced that it had fallen to earth about 40 miles north of Roswell...."

Woody wasn't the only one to report something like that. Corporal E.L. Pyles was stationed at the Roswell Army Air Field in July 1947 and was assigned to the 101st Airways and Communications Service Squadron. Don Schmitt was the first to interview him and wrote in the notes he supplied to me that Pyles was off duty that night. He and a friend, whose name he no longer remembers, was walking across the drill field when he saw what he first thought was a shooting star, but somehow larger. According to the notes, it traveled across the sky, had an orange halo, and arched downward.

Karl Pflock interviewed Pyles some years later and the story, as reported by Pflock, isn't all that dissimilar to what I had written first. Schmitt and I assigned a date, given what we believed were the true statements of Frank Kaufmann, but Pflock makes a big deal out of one of Pyles' comments about the date. Pyles, according to Pflock, said, "I don't even remember the month or the date I saw it.... It seems to me like it was summertime."

Then Pyles mentioned to Pflock that a few days later he saw the newspaper article about the "RAAF Captures Flying Saucer" (July 8, 1947). That pinpoints the date as early July 1947. And though Pyles told Pflock that it was sometime after eight that night, and, given the confusing nature of Pflock's statement, it could have been as late as eleven, though before midnight, what Pyles had told Schmitt and what I reported were essentially the same thing that he told Pflock.

There are, then, two reports of something bright in the sky, and it is quite possible that both witnesses had seen the same thing. It suggests that something was in the sky in the right time frame, but frankly, neither witness saw it hit the ground. It could be a coincidence.

Mack Brazel, after he found the debris, wondered who was going to clean up the mess and finally traveled into Roswell to talk with the local sheriff, George Wilcox. Brazel carried some of the debris with him and showed it to the sheriff, who wasn't sure what to do about it, but suggested he call out to the base. They were responsible for the things in the sky and maybe responsible for cleaning up the messes they made.

On Sunday, July 6th, according to the time lines worked out by UFO researchers, and based on the testimony of Major Jesse Marcel, the air intelligence officer at the Roswell Army Air Field, Brazel drove into Roswell to see the Chaves County Sheriff George Wilcox.

Wilcox's daughter, Phyllis McGuire, told me in a number of interviews that her father dispatched two deputies out to try to find the scene. Here we could run into a jurisdictional problem, because the ranch Brazel managed was in Lincoln County, but Roswell is in Chaves County. McGuire said the deputies came back talking of a burned area on the ground, but no real discussion of metallic debris. They apparently found a site different from the one that Brazel had been describing.

Wilcox wasn't sure what Brazel should do about the debris, but suggested they call out to the base and talk to them. After all, what had fallen was from the sky, which meant it belonged to the Army. Marcel, according to what he would tell interviewers decades later, said that he was finishing his lunch when the call came into the Officer's Club.

*3.4. Sheridan Cavitt. Author's photo.*

Marcel said that he had gone to the sheriff's office to talk to Brazel and then returned to the base. Brazel had some errands and Marcel wanted to talk to his boss, Colonel William Blanchard, the commanding officer. Blanchard would tell Marcel to work with the counter-intelligence corps officer, then Captain Sheridan Cavitt. In two cars, Marcel's convertible and an Army "carryall," they followed Brazel out to the ranch. According to Marcel they stayed that evening in a small outbuilding and the next morning were taken to the debris field. Cavitt would later deny to me that he had spent the night out on the ranch. He would deny that he went anywhere with Brazel. He would deny that he had ever participated in any type of balloon recovery. He would later reverse himself on all of that and more.

Marcel would talk about the strange properties of the debris. According to him, there was a parchment-like substance that would not burn when he held his lighter to it. He talked of some metallic material that was very thin, but they couldn't dent with a sledgehammer. He was quite puzzled by what he was seeing and stumped about the origin of it.

Marcel would later, in a recorded and videotaped interview, say, "It came to Earth but it was not something from Earth.... I was amazed by what I saw."

Cavitt, on the other hand, insisted to me originally that he had not been a participant in any such off-base activities. He told me that he had never bothered with a balloon recovery, and that he and Master Sergeant Lewis Rickett, the NCOIC (Noncommissioned Officer In Charge) of their office, had been too busy with important work (security investigations and the like) to worry about weather balloons. In fact, according to Cavitt, he hadn't even been in Roswell when all these events took place in early July. He insisted that someone had gotten the dates of his arrival in Roswell wrong.

But then his story began to evolve slowly, and he even showed me records documenting that he had just finished his counter-intelligence training and had been assigned to Roswell in June 1947. Given travel time and leave, he said that he wasn't there until the middle of July, but his wife had been there in early July to pick out an apartment and get ready to receive him. Eventually he admitted that he had been there when Brazel went to the sheriff and Marcel went out to the debris field. Cavitt would tell Colonel Richard Weaver, who conducted an official Air Force investigation in the mid-1990s, that he was the man who accompanied Marcel.

When the Air Force investigated the Roswell crash (Weaver visited Cavitt at his home) Cavitt had a new story: Yes, he had gone out with Marcel and found a field filled with strange metallic debris, but he had recognized it immediately. There was no doubt in his mind that it was a weather balloon of some kind.

3.5. *Walter Haut.*
*Author's photo.*

Remember here that this was before Lieutenant Walter Haut had been called by the commanding officer, Colonel William Blanchard, and told to create the press release. This was, according to the reconstructions of the time line, Monday, July 7th. No one had heard that something had fallen near Roswell. No one was talking about a flying saucer near Roswell, though the newspapers were filled with stories of them in many other places. Roswell was just another dusty, dry desert town then.

Standing on that sun-drenched field with the temperature in the high 90s, Cavitt didn't say a word about the identity of the debris to Marcel. He didn't say that he knew it was a balloon. Instead, he returned to the base and kept his mouth shut. He would suggest, as a counter-intelligence agent, that he was outside Blanchard's chain of command, and, though technically correct, it seems that Blanchard would have spoken to both Marcel and Cavitt upon their return. Marcel would be enthusiastic about the strange metallic debris and stumped by its identity. Cavitt, however, told Weaver that he knew immediately that it was a balloon. So why didn't he mention this to Marcel on the field, or to Blanchard when they reported what they had seen? Why would Cavitt fail to let his superiors know that what he had found with Marcel was nothing more dramatic than a balloon? Why let the controversy go?

Blanchard told Haut to alert the local media, and later Haut would not remember if Blanchard gave him the details or had dictated the press release to him. In fact, he wasn't sure whether he talked to Blanchard on the telephone or if he had visited him in his office. That matters little now. Blanchard ordered a press release, and Haut took it into town on July 8, 1947, delivered it to both newspapers and radio stations, and then went home for lunch.

It was a simple and short press release, mentioning that a flying saucer had been captured. No real details available, other than a local rancher had told Sheriff Wilcox who in turn had told Jesse Marcel. Marcel was on his way to his higher headquarters with the wreckage.

Years later, the wording of the release would come into question because it said the saucer was being flown to higher headquarters, and some wanted to know how Marcel had known how to fly it. Haut told researchers that he had meant that Marcel was escorting some of the debris to Fort Worth in one of the 509th's bombers.

Hours later, or sometime around dinner time, Brigadier General Roger Ramey, photographed in front of some debris in his office, said that all the excitement was not warranted. All that had been found was a weather balloon with a rawin radar target. It was made of aluminum foil, balsa, twine, and some fancy tape.

Reporters may have searched for some of those involved in the story. Haut reported that he received telephone calls from around the world, as well as postcards and letters. The phone lines to the base were tied up with incoming calls. Brazel, however, was in custody at the base, Marcel was gone to Fort Worth, and the sheriff refused to answer any questions, telling those who called him to contact the Army.

On July 9th, the *Roswell Daily Record* ran follow-up stories about the crash. In one article, General Ramey explained that debris was merely the remains of a weather balloon that had been misidentified. In the other, Mack Brazel told how he had found the object not a couple of days earlier, but a couple of weeks earlier. He said that the wreckage was made up of "rubber strips, tinfoil, a rather tough paper and sticks." Two weeks later, he, his wife, a son, Vernon, and his daughter, Bessie, went back out to the field and cleaned it all up. In fact, Bessie, interviewed decades later, said that they stored it all in burlap bags under the front porch. There had been nothing in the field for Marcel and Cavitt to find, according to her, and her father had not gone back to Roswell after the initial trip.

The article said that on Monday, July 7th, after learning about flying saucers, Brazel, thinking he might have found parts of one, took it to Roswell to show the sheriff. He had gone to town to sell some wool and had gone over to the sheriff's office. The sheriff, in turn, alerted the Army and Jesse Marcel.

Brazel, according to the interview, had not seen anything fall from the sky, and there was no talk of a strange explosion in a thunderstorm. He didn't know what size or shape the object had been, but thought it must have been about 12 feet long. The rubber was smoky gray and scattered over an area of about 200 yards.

According to the article, "When the debris was gathered up the tinfoil, paper, tape and sticks made up a bundle about three feet long and 7 or 8 inches thick, while the rubber made a bundle about 18 or 20 inches long and about 8 inches thick. In all, he estimated the entire lot would have weighed maybe five pounds."

Brazel said that he had found weather balloons on two other occasions, but what he had found that time didn't resemble them in any way. He added, "I am sure what I found was not any weather observation balloon."

That was the way the Roswell case stayed for decades: some kind of balloon that had been misidentified by the rancher, the sheriff, and the officers at the air base. There were a few brief mentions of it in some obscure publications or in books that reached researchers and investigators, but always with the exposé of *Behind the Flying Saucers* in the background, suggesting that stories of UFO crashes were untrue. No one was interested.

Except Len Stringfield, a UFO researcher from Ohio. Stringfield began to collect tales of flying saucer crashes. Then Jesse Marcel, living in Houma, Louisiana, and retired from repairing TVs and radios, began to tell friends and ham radio operators that he had picked up pieces of a flying saucer many years earlier. One of those was a station manager in New Orleans who mentioned to Stan Friedman, who was being interviewed about his UFO research, that he should talk to Marcel. This was 1978, more than 30 years after the events in Roswell.

Marcel said that he couldn't remember the exact date, but provided enough details that research could begin. Friedman told both Len Stringfield and William L. Moore, a fellow investigator. The research began with the newspapers in June 1947 and worked on from there. On July 9th, there were pictures of Jesse Marcel in Brigadier General Ramey's office, holding the remains of what looked exactly like what Ramey said it was: a rawin target and a weather balloon.

Now there was some documentation about the event. True, the newspapers, and the military, quickly accepted the weather balloon story, but, unlike so many other crash retrieval stories, here was evidence that something had happened and that something dealt with a craft that might have come from another planet.

But those leads, from Marcel and from the newspapers, took us in a new direction. We learned that Mack Brazel had been interviewed for a report for the radio. Judd Roberts had been the minority owner of radio station KGFL in 1947, and he told me on several occasions

that the first, most interesting interview with Brazel was never broadcast. Orders from members of the New Mexico congressional delegation called majority owner Walt Whitmore and warned that if they played the interview with Brazel then they could begin looking for something else to do. Their license to broadcast would be pulled.

*3.6. Judd Roberts, Roswell. Author's photo.*

Roberts said that the interview contained information about the crash. He said that, once they had finished the recording, Whitmore took Brazel out to the base because he thought they might be interested in talking to him. And that would be when they decided to keep Mack Brazel on ice.

It was on July 9th that Brazel, now under military escort, was taken to the offices of the *Roswell Daily Record,* where he was interviewed and gave the description of the weather balloon. It was during this trip to the newspaper that Mack Brazel's friends, including Floyd Proctor, saw him in town. Proctor suggested that Brazel didn't seem happy about it.

Bessie Brazel, a daughter, interviewed years later by John Kirby and Don Neuman, said that her father had not gone back into Roswell, that he hadn't been alone at the ranch in July, and that she, with her father, had gathered up all the debris. They put it all in burlap bags and stored them under the porch.

Skeptics have reported, frequently, on what Bessie Brazel said, never questioning her testimony on this point. It made no difference that others— Jesse Marcel, Sr., Edwin Easley, Judd Roberts, and the Brazel neighbors—all said that Mack Brazel had been in town. Even the newspaper story written at the time proved that Mack Brazel had been in town on the days that she said he was at home. Bessie said no, and her word, because it was what they wanted to hear, ruled.

In fact, many years later, in discussions with her brother, Bill, she would suggest that maybe she had been confused. The recovery of the balloon was something that happened on another occasion. And the evidence and testimony suggested that she had been confused.

Now we return to William Woody, the young man who said that he had seen the object, or rather an object, in the air. He told me that a couple of days later, when they had the chance, he and his father had driven out, north of Roswell, looking for the object, whatever it was. He said that off to the west, along the dirt roads leading into the desert, they saw a military cordon. Soldiers were stopping the traffic and turning the cars around.

Woody wasn't the only one to report this. Judd Roberts said that he and Whitmore, the radio station owners, had tried to do the same thing, but came to a military car and soldiers blocking the road. They were turning back everyone.

Lewis Rickett, the NCO who worked with Cavitt, said that they too had run into a military cordon, but because of who they were, they were allowed to pass. Cavitt would later claim that there had been no military cordons when interviewed by Colonel Weaver, but it is clear from the testimony of many others that the cordons did exist and that those not authorized were not allowed to pass. These witness, all of whom made statements on tape, included Rickett, Woody, Roberts, and Dr. Bertram Schultz, who had been in Roswell doing research and noticed the cordons off the road to the west. Because he didn't want to go in that direction, he didn't care about them. He just had seen them and wondered what was going on.

Rickett, in fact, would go farther than just talk of the cordon. He said that he had seen some of the metallic debris. When they had reached one of the crash areas, this one about 45 minutes or so north of Roswell, they got out of the car. Laying around was some of the metallic debris. Rickett asked Cavitt if the metal was "hot"—meaning, was it radioactive? He was told that no signs of radioactivity had been detected.

Rickett said that he found one piece that was about 2 feet square and he crouched to pick it up. It was slightly curved. He locked it against his knee and used his arm to try to bend it. The metal was very thin and lightweight, but he could not bend it.

So, suddenly, the number of people who were in Roswell in July 1947 and who had both handled the debris and who had seen the military cordon grew to include members of the military. These were reliable witnesses who reluctantly told their stories and whose descriptions of events generally matched one another. Unfortunately, as the case became bigger and received more attention, others came forward to tell their tales. But they were inventing them.

A witness with a story that I originally found plausible was Frank Kaufmann. I called Kaufmann for the first time on January 4, 1990, told him that I was looking into the flying saucer event of July 1947, and asked if he had been involved in some fashion.

His response, which would become typical of him, was, "Well...I don't know."

*3.7. Frank Kaufmann.*

He hinted during that first conversation *Author's photo.* that he knew a little more and for the first time introduced a warrant officer named Robert Thomas, who would eventually evolve into a general who had been traveling in 1947 as a warrant officer. A general arriving at Roswell, especially after the announcement they had found a flying saucer, would be big news. A warrant officer coming in wouldn't stir much interest.

Kaufmann was cagey, though he admitted to having seen the 1989 *Unsolved Mysteries* broadcast about the crash. He suggested that they were mostly right, but he objected to the Jesse Marcel story of taking debris home to show the family. Kaufmann said that it would have been classified before Marcel went to pick it up. He was saying the military had more information than they had admitted.

Over the next several years, Kaufmann granted more interviews and finally said that he had been deeply involved, that he was on the inside, and that he had helped plan the retrieval and the cover-up. He would provide some documents to prove his case, and suggested that he had more and better documents that he would release some time later. He did show me a couple of those and one of them, if it could be believed, was the smoking gun. It was from Major Edwin Easley, the provost marshal, and it discussed the retrieval operation and suggested the craft was from another world. The date was late 1947, and there would be no way to counter such an explosive document if it could be authenticated.

Kaufmann's tale unraveled after he died. Among his papers were found original documents, as well as the forgeries that proved he was lying. For example, he had made it clear that he was a former master sergeant who had specialized intelligence training. His military records showed that he had been a staff sergeant with training in administration, but no intelligence courses. The document he had showed to prove his claims was not the same as the original found later. Clearly he had fabricated one.

And the letter from Easley? It too was bogus. Office symbols (by office symbols, I mean the acronyms that designate various government and military organizations) used in it, though accurate, were agencies that had not existed in 1947. This became just one more bit of misinformation to clutter the landscape.

So Kaufmann's story fell apart. The details didn't match his claims, and there was no reason to believe that he had been an insider. None of those he named as having been with him were ever found, though he had given us some names and even provided the hometowns of a couple. No corroboration for his wild tales meant that we could now reject his story as pure invention. I mentioned it here because the record on Kaufmann needs to be set straight.

That doesn't mean that other witnesses can't be found and that the stories of some of those earlier witnesses can't be corroborated, at least to some extent. The investigation has continued with new revelations about some of the old witnesses. Frankie Rowe, for example, has been attacked for years with all sorts of allegations being made about her story, what her father told her, and even what her father did for a living.

In 2008 and 2009, Tony Bragalia and I had been exploring various facets of the Roswell UFO crash case with an eye to verify and corroborate some of the testimony that witnesses have offered. New information from a Roswell firefighter has surfaced that not only corroborates part of what Frankie Rowe reported, but that confirmed that he, the firefighter, believed that what crashed had not been built on Earth. It also suggests that others in Roswell, including Sheriff George Wilcox and City Manager C.M. Woodbury, knew about the event.

The firefighter, once part of Karl Pflock's attempts to reduce Rowe's testimony to nothing, and who is now 90, told both Bragalia and me, in separate interviews, that he remembered the incident. Contrary to what had been reported by other researchers, including the late Karl Pflock, there had been a crash and there had been a visit from an Army officer to tell the firefighters their help wasn't needed.

J.C. Smith told us that a colonel from the base had come into the fire department and told those on duty that "an unknown object from some place else" had crashed outside the city. He told them that the military would take care of it and that they were not to tell anyone what they had heard. He told them that no one needed to go out to the site. This, of course, explains why there is no record of a trip out to the site. They were told not to go, and the majority of them didn't.

When I interviewed him, he was more than a little irritated that I seemed to be asking the same questions over and over, but it was only to verify the information. What he was saying to both Bragalia and me was that the fire department hadn't been involved in the retrieval operation, but that some of them knew it had taken place.

Then I asked a question that Pflock might not have asked. I wanted to know if he knew Dan Dwyer, Rowe's father, and learned that he did. I asked about Dwyer making a run outside the city, and that was when I learned of the "colonel" who had advised against it.

Then he said that Dwyer, in his personal car, did drive out to the crash site. Dwyer, and not the fire department, went out there, which explains why there is no record, and why some of the other fire fighters didn't remember it.

Pflock had used him as a witness to prove that the Roswell Fire Department had not made a run outside the city, and that Frankie Rowe's story could not be corroborated. It seemed that I was getting the same story until I asked about Dan Dwyer, and it was then that he told me that Dwyer had gone out in his personal car. Pflock, apparently, didn't ask that question.

The retired firefighter was quite clear about these points. They had been visited by an officer from the base, they had been told not to go out there, and Dwyer, in his personal car, did.

He then said that the Roswell Army Air Field Fire Department was involved in the crash recovery. The firefighter said that this was where the confusion comes from. The city department didn't go out, but the base fire department did.

What is surprising here is that this man is cited by Karl Pflock as one of those he interviewed. Pflock accurately reported that the city fire department hadn't made a run, but that wasn't the whole story. Somehow Pflock missed the part of Dan Dwyer driving out in his own car, and that Dwyer later told the firefighter what he had seen. That information tends to corroborate, independently, the story that Frankie Rowe has been telling for nearly two decades.

Bragalia has his notes on what the firefighter told him, and I have my interview on tape. When someone says I misquoted the firefighter, I can play the tapes. When someone challenges what I have written, I can play the tapes. More than once I have proven my point with tapes.

Another woman who has been attacked by the skeptics is Lydia Sleppy, secretary of radio station KOAT in Albuquerque, who was taking some dictation over the telephone from Johnny McBoyle, a reporter for the station. McBoyle was telling her of a crashed flying saucer that he said looked like a crushed dishpan. As she was putting the information on the wire, that transmission was interrupted with an order to cease immediately.

The first known publication of the Sleppy story came in 1974 in the old *SAGA UFO Report*. That article said, in its entirety, "...[I]n New Mexico, a woman with a responsible position at a radio station received a call from the station manager. He had been out checking reports of a UFO which had crashed in a field and was trying to track down the rumor that pieces of the object were supposedly stored in a local barn. In his excited call to the newsroom, the station manager verified the UFO crash report, and also claimed he had seen metallic pieces of the UFO being carried into a waiting Air Force plane which was destined for Wright-Patterson Air Force Base.

"As the woman began typing out the fantastic news item over the teletype to their other two radio stations, a line appeared in the middle of her text, tapped in from somewhere, with the official order: *'Do not continue this transmission!'*"

The next appearance of Sleppy, as far as I know, was in *The Roswell Incident* by Charles Berlitz and William Moore. They write:

Understandably bemused, Lydia placed the phone in the uncomfortable position between ear and shoulder and started to type McBoyle's startling statements into the teletype. But after she had typed only several sentences the machine suddenly stopped itself. As this was a common occurrence with teletypes for a variety of reasons, Lydia was not concerned, though she had never been cut off the air before in the middle of a transmission....

...Moving the telephone from her neck to her hand, she informed McBoyle that the teletype had stopped at her end.

This time, according to her recollections, he seemed not only excited but under pressure and apparently speaking to someone else at the same time. His voice seem strained. "Wait a minute, I'll get back to you... Wait... I'll get right back." But he did not. Instead the teletype went on again by itself and started addressing Albuquerque, or Lydia directly. The sender was not identified and the tone was formal and curt: ATTENTION ALBUQUERQUE: DO NOT TRANSMIT. REPEAT DO NOT TRANSMIT THIS MESSAGE. STOP COMMUNICATION IMMEDIATELY.

Note here that the FBI has not entered the case and, although there are people quoted by Berlitz and Moore, it is not indicated if those people said those things, if it was one person quoting someone else, or if it was exactly what Sleppy had told to Moore and Berlitz.

In *Crash at Corona* by Stan Friedman and Don Berliner, we learn something interesting. They write:

While he [meaning Johnny McBoyle here] refused to discuss the matter even after almost half a century, another principal has been found. Lydia Sleppy, the teletype operator whose message was interrupted so mysteriously. Long thought to have died, she was located by Stanton Friedman in October 1990 and interviewed.

Apparently Friedman had forgotten that he and Bobbi Slate had used the Sleppy story long ago (or even he failed to make the connection after he began his Roswell research).

The critical paragraph in that interview is:

I went back and asked Mr. [Karl] Lambertz (he came up from the big Dallas station) if he would come up and watch. John [McBoyle] was dictating and [Karl] was standing right at my shoulder. I got into it enough to know that it was a pretty big story, when the bell came on [signaling an interruption]. Typing came across: "This is the FBI, you will cease transmitting."

Now we have the FBI involved, but there is nothing to suggest where that came from. Sometime between the publication of *The Roswell Incident* and the investigations that began in the 1990s, Sleppy became convinced that it was the FBI who had interrupted her.

When I interviewed Sleppy, she told me:

> *I called Mr. Lambertz, Karl Lambertz, who was acting in Mr. Tucker's place [that would be Merle Tucker, the station owner who was away on business].... He was the program director. I called Mr. Lambertz up, there was something coming through and I had just started—I don't know how much I typed but I was typing what John [Johnny McBoyle] dictated when the signal came on that this was the FBI and we [should] cease transmitting.*

I asked if she knew what FBI office, but she didn't. She said, "It was the FBI that stopped us."

Karl Pflock, in his *Roswell: Inconvenient Facts and the Will to Believe*, wrote:

> Subsequently, I did some further investigating. Merle Tucker told me the Teletype in KOAT's office [that is the Albuquerque office of his fledgling radio empire] had both a send and receive capability, but did not know if it was possible for an incoming message to be automatically printed on it without some enabling action being taken first. I was told by several journalistic old-timers that in the 1940s send-and-receive Teletypes definitely had to be manually set in one mode or the other. If a machine was set to send, it could not receive an incoming message. A bell would ring to alert someone to switch over to receive.

The implication here is clear. The Sleppy tale can be discounted because there had to have been a warning bell, and she would then have to flip a switch.

Sometime between Sleppy first appearing in the old *UFO Report* and later in *The Roswell Incident* and the 1990s, she added the note about the FBI. I don't know if this was something she remembered, if it was something someone suggested to her and she incorporated into her story, or if it is a bit of confabulation. In the end, it might not be an important fact, other than to suggest that memories are fallible and we must be careful when interviewing witnesses after decades have passed.

The important facts, though, are these. Lydia Sleppy told this story to researchers prior to the publication of *The Roswell Incident,* and she was quoted in that book, and in the magazine article. She told us all that her transmission was interrupted and she was told to cease that transmission. Karl Pflock and Kal Korff told us there was a mechanism for interrupting transmissions, but it required that the operator then make a manual change. Sleppy told Friedman, prior to Pflock's and Korff's criticism, "*...when the bell came on [signaling an interruption]* [emphasis added]."

In fact, in the affidavit, published in Pflock's book (and gathered by the Fund for UFO Research) Sleppy said, "As I typed McBoyle's story, a bell rang on the teletype, indicating an interruption. The machine then printed a message something to this effect, "THIS IS THE FBI. YOU WILL IMMEDIATELY CEASE ALL COMMUNICATION."

In other words, Pflock and Korff were right about a signaling bell, and Sleppy mentioned that in her interview with Friedman, and later in her affidavit. She would have then made the manual switch and the result would have been the message typed out in the middle of the story that she was putting on the teletype. The fact that she mentioned that bell in two separate interviews is important. Both Pflock and Korff who wrote their books after this information was available, and that Pflock actually has it in his book is interesting. It suggests they were interested in dismissing testimony rather than finding facts.

Nothing has been offered that disqualifies the Sleppy testimony. She told the tale prior to the overwhelming interest in Roswell and that is documented. She told us that her transmission was interrupted and said that there was a bell to alert her to incoming transmissions. No, she didn't say that she flipped the switch, but clearly she did.

There is also testimony from new witnesses that provides more insight into the Roswell case. In fact, there are so many witnesses now that it seems impossible to reject the idea that something highly unusual fell outside of Roswell. One of those new witnesses, discovered recently, is Harry Cordes.

We know that 1st Lt. Harry N. Cordes served with the 509th Bomb Group in Roswell in 1947, specifically with the 393rd Bomb Squadron. His picture is in the yearbook that Walter Haut prepared. According

3.8. Brigadier General Harry N. Cordes, Roswell. Photo courtesy of the U.S. Air Force.

to his official Air Force biography, in 1946 General Cordes [as a lieutenant] participated in the first atomic bomb tests at Bikini Atoll. From 1946 to 1949 he was assigned to the 509th Bombardment Group, Roswell Air Force Base, New Mexico, as a radar observer on a B-29 crew. His crew won the first annual SAC bombing competition in 1948. He entered pilot training in August 1949 and when he graduated in 1950 returned to the 509th Bomb Group as a pilot, and he was later aircraft commander of a B-50 (which is a glorified B-29). He served in a variety of assignments after he left Roswell, and eventually, as a brigadier general, assumed duties as deputy chief of staff, intelligence, at the Headquarters of the Strategic Air Command (SAC), Offutt Air Force Base, in April 1970. He retired on July 1, 1973, and he died on May 10, 2004.

Cordes has been reported as saying that when he was assigned to the CIA, one of the first things he had done was look for the Roswell files, but they were missing. It is an interesting statement, but by itself means little.

Tony Bragalia decided to follow up on this. He located Cordes's widow, who told him that she was surprised that Cordes would say anything like that to anyone outside the family. But then she went on and confirmed the fact, saying that he told her that he had unsuccessfully tried to find the Roswell crash file back in the 1950s.

According to the notes that Bragalia shared with me, as a lieutenant, Cordes admired Jesse Marcel, Sr. (who was an intelligence officer, and Cordes would find himself assigned to intelligence later in his career) and said that there was no reason for him to lie about anything. She said that Glenn Dennis's nurse had been committed to a home before she died. She told Bragalia in her discussions with him that Blanchard was "a believer and anyone in the military who wanted to stay in didn't talk about it (meaning the crash retrieval operation)."

Because she had grown up on a farm near Roswell and had worked in the First National Bank there, she knew many of the players in this story, knew some things about the case outside the military. She said that she had lived two doors down from the Wilcox family and said that they "were threatened and were afraid for their own reasons."

Working in the bank she heard things from the ranchers and wrote in an e-mail about some of this to Bragalia. "At the bank I heard the ranchers discussing Mack Brazel and they thought his new red pickup was his payoff."

But her story wasn't just about what she had heard in the bank. She wrote:

My story begins the night of July 3rd with my family in Ruidoso where we always celebrated the 4th and I had to close the bank and was tasked with icing the soda and beer and driving to meet them. As I made the usual rounds for ice I was told that the Air Base had bought all the ice so I went to the train station looking for dry ice but was told the AFB had wiped them out....

She added:

Then when our family returned that week to go back to our ranch to attend to our stock we were barred from the Pine Lodge hiway by camaflogued [sic] airmen with machine guns that some fear entered the picture. Many stories at the bank from early rising ranchers about long trucks covered in canvas going to the base before dawn!!

She also said:

My husband flew 25 different planes including the U-2 and Airborne [sic] Looking Glass [which was the airborne command post during the Cold War] and said there was nothing hidden at Area-51 except planes. He also wondered his whole life why there was a cover-up and yes, he did tell me that he perused the files as a CIA agent but found everything empty.

I will note here that there is nothing in Cordes official biography that suggests he was detailed to the CIA, but, by the same token, there are gaps in it. However, after his completion of Command and Staff School, he was assigned as an intelligence staff officer, which could mean he worked with the CIA and would have had some access to their records.

In the end, we have an intriguing story that begins with a quote from a former Air Force brigadier general and then we have additional information from his wife. Firsthand quotes from the general, firsthand quotes and observations from the wife, and then her memories of things her husband had shared with her. Maybe not the smoking gun, but certainly interesting testimony to add to the stack.

There are still other avenues of corroboration for some of this story. As mentioned earlier, I interviewed Loretta Procter a number of times on both audiotape and videotape. She told me, as she told many others, that she, along with her husband, Floyd, had a chance to see a small piece of the debris recovered by Mack Brazel, but had never bothered to drive down to the debris field. So, she didn't see the field in 1947, but there are indications that her young son, William "Dee" Proctor, who was with Brazel on the morning he found the debris, did. In fact, all this might have happened as Brazel took Dee home that day so that he had a chance to talk to the Proctors about the crash.

Dee Proctor never really talked to investigators about the event. I spoke with him twice, both times briefly and both times by accident. He did confirm that he had been with Brazel and that military authorities had talked to him in the days that followed the discovery. In fact, it was clear that he had not only been there, but he had taken some friends out there with him. He would not say what the military told him, nor would he say much about what he had seen, other than to say that it was a field with metallic debris and the remnants of a craft. It was clear that these experiences with the military left a lasting impression on him, which guided what he said for the remainder of his life.

Of course, these vague descriptions tell us nothing of the nature of the object that crashed. He also said that the craft was of extraterrestrial origin, though those words came from the older man 50 years later and not the 7-year-old boy in 1947.

Proctor died in January 2006 at age 65. He had always been a somewhat reclusive man, quick to anger and reticent to talk about these events. In 1996, he took his mother to a bluff about 10 or so miles from their ranch house and about 2 1/2 miles from the debris field. He told her that was the field in which more than just debris had been found. Any trace of the craft or its impact was long gone in 1996.

In this case, we have talked about strange debris, the number of witnesses who saw it, military reaction and cordons around the area, and a changing story that smacks of something bigger. In fact, a review of the newspapers of the era show that prior to July 8th, there is discussion about what the flying saucers might be. There is speculation from the highest levels of government and the military, to the scientific community, and almost anyone else who has anything to say. Everyone has an opinion, and those run from spots in front of the eyes to alien creatures from other worlds. There is no single theory about this.

But then, suddenly, on July 9th, there was a new crop of stories reported by the Associated Press. The lead suggests that "The Army and Navy moved today to suppress the stories of flying saucers whizzing through the atmosphere." The question becomes: "Why, on that date, did they suddenly care about the speculation in the newspapers?"

The answer is simple. They had an alien spacecraft and they knew that it was not something built on the Earth. We know, for example, that Jesse Marcel, Sr., said that it was something that had come to Earth, but that was not built on Earth. We had the descriptions of the debris that seemed to defy analysis. What we didn't have was much of a paper trail that lead to that conclusion.

To move directly to the extraterrestrial, we need something more than strange metallic debris and government reaction to the report of a UFO crash. Most of the stories that mention bodies are either secondhand or have been discredited. One of the few to withstand scrutiny is that of Thomas Gonzales, a sergeant stationed in Roswell in 1947.

Gonzales told John Price and Don Ecker that he had seen the bodies of the alien creatures. He was a sergeant in the transportation section, but, as the military swept through the base looking for all available men for guard duty, Gonzales was drafted.

Gonzales described the craft as looking more like an airfoil than it did like a saucer. He said that the bodies were like "little men" but not like the "greys" of the more recent abduction literature. He was careful to make that distinction.

Gonzales, when I interviewed him, was reluctant to talk, and I fear that my style in this particular interview was more forceful than it needed to be. I was attempting to verify his credentials, though his picture in the Roswell Yearbook certainly put him at the base at the right time. And I wanted to make sure that the information that I had was correct. It had been filtered a couple of times, and sometimes during the passing of information, it becomes distorted. That didn't seem to be the case here.

Unfortunately, Gonzales was not an articulate man, and, when I talked to him more than a dozen years ago, he was 78. His son said that his father had been telling the story for years, long before the information about Roswell became well known. Gonzales's son verified a date in the 1960s as being one of the first times he'd heard his father mention the Roswell case.

Gonzales also mentioned that he had trouble with the military after he was involved there. He suggested he was transferred quickly and, in the process, lost some personal property. The rumor is that many of those involved were quickly transferred from the base. However, the unit history provides information about transfers into and out of the 509th. The records seem to indicate that there was not an appreciable increase in transfers in July or August. The numbers remained consistent with those of earlier months. This does not mean, however, that specific people weren't transferred out.

It is clear from the description that Gonzales gave that the occupants of the craft were not human, and they certainly weren't some kind of primate that had been shaved and stuffed into a flight suit.

*3.9. Gonzales alien wood carvings, Roswell. Photo courtesy of Don Ecker.*

The Roswell crash case, as seen here, is the biggest, is the best researched, and has many reliable witnesses. There is documentation for it, some of it just coming out, as Tony Bragalia has found in a FOIA request from the Battelle Memorial Institute. His information, released in August 2009, suggests that some of the metallic debris that had been taken to Wright Field was passed on to scientists at Battelle for reverse engineering.

In a special report Bragalia posted to the Internet and shared with UFO researchers, he wrote:

> A research study that has recently been obtained through FOIA offers stunning confirmation that Wright-Patterson Air Force base contracted Battelle Memorial Institute to analyze material from a crashed UFO at Roswell in 1947. Remarkably, the co-author of this very metals study is the same scientist who decades ago had confessed that he had examined extraterrestrial metal from a crashed UFO while he was a research scientist at Battelle!
>
> This just-received document also reveals that another one of its metallurgist authors reported directly to a Battelle scientist who was conducting secret UFO studies for the USAF. It appears that the study represents first-ever attempts in creating highly novel and advanced Titanium alloys. Some of these alloys were later associated with the development of "memory metal" of the type reported as crash debris at Roswell.
>
> This 1949 Battelle research study had never before been publicly available until earlier this month. Its release was compelled under the Freedom of Information Act (FOIA.) It was sought because references to it had been found as footnotes within later military-sponsored studies on shape-memory alloys such as Nitinol. It was previously believed to be "missing" because both Battelle and Wright historians were unable to locate it. Earlier research had revealed a paper trail that led from Roswell to Wright Patterson, to the doors of Battelle—and to this 1949 study.
>
> Once received, investigators were astounded to learn that the sought study was in fact co-authored by none other than Elroy John Center. Center was a Battelle scientist who—in June of 1960—had privately related that he had analyzed metal from a fallen UFO when he was at the Institute. Citations that had been found to this Battelle report had not listed Center as a co-author. When the report was finally received, Center was revealed to be an "et al" or "and others" author of the study. Center's story about examining ET debris was first publicly told in 1992. But it was not known that Center was the co-author of this Battelle study until it was obtained under FOIA in August of 2009!

The trail, then, is becoming cluttered with evidence. Witnesses are telling what they saw. Documents are surfacing, giving us a glimpse into the workings behind the scenes. And the Air Force is working to prevent us from reaching the truth.

We are left with this story, told by reliable people who corroborate one another. These range from the people who had the experiences to family members who relate what their fathers, brothers, and husbands saw. A story of highly strange material that isn't explained by either a weather balloon or the Project Mogul solution, which is, in essence, the weather balloon answer in a different form. Something strange fell, and it has yet to be identified. There is a very good chance that it was extraterrestrial. We have yet to find the absolute solution, or the absolute smoking gun, but someday we will.

## July 5, 1947

### PLAINS OF SAN AGUSTIN

The connection between the crash of an alien spacecraft near Roswell, New Mexico, and events on the Plains of San Agustin in July 1947, was drawn by Barney Barnett. Or rather, the connection was drawn by the original investigators talking to friends and relatives of Barnett, who then assumed that the Barnett report had something to do with the Roswell case.

During those early investigations, the only story of crashed craft and bodies came from Barney Barnett. Witnesses to the debris field, the area 75 miles northwest of Roswell, included Mack Brazel and Jesse Marcel, Sr., and witnesses to the material picked up there included Brazel's neighbors and Marcel's fellow officers. There are, literally, dozens of people who saw and handled the debris, but only Barnett talked of seeing a craft and the bodies of the alien flight crew.

Unfortunately, Barnett died before anyone had the opportunity to interview him. Investigators were forced to rely on the information as reported by family and friends of Barnett. Alice Knight, Vern Maltais, Harold Baca, and J.F. "Fleck" Danley all reported that Barnett had mentioned the story of the crashed alien ship to them. All of them spoke of Barnett in the highest terms; all said that he was a reliable, fine man who was not given to practical jokes or one who told tall tales.

According to those friends, Barnett said that he had been driving through the desert when a flash of light caught his attention. He turned toward it and came upon a crashed, disk-shaped object. Maltais said that Barnett told him that the craft was metallic, dull gray, and "pretty good sized." According to Maltais, Barnett thought it had burst open as it slammed into a low ridge line. There was almost no wreckage scattered around the damaged ship. Barnett also said that he saw the flight crew. The beings were small, with pear-shaped heads, skinny arms and legs, and no hair. All wore metallic-like, form-fitting, silver "flight suits" without buttons or zippers.

While on the site, Barnett said he was joined by a handful of archaeologists. They did not approach the craft or the bodies as he had. He'd gotten closest, standing over one of the bodies. Before they could do much more, the military arrived, warned them that what they had seen was classified top secret, and then escorted them from the site.

It is not clear if Barnett ever told anyone exactly where he'd seen the craft. Those he did speak to thought that he'd mentioned the Plains of San Agustin, west of Socorro, New Mexico, and about 125 miles from Corona and the debris field discovered by Mack Brazel.

That was where the story ended. Investigation failed to find a single, first-hand witness to an event on the Plains. There were others, such as Robert Drake, who told of a trip into the Plains area in the summer of 1947. Drake, though he didn't see anything himself, did speak to a cowboy who told him of the crash of some kind of spacecraft out, somewhere, on the Plains.

Drake provided two other sources of information. According to him, students at Chaco Canyon, an archaeological site about a hundred miles north of the Plains, returned from a July 4th holiday talking of a spacecraft crash. He also mentioned Roscoe Wilmeth, a document clerk who worked at the Los Alamos National Laboratory, and who claimed that he'd seen a file that mentioned a crashed craft and alien bodies. Wilmeth told Drake that he wanted to travel to the "body" site. Drake, as well as others, interpreted that to mean he wanted to go to the Plains of San Agustin.

According to Drake, he had been making a preliminary survey of the Bat Cave on the southeastern edge of the Plains with Dr. Wesley Hurt, Dan McKnight, and Albert Dittert in July 1947. On the way back to Albuquerque, they stopped at a ranch. Drake, while searching for land snails, talked to a cowboy who told him of the crash. On the way back to Albuquerque, Drake, along with the others, discussed the story told by the old cowboy. Drake no longer remembers who that cowboy might have been.

But Hurt, McKnight, and Dittert, all interviewed by Kevin Randle or Tom Carey, said they remembered nothing about such a conversation. In fact, Hurt said that he'd heard nothing about an alien spaceship crash on the Plains until researchers began to call him around 1980. Neither had McKnight nor Dittert. Only Drake recalled the event. When questioned about it, Drake said that it hadn't been a topic of discussion on the way back to Albuquerque, as he had originally said. Of course, no one had a clue who the anonymous cowboy who talked to Drake might be.

3.10. Tom Carey (center) at the Brazel crash site. Author's photo.

Carey, in his research, also located a number of students who had been at the Chaco Canyon site in July 1947. Flying saucers and crashed disks had not been discussed. Instead, they all had engaged in a cooling-off period. There had been an incident involving fireworks that had angered some of the students. That had been the topic of discussion.

When all the data about the Drake testimony is examined, it is clear that it fails to meet even the most lenient standards. Of all those interviewed, only Drake remembers the events he speaks of, even though others were involved. Those others fail to recall the events the way he does.

The other corroborating witness, Roscoe Wilmeth, was never interviewed. He died days before he returned from a vacation that would have allowed researchers to speak with him. His secondhand testimony doesn't corroborate an event on the Plains because he spoke of going to the body site; it was others who made the assumption that he was talking about a site on the Plains.

It wasn't as if there hadn't been a search for archaeologists on the Plains. Several were identified as having worked on the Plains during the summer of 1947. Herbert Dick, making a preliminary survey of the Bat Cave, arrived in the very beginning of July, according to records found at Harvard. He told various researchers that he knew nothing of a flying saucer crash. He also knew many of the ranchers in the area and spoke to them frequently, but none of them mentioned any crash of a spacecraft.

*3.11. Don Schmitt on the Plains with Bat Cave in the ridge behind him. Author's photo.*

In a letter dated December 14, 1947 to his colleague, Dr. J.O. Brew, and now housed in Peabody Museum of Archaeology and Ethnology at Harvard University, Herbert Dick wrote, "Our party proceeded to the Plains of San Augustin (sic) on July 1, 1947. We went immediately to the 'Y' Ranch, owned by the Hubbell Cattle Company...."

What this tells us is that Dick would have been in a position to see anything going on over on the Plains in July 1947, because he was at the Bat Cave. This was on the "Y" ranch, and, according to the information available, Dick and his party camped on the flat ground about 150 yards from the cave, which, itself is about 100 feet above the Plains. The campsite provided a 180-degree view for miles that included Datil, the Tularosa Mountains, and the San Francisco Mountains. In other words, they were on the eastern side of the Plains and could see across them to the Horse Springs site that Gerald Anderson had selected as the spot the UFO crashed.

Dick and group were there from early July and, although he was contacted by several UFO investigators, including Tom Carey and me, he denied that he had seen anything.

No firsthand sources were located who saw anything on the Plains. All the archaeologists who were there in the summer of 1947 said they had heard and seen nothing. The ranchers in the area, including Dave Farr, who owns the ranch where Gerald Anderson claimed the saucer crashed, say they had heard nothing about a crashed saucer until recently. The single exception was John Foard, who told me that he knew nothing firsthand, but remembered someone, at some time, talking about

*3.12. Anderson crash site, plains of San Augustin. Author's photo.*

a flying saucer crash. In other words, his information was secondhand, at best.

With the elimination of Drake, Anderson, and the archaeologists, the only source for an event on the Plains was Barney Barnett. Then the Barnett story suffered a major set back.

Alice Knight, a niece of Ruth Barnett, found a diary for 1947 that had been kept by her aunt. There is nothing in it during the month of July that gives any hint that Barney was involved in, saw, or was chased from the site of a flying saucer crash. He had been out of the office on July 2nd, and as far west as Pie Town, which is west of Datil and close to the Arizona border, on July 8th. On the other days, Barnett was in his office or at home in Socorro.

What this means is that the story about Barnett, related by others, does not track with the established facts. The diary takes Barnett out of the picture. What it doesn't do is explain how Barnett knew about the archaeologists. Clearly archaeologists were involved in the case. They weren't on the Plains, but they were involved.

This however, is a minor point. There were articles about flying saucer crashes published in the news magazines in 1950. The stories related to Frank Scully's *Behind the Flying Saucers*. It's not known if this is the source of Barnett's tale, or if he actually saw something on the Plains in 1947. That book could be the source of the contamination.

For a while it seemed that there was new life in the Barnett story. A firsthand witness had been found. Responding to the request for more information that followed the *Unsolved Mysteries* segment about Roswell, Gerald Anderson telephoned the call center and said that he might have some information that would be helpful. He was given my address, and he sent me a letter telling me that he might be able to help with the names of the archaeologists and he could provide some information about the crash site. He said that he had been there.

Some of the most damaging evidence added to Anderson's story is Dr. Buskirk. Anderson claimed his name was Adrian (or rather, that was the name in the diary) and that he had been the leader of the archaeological expedition. Not content with providing a name, Anderson made an identikit sketch of Buskirk.

In June 1991, Tom Carey located the only Dr. Buskirk in anthropology or archaeology. His name was Winfred and not Adrian, but he was the only Buskirk who had any sort of anthropological credentials.

Carey discovered that Buskirk had published a book on the western Apache in 1986 and wrote to the publisher, asking for a copy of the dust jacket. Using the photo on it, and Anderson's identikit sketch, Carey discovered that Winfred Buskirk was the man that Anderson had been describing.

When Buskirk was contacted in June 1991, he denied that he had been on the Plains of San Agustin during the summer of 1947. In fact, he had been on the Fort Apache Indian Reservation in Arizona from late June until September. A July 4, 1947 photo that appeared in his book showed that he was on the reservation on that day. And Buskirk, who was working on his PhD, confirmed that he had been on the reservation solidly from late June until he returned to Albuquerque in September.

Stan Friedman and Don Berliner, two advocates of the Anderson story, issued a belated and very brief statement several months later. In the *MUFON UFO Journal* for January 1993, they wrote:

> ...[we] no longer have confidence in the testimony of Gerald Anderson.... Anderson has admitted to falsifying a document, and so his testimony about finding wreckage of a crashed flying saucer near the Plains of San Augustin [sic] in western New Mexico and then being escorted out by the U.S. military, can no longer be seen as sufficiently reliable.

The Anderson tale is just one more example of the aberrations that dot the Roswell case and should become little more than a footnote. He was an opportunist who cashed in modestly on his imagined tale, took a few trips at the expense of researchers, and appeared on a number of television shows. But he provided nothing but confusion for the Roswell case.

All of this tells us that the idea of a crash on the Plains of San Agustin in early July 1947 has no solid evidence. Barney Barnett clearly couldn't have been there, based on the diary that Ruth Barnett kept, Gerald Anderson's tale, which at first seemed to corroborate Barnett, collapsed under a mountain of lies and forged documents, and those who told me they remembered something about this from years earlier, couldn't remember if it had been in the 1950s or 60s, or if it was after the publication of *The Roswell Incident* in 1980. In other words, they provided nothing in the way of corroboration.

## July 6, 1947

### SAN DIEGO, CALIFORNIA

I was reviewing some of the old cases in my files and I came across the notation for a UFO crash near San Diego in 1947. I had published all the information I had in *A History of UFO Crashes* and was looking for additional data.

In that book I wrote:

> Unidentified witnesses reported that a flaming object was seen to fall into the ocean west of San Diego. A check at the local observatory suggested that it wasn't a meteorite and there were no aircraft reported missing. Recently declassified documents suggest an investigation by the military into the unidentified flaming object, but the case file itself has not been discovered.

Okay, that's not much. There were a couple of sources on this material. One of them was *Flying Saucers on the Attack* written by Harold T. Wilkins and published by the Citadel Press (under the Ace Star Books imprint, page 72) in 1967. The only additional and probably irrelevant information contained therein was that someone had checked with the Observatory at Griffin Park, which is in Los Angeles and not San Diego, and the person there didn't think it was a meteor.

The footnote for the case relates it to Sherman Brown, who had an unpublished manuscript called *UFO Crashes* and was dated 1990. I actually reference that book several times, but could find nothing in my files that tells me anything more about it.

The other thing is that I have several letters from people attempting to track down the original sources of this information and trying to find

Sherman Brown. One of those writers said that he had looked through the San Diego newspapers of the time. He found nothing there that related to an event in October.

All this led to one important point. In the book, I dated the crash on October 20, 1947, but the other sources suggest, instead, September 20th. I don't know the source of the error in my book, but would guess that it belongs to me.

None of this matters for those trying to run this down in San Diego. They checked the newspapers, starting with the Arnold Sighting of June 24, 1947, and ran through the end of October. One man sent me a list of people who had made sightings in 1947.

I tried some other sources, including the J. Allen Hynek Center for UFO Studies. They checked through their records and they found nothing to relate to either Sherman Brown or a crash near San Diego. I have believed, since there was nothing in my files on this, I had picked this up or researched it further at the Center. Unless something strange happened there, they were not the source of Sherman Brown.

I did find that the *San Diego Union* carried an article about John Kuder, who said he had seen "a luminous flying disc" circling about a half mile off Mission Beach. It dipped into the ocean and there was a ball of fire visible for a few seconds after the disk disappeared. This could be the source of the original story. The date isn't close, but the location is, and the description of the event would fit with the idea that there had been a crash of some kind.

Here's where we are on this one. I have located some of the sources about this event. I can now correct the date to the proper time or, at least, to another date in those sources that suggest September 20th. Other sources, including one newspaper, suggest July 6th because the story was reported on July 7th. Given the story, I would opt for July 6th.

The thing to do now is leave it as insufficient data. We have found a UFO sighting that goes with the report, we have a suggestion that the object might have dropped into the sea, and we have the report of a fireball moments later. At the moment, this is a single witness case and, for that reason, I leave it as insufficient data, though I suspect that a mundane answer would be found with additional information.

## July 7, 1947

### SHREVEPORT, LOUISIANA

This case resulted in a confusion that lasted for a number of years. There is no doubt that it originated as a hoax, but it came to the attention of the FBI and J. Edgar Hoover, who believed it proved that his organization was being left out of an important role in national security.

According to a report dated July 23, 1947, the intelligence office at Barksdale Field, near Shreveport, had received a report that a flying disk had been located, or crashed, in Shreveport. A witness told the Army officers that he, a man named Harston

> had heard the disc whirling through the air and had looked up in time to see it when it was approximately two hundred feet in the air and coming over a sign board adjacent to the used car lot where he was standing.... [witness] stated that smoke and fire were coming from the disc and that it was traveling at a high rate of speed and that it fell into the street....

The following day, the Army investigators talked to another witness who told them in an interview "that he had made the disc in order to play a joke on his boss and that the starter had been taken from a florescent light and two condensers from electric fans."

The witness described how he put it together and then

> sailed the disc in front of his boss's car, but that his boss failed to notice the disc and drove away. [The witness] further stated that some man (presumably Harston) saw the disc fall into the street.... [H]e [the witness] was of the opinion that anyone who examined the disc could readily tell that it was not dangerous, and that it was the work of a practical joker.

With that, the Army closed their investigation. But the FBI was still interested and the importance of that interest would be learned later. The FBI document covers the same information. The report added one detail: According to the document, "Harston stated that the disc made a sound when traveling through the air similar to a policeman's whistle and that the smooth side was toward the earth while in flight."

There was a handwritten note that said, "10 July 47—Maj. Carlau (US Br of ID) [whatever that means] says FBI advises this was a hoax."

It was also in July that the military asked the FBI for assistance in investigating the flying saucers. J. Edgar Hoover responded to the request, which came from the Army Air Forces' Brigadier General George F. Schulgen, at the time Chief of Requirements Intelligence Branch, by writing, "I would do it but before agreeing to it we must insist upon full access to discs recovered. For instance in the La. case the Army grabbed it and would not let us have it for cursory examination." This statement, which seems to suggest the recovery of a flying saucer, did, for many years, become the focus of a dispute as to exactly what Hoover meant when he wrote it in 1947.

First, the "La." is written in such a way that it could just as easily be "Sw." or "gov." or "Sov." or even "2a." Hoover's handwriting was sloppy enough that each of these interpretations might be accurate. However, in another document completed at the end of July 1947, the statement has been typed, and it was interpreted by the typist in 1947 as "La." Because this document was an FBI creation, and was typed at the FBI headquarters by a secretary familiar with Hoover's handwriting, it would seem that the interpretation is accurate. The real question is, then, to what did La. refer?

Skeptics and debunkers point to Shreveport. If this is the case to which Hoover referred, then the mystery is solved and the Hoover note does not support the case of a crashed flying saucer.

The problem here is that the case file for the Shreveport crash is readily available from Project Blue Book. The FBI was not cut out of the case, and the Army didn't grab the saucer or refuse to allow the FBI to inspect it. In fact, just the opposite is true. The FBI had seen the file, seen the disk, and seen the pictures taken of it.

What is noted is an ambiguous statement by the director of the FBI, who had been fighting a turf war with other intelligence establishments for six or seven years. When "Wild Bill" Donovan set up the Office of Strategic Services (OSS) at the beginning of the Second World War, it was understood by Hoover and Donovan that Donovan would have the responsibility for foreign intelligence gathering, while Hoover would retain it on the domestic front. Hoover had always viewed the FBI as the ultimate intelligence organization and saw Donovan's OSS as a threat to his empire. FBI agents worked outside the United States during the war and that tradition has continued until today.

In 1947, the flying saucers appeared in a domestic environment, which, to Hoover, suggested that the FBI was the agency responsible for gathering intelligence about them. The Army Air Forces, however, charged with the defense of the skies over the United States, thought otherwise. That would give rise to another "turf war." That seems to explain Hoover's demand to be allowed access to the disks recovered and his complaint that the FBI had been "cut out of the loop."

The Hoover document, then, is understandable in the context of the times. Hoover was fighting a turf war with the Army, trying to pry into what military officers considered their areas of responsibility. Hoover wanted to be on the inside of the discussion. He would require information in response to his assistance in background investigations of those who saw flying saucers. From Hoover's point of view, this was empire building and had nothing to do with the reality of flying saucers.

Even understanding the context of the time doesn't explain the cryptic "La." in the note. Nor does it explain the "discs recovered" reference. While no one seems to know, at this point, what "La." means, it is quite clear what "discs recovered" means: It means that a flying disk, or two, had been recovered by the Army by late July 1947. For those asking for some kind of documentation about the UFO crash, this is it. The fact that Hoover's note is ambiguous only deepens the mystery rather than solving it.

## July 7, 1947

### BOZEMAN, MONTANA

The first of the modern crashes to receive any sort of national publicity was the crash of a clamshell-shaped object in the Tobacco Root Mountains of western Montana. Vernon Baird, the pilot of a commercial photographic plane, said that, while he was flying at 32,000 feet and at about 360 miles any hour, one of the "flying discs" appeared behind him. According to Baird, it got caught in the prop wash of his aircraft and came apart, spiraling down into the mountains.

In newspaper reports, he said that the object was a "pearl gray, clam-shaped 'airplane' with a plexiglass down on the top." The one that crashed had been part of a formation of several that Baird and one of his photographers, George Suttin, had seen. Suttin, though a commercial photographer who was on a photographic mission, was so excited by the sight that he didn't think to take any pictures of the flying disks.

The next day, the solution for the case appeared in the various newspapers when Baird's boss, J.J. Archer, said that the whole thing was a hoax. Archer, Braid, and other pilots were sitting around the hangar and invented the tale for something to do. It had snowballed from there, they said, and somehow it had reached the newspapers and wire services. They didn't explain how that happened, but clearly someone had to call the newspaper after they had finalized the tale. Given the admission and the lack of any sort of corroborating evidence, there is no reason to suspect that this is anything other than a hoax.

## July 7, 1947

### OELWEIN, IOWA

According to the *Chicago Daily News* on July 8th, Lloyd Bennett, a wholesale tobacco salesman, said that he heard something crash through the trees the night before, and the next morning found a small disk. He said it was about 6 1/2 inches in diameter and about 1/8 inch thick. He said he was going to notify the Army authorities and claim the reward.

Bennett was talking about the offers made over the July 4, 1947 weekend by various organizations for proof of, or a solution to, the mystery of the flying saucers. There were three $1,000 rewards, but one of them expired after the weekend was over, and I know of no one who successfully claimed any of them.

## July 10, 1947

### BLACK RIVER FALLS, WISCONSIN

Sigurd Hanson found a small flying saucer on the afternoon of July 10, while working with two other city employees installing lights on the fairgounds. He found it in some tall grass and was accused of making it himself.

The newspaper *The La Crosse Tribune* reported, "One of the flying thingmajigs, which have kept the nation on edge for the past several weeks, was found on the fairgrounds at Black River Falls Thursday afternoon and the entire community is as excited as though Orson Welles himself were here to direct another invasion from Mars."

The saucer weighed about 1 1/2 pounds, was made of cardboard, and was 15 inches in diameter. It had a vertical fin and was topped by a small propeller that was connected to a tiny motor and was wired to a photoelectric cell.

Some thought the photoelectric cell powered the craft, if that's the right word for it; others thought there was some kind of jet or rocket propulsion because of a burned area near the fin.

In an article published in 1997, the newspaper reported that the jokester who had created the saucer was still alive and "chuckling."

## July 11, 1947

### TWIN FALLS, IDAHO

Another small saucer, described as looking like cymbals on a set of drums, was found and turned over to the FBI. The object was just more than 30 inches in diameter with a metal top that was anchored in place by what appeared to be stove bolts. It was gold on one side and silver on the other. It was sent on to Fort Douglas, Utah, for examination. At Fort Douglas, a high-ranking officer who didn't want to give his name said he could neither confirm nor deny that Army authorities had heard of the reported find.

## July 1947

### TULAROSA, NEW MEXICO (INSIDE WHITE SANDS MISSILE RANGE)

A master sergeant reported that the base commander at Alamogordo Army Air Field, Colonel Paul F. Helmlek, had ordered him to print a special report concerning a crashed object. He was to print it himself so that no one else would be able to read it or see the photographs. The pictures he did see suggested a shiny, metallic object had crashed. Once the project was completed, Helmlek collected all the documents and took them away.

# Chapter 4

## October 1947

### PARADISE VALLEY, ARIZONA

It was Frank Scully in his *Behind the Flying Saucers* that told about the crash outside of Paradise Valley, Arizona. Scully suggested it was the smallest of the three craft recovered, the most famous being that found outside of Aztec, New Mexico. There were two bodies and one of them was found half out of the escape door. He was, of course, dead. The other was sitting in his seat at the "control" board.

This ship was only 36 feet in diameter and had some kind of size relationship that worked out in what Scully called the "system of 9's." He said that there were no sleeping quarters or toilet facilities on the ship, and to the scientists who had inspected the craft it meant that the trips it took were very fast and very short. That ship, according to Dr. Gee, the scientist responsible for investigating the craft (more on him later), was at one of their laboratories.

When the Scully story collapsed (more on that later) this report was rejected with the others, and no one thought much more about it. In 1988, Timothy Good, a British writer, published his *Above Top Secret,* and he seemed to breathe new life into the Paradise Valley crash. Good said that in 1987 he had spoken to a former businessman and a private pilot named Selman E. Graves, who said that he had witnessed part of the recovery operation that had taken place at Cave Creek, which is north of Paradise Valley.

According to what Good reported, Graves said he had been in the Cave Creek area and was planning on a hunting trip. A friend, Walt Salyer, arrived and told them they couldn't go due west, that it wasn't a good time to go hunting, and that the Air Force had restricted the area.

They did go out to a place that Graves called the Go John Mine, and rode up into the hills. They could look back and see everything, and from that point they could also see what Graves called a large, aluminum dome-shaped craft that was about the size of a house, or, according to Graves, about 36 feet in diameter.

Reading this, I thought immediately of contamination. The diameter of the craft, for example, was too precise for a distant observation. Good reported that Graves said he had thought little of the incident until he read Scully's book.

He also mentioned that there were some small creatures recovered, but apparently neither he nor the two with him saw of them. He thought that his friend, Salyer, might have had a hand in helping the military get the bodies off the site and into a freezer.

Graves and the men watched the retrieval for about 10 hours, according to Good. They then left their perch and headed back to Cave Creek and Salyer's house.

## October 12, 1947

### SAMALAYUCA MOUNTAINS, MEXICO

According to a newspaper article published in El Paso, Texas, a flaming object "soared over the Texas-Mexico border" and apparently crashed into the mountains south of Juarez, Mexico, with a loud explosion and a expanding cloud of smoke. This site was about 10 miles from the point where a V-2 rocket had crashed on May 29, 1947.

The public information officer at White Sands said that none had been launched since October 9th, and it was clear that none were missing. The commander of Fort Bliss (El Paso) said that no missiles had been launched from his facility so it hadn't belonged to him.

On October 15, 1947, in a letter to the Chief of Staff of the U.S. Army in Washington, D.C., the Commanding General of the Fourth Army at Fort Sam, Houston, Texas, wrote:

> Reference previous unverified report of aerial object landing in Mexico opposite town of Fabens, Tex, reports received this date from CG AAA and GMC and Branch Intelligence Officer Ft Bliss Tex to effect Mexican Garrison of Juarez still searching suspected area of impact. No results reported. No verification of report. Investigation continuing.

Interestingly, there is a teletype message that was from the "Helmick Co AAFLD, Alamogordo, NMEX 151725Z," that went to the "CG AMC Wright FLD Dayton Ohio ATTN TSNAD Analysis Div T-2," that said:

> CITE URTEL TSNAD-10-1 PD LAST MISSILE LAUNCHED FROM THIS STA 8 OCT AND RECOVERED IMMEDIATELY PD LAST MISSILE LAUNCHED BY WHITE SANDS PROVING GROUND WAS 9 OCT AND RECOVERED ALMOST IMMEDIATELY PD THE MEXICAN GOVERNMENT FROM MEXICO CITY CMA MEXICO RELEASED A WNHIS MORNING THAT THE UNIDENTIFIED FLAMING OBJECT THAT LANDED ABOUT 35 MILES FROM JUAREZ MEX WAS DEFINITELY A ROCKET TO HAVE BEEN LAUNCHED FROM SOME TEXAS BASE.

There is one other document that I have that is relevant here. A news report from El Paso said that the officer in charge of the Juarez military garrison had blamed a false report from the Mexican Department of War announcement that an American rocket had crashed. He said that they were continuing the search for whatever had hit.

It's clear from the reports that there were multiple witnesses to the object in the sky, and there was enough evidence that a search was mounted for the object, whatever it might have been. It's also clear that the records available have ruled out any sort of a missile or rocket, which means that whatever fell, it remained unidentified.

## March 25, 1948

### AZTEC, NEW MEXICO

The first hint of a crash in New Mexico came from a Hollywood *Weekly Variety* columnist named Frank Scully. True, the Roswell story had appeared in national newspapers in July 1947, but they said only that a flying saucer had been captured, and within three hours it was suggested that it was a weather balloon instead. Scully's tale, published in 1949, eventually made it clear that the object had crashed in New Mexico.

On October 12, 1949, Scully wrote what can only be described as tongue-in-cheek column by a generous writer. It contains all the basic information that would haunt the UFO world from that moment forward. That is, it tells of the crashed saucer in the Mojave Desert with information of a second, smashed disk in the Sahara. Neither of these two crashes would be explored again and the locations would be changed, but the craft were found on the ground and they hadn't landed.

According to Scully, "The one that landed in Africa was more cracked than a psychiatrist...," which, of course, provides a glimpse of the tone of the whole story as Scully originally saw it. It seemed that, at that point, Scully really didn't believe anything about crashed flying saucers, but it made for an interesting column if nothing else.

Scully noted that there had been 16 men inside the saucer (but no women), all small, and added, in his *Variety* column of October 12, 1949, that they were "about the size of Singer Midgets. They weren't Singer midgets because all these have been accounted for. Neither were they pigmies [sic] from the African jungle."

Scully suggested that the interior of the saucer was loaded with push-buttons and control instruments but that no one, after they entered the craft, had wanted to push anything for fear of blowing themselves up. He also said they had bombed the ship with cosmic rays and Geiger devices to make sure there was nothing lethal hidden inside. Yes, I find that whole idea to be strange, but then the information was coming from a man who had little scientific training, and certainly didn't understand either cosmic rays or Geiger counters. He would prove this time and again as he tried to talk about scientific subjects and mangled the terms and concepts.

About a year later, Scully would publish *Behind the Flying Saucers,* which greatly expanded on all of this, and a couple of other columns he had written. Now we learn more about this flying saucer crash, which was located outside tiny Aztec, New Mexico, and of a couple of others that had taken place in Arizona, including one in Paradise Valley mentioned earlier.

According to Scully's sources, one of which was later identified as Silas Newton, and according to

*4.1. Near Aztec crash site. Author's photo.*

Newton's sources, one of which was a man identified only as "Dr. Gee," in the beginning, three radar stations, including an experimental site situated on a mountaintop, spotted one of the saucers traveling at 18,000 mph at about 90,000 feet. One of the radars was a special, experimental station with a high power beam that, according to some sources, interfered with the power generation of the saucer, knocking it down.

Because there were three radars involved, they could triangulate the position of the crash, and the military was dispatched for the retrieval. They spent two days observing the craft before they ventured close to it. Through portholes, they could see the bodies inside and, probing with a long stick through a small hole in a porthole, they hit a button or knob that activated the hatch.

The bodies, all 16 of them, as Scully had noted in his October 1949 column, were laid out on the ground. They were between 3 and 3 1/2 feet tall (36 to 42 inches), perfectly normal—meaning they were well-proportioned humans except for their small size—and were wearing old-fashioned clothes made of some strange cloth that was nearly indestructible.

The skin was a dark brown, but according to Scully and his sources, that was a result of a burning inside the craft. Apparently the damage in the porthole caused some sort of atmospheric imbalance inside the saucer, causing the burns, or rather that was what Dr. Gee thought—or maybe more accurately, that was what Dr. Gee said.

Except for the damage to the porthole, there was nothing else wrong with the craft. It was dismantled, the scientists or soldiers having discovered that it had been manufactured in pieces, and trucked from the scene. All of this—the craft in segments and the bodies—was taken then to Wright-Patterson Air Force Base in Dayton, Ohio.

The bodies, or at least some of them, were dissected and were found to be human in every way, except they all had perfect teeth. When the study was completed, some sources suggested that the bodies were buried, though I doubt you'd dispose of what could be thought of as unique biological specimens. How many representatives of an alien race could you expect to recover? (Though if I wanted to be cavalier about this, I would suggest a nearly endless supply, given the number of crashes that have been reported in the last few years.)

Scully said that he had been able to examine some of the material recovered. He said he had seen a "tubeless" radio and some small gears. Scully said that the metal had been extensively tested, but no one had been able to identify the material.

Scully was sure of his information and produced his book, which was published in September 1950. Earlier that year, Silas Newton was identified as one of Scully's sources because he (Newton) gave a lecture at the University of Denver in which he discussed, to some extent, the Aztec crash. This lecture, it seems, was Scully's attempt to learn the truth and, because of the positive reaction, he decided to go ahead with his book.

Several different writers have covered the Denver lecture aspect of the story, and many of those accounts are accurate. J.P. Cahn wrote, in a 1952 expose in *True,* that:

> To test public receptivity to the saucer revelation, the oil man-geophysicist appeared as an anonymous guest lecturer before a University of Denver elementary-science class on March 8, 1950, escorted by George T. Koehler, who is a salesman for Denver radio station KMYR. The lecturer told in detail of Dr. Gee's findings and drew some blackboard diagrams. News of the lecture leaked, of course, beyond the cloistered walls, and the how-come of university sponsorship raised a local tempest that blew off the lecturer's cloak of anonymity. His name was Silas M. Newton....

William Steinman, in his "privately published" book, *UFO Crash at Aztec,* reported on the same lecture. He wrote:

But, lo and behold, a college student at the University of Denver, who worked part-time at KMYR Radio Station remembered Koehler telling a saucer story.... This student's class instructor, Francis F. Broman, was looking for someone to give a lecture to the class, on a subject bordering on the fantastic, before his class as an object lesson for the students. His class had been studying how to verify truth in such situations... Koelher, remember all the hassel [sic] he had with AOSI [meaning here AFOSI or the Air Force Office of Special Investigation], FBI and ACID (Army Counter Intelligence Division [meaning here the Army CIC], had asked Newton to perform the lecture in his place on the premis [sic] that Newton knew more about the saucers....

Steinman went on, writing:

Someone from an unidentified intelligence group in Washington, D.C. (probably an MJ-12 staffer [which is the mythical group that some believe controls UFO information at the highest level]) called Francis Broman within a few days after the lecture was given. He was quizzed whether he believed what the lecturer had said or not. Borman told the presumed investigator that he was very doubtful, which seemed to satisfy him.

In 1991, William E. Jones and Rebecca D. Minshall, from the MidOhio Research Associates, published a preliminary study on their investigation into the Aztec crash in the *International UFO Reporter* for September/October 1991. They acknowledged Steinman and his claims about Newton's Denver lecture. They thought it would be a good idea to talk with Broman, and in June 1991, they located him. They wrote, "...Mr. Broman essentially verified what Steinman had written about the incident. For the record, the class was entitled, 'Science and Man'."

So, Steinman got that information right, but then it isn't of overwhelming importance. The topic of the lecture is confirmed, but that doesn't mean that the information included in it has been confirmed, and, in fact, looks as if it wasn't of much use except as an exercise in critical thinking.

With Scully's book climbing the best-seller list and with people talking about it, several newspapers and magazines were interested in verifying the information. After all, if it could be proven, it would be the biggest story of the last 1,000 years. We were not alone in the universe, and the intelligence creatures had found a way of traveling through space to get here. Dr. Gee believed that they had come from Venus and had some theory as to why. In 1950, no one knew that Venus had a surface temperature that could melt lead. Most thought of it as a planet covered with tropical oceans, which accounted for the impenetrable cloud cover.

J.P. Cahn, then a reporter for the *San Francisco Chronicle,* was commissioned by *True,* which had published much of what Major Donald Keyhoe had to say about flying saucers, to learn what he could about Scully's claims and the mystery men he cited as his sources. Cahn lost no time in beginning his investigation into Scully, Newton, Dr. Gee, and the flying saucer crash at Aztec, not to mention the two, or possibly three, others.

The first thing that came out was that Newton's background was not very good. He had boasted that he had rediscovered the Rangely Oil Fields in Colorado, but others said this simply wasn't true. Other oilmen said that there was no evidence for this claim, and I confess it makes little sense to me. All I know is that Newton, and Dr. Gee, would eventually be convicted of fraud in some kind of scam that involved a device to locate oil and the rediscovery of the fields, but that came after Scully's book and Cahn's exposé, and might be irrelevant here except as a testament to character.

Cahn arranged a meeting with the seemingly reluctant Newton and told him that he (Cahn) was authorized to pay up to $35,000 for the story, providing that Newton could verify his claims. Newton then showed Cahn some photographs and several small disks that Newton said were of some mystery metal.

Cahn, of course, wanted one of the disks for analysis, but Newton was reluctant to let any of them go. If this was truly metal from an alien spaceship, then Newton might have trouble getting more. He said he would provide documentation to prove they were pure, but he wouldn't allow Cahn to have one.

Cahn, instead, had several small disks made, based on his memory of what they looked like. He figured that at some point he might have the opportunity to make a switch. During one of their meetings, Newton displayed the disks again and Cahn was horrified to see that none of his fakes looked much like those Newton had, but he used the one that resembled them the most and made a switch. Newton noticed nothing and wrapped up the fake with the others (which is to say, the original fakes brought by Newton).

Cahn took the disk to Stanford laboratories for analysis. They found it to be rather poor grade aluminum that contained no traces of anything they couldn't identify. Instead of withstanding temperatures up to 10,000 degrees, as Newton claimed, it melted at 650 (F) degrees. For those who don't know, lead melts around 800 (F) degrees so that, if the object came from Venus, it would have been molten just sitting on the surface of the planet.

Cahn was able to learn the identity of Dr. Gee, apparently by accident. He was checking the telephone calls made by Newton and noticed that many went to Leo GeBauer in Arizona. A check found that GeBauer had a degree in electrical engineering from Louis Institute of Technology in Chicago, but he had never been in charge of 1,700 scientists, as claimed, and it's doubtful he'd ever seen 1,700 scientists. In fact, while he was supposed to be running these highly classified projects, he was actually working in AiResearch, where he was responsible for keeping the lab machinery working. It other words, he wasn't much more than a glorified maintenance man.

GeBauer admitted to Cahn that he was the mysterious Dr. Gee, though Scully would suggest that Dr. Gee was a composite of eight men. Not that it matters: GeBauer tried to retract his statement later.

With all that, Cahn was satisfied that the story was a hoax concocted by Newton and GeBauer. Cahn didn't think that Scully was involved, but he must have had some suspicion, especially when the truth about Newton began to surface. Reportedly, Scully was annoyed when he learned that the story was a lie—at least some have suggested that.

Scully, however, published a piece just prior to the publication of the Cahn exposé and after he had received many negative reviews of his book. Not that the negativity mattered much, because the book was a national best-seller and Scully claimed he was offered $75,000 for the film rights. Scully told the studio they'd need a lot more money because Dr. Gee had said he would not talk for $20 million.

This seems to contradict the claim that Dr. Gee is a composite of eight scientists. There were, in fact, many such contradictions in the various stories told by Newton and GeBauer—not that it mattered all that much, because the killer blow was their convictions for fraud. If nothing else could stop the Aztec story, this was it. Two of the principals were convicts.

With that, nearly all reports of flying saucer crashes were rejected by UFO researchers as well as nearly everyone else. This one tale, which had given so much hope to researchers, had been jerked away, and I think the blowback from that infected UFO research for decades. No one was interested in tales of flying saucer crashes, regardless of the source or the evidence.

But this tale was not dead yet. At a press conference in 1974, a retired professor, Robert Spencer Carr, claimed that he had talked to five people who had inside knowledge of a flying saucer crash and

he believed it to be the Aztec case. Carr refused to reveal his sources, which right there made all this suspect, but he did manage to intrigue the national press for a couple of weeks with his story.

*4.2. Road near Aztec, New Mexico. Author's photo.*

As he told it, the facts matched those that Scully had reported two and a half decades earlier—well, sort of. He did talk about the radar stations and the triangulation. He suggested the landing was a soft one, on a triangular gear. Carr said law enforcement got there with guns drawn and approached the 30-feet-in-diameter ship. Through a thumb-sized hole in the dome of the disk, they could see 12 little men slumped near their instruments.

Carr said the military and the scientists, who had arrived after the sheriff managed to open the door, removed the bodies. They were muscular and solid, with light hair and blue eyes. They all wore the same clothes, which were not from the 1890s as suggested by Newton and GeBaur, but some kind of blue uniform.

These bodies were taken to Edwards Air Force Base rather than to Wright-Patterson but were later moved, along with their craft, to Wright-Patterson. One of the bodies was dissected, with surgeons flown in from Washington, D.C. Their blood type was O. Carr claimed to have received the information from a nurse who was involved with the dissection, and she said that she could think of no reason to take this to her grave. (I, on the other hand, can think of one, which is that she was probably told never to tell, if we are to believe the story.)

The problem here was that Carr refused to name any names. He claimed five sources, but he was going to hold those names in confidence because he had promised to do so. At that point, for me and for many others, Carr's tale moved into the realm of fantasy. There was no way to verify anything that Carr said, and he was repeating, to some extent, the Scully tale, which we all believed to have been discredited.

In 1975, Mike McClelland wrote an article for *Official UFO*, claiming that "The UFO Crash of 1948 is a Hoax." He provided a look at both Carr's new story and Scully's old, and found they were generally similar, but had some sharp disagreements.

McClelland also wrote that he had interviewed several "highly reliable 'old-timers' from Aztec," including Deputy Sheriff Bruce Sullivan who would have been in high school at the time. According to McClelland, "He has lived in Aztec all his life and 'never knew or heard anything about it.'"

McClelland also interviewed Lyle McWilliams, who had been in business in Aztec his whole life and was 32 in 1948. According to McClelland, "He recalls nothing of the incident except for the original claim and has always treated it as a joke."

That testimony is interesting because McWilliams does not remember the first story to appear in Scully's book, and that was only about a year or two after the crash. Surely, had something happened, McWilliams would have known about it at the time.

Coral Lorenzen, at the time one of the leaders of the Aerial Phenomena Research Organization in Tucson, Arizona, made her own investigation. According to the January/February 1975 issue of *The A.P.R.O. Bulletin*:

> Mrs. Lorenzen called and interviewed Sheriff Dan Sullivan at Aztec, who told her there was absolutely nothing to the tale. He

further said that he had had deputies on extra duty running around the country trying to locate the alleged site (identified as Hart Canyon by one news release) and they were unable to find anyone who could given [sic] any kind of lead to follow concerning the alleged crash landing. In fact, the family which has had residence at the mouth of Hart Canyon for the last 40 years which was in residence for all of the year of 1948, said categorically that there were no UFOs, helicopters, or any kind of military activity during that whole year nor during any of the preceding or following years.

That seemed to end it, once again. Carr said he had sources, but didn't name them. Residents of Aztec who had lived there during the 1948 crash knew nothing about it, nor remembered the rumors, and had seen nothing themselves. No newspaper articles about the crash in 1948 could be found. The issue disappeared again.

But like the vampires of old, the story came back again. This time William Steinman, who found a copy of Scully's book in an old used bookstore, was intrigued by the tale. He wrote to and telephoned a number of the old-time UFO investigators, researchers, and authors, and was appalled to learn that no one had actually investigated the Aztec case—at least, to the best of his knowledge. He did find a copy of the J.P. Cahn exposé, so he knew why most of us had rejected the story. He found more leads.

He eventually drove to Aztec, first stopping in Durango, Colorado. This was supposed to be the staging area where the scientists and a team from the I.P.U. (Interplanetary Research Team according to one bunch of MJ-12 documents) gathered before moving onto Aztec. He found no one at the airfield who knew anything about this, and to be fair, none of them had been there in 1948, so it isn't all that surprising.

Steinman said he followed their route, though he didn't know it at the time, into Aztec. He went to the newspaper office and looked at the back issues of the newspaper for the months around the crash, but found nothing there to suggest that anything unusual had happened. While there, he placed an ad asking that anyone who had information about the crash contact him at his residence.

Then he went to a garage sale—well, again, not quite fair. He happened to see one and stopped to shop. He asked the woman there,

Vivian Melton, about the crash, and, according to Steinman, she said, "We know about that; in fact we know exactly what happened!!"

Steinman then wrote in his book, "Harvey and Vivian Melton moved into the Aztec area around 1970... They first heard of the Aztec crash from Mrs. Alda Wild."

That seemed to me to be a dead lead. If they hadn't been there in 1948, the best they could be is secondhand witnesses. They wouldn't have seen anything themselves and, by the time Steinman arrived in July 1982, the story had been circulating for years. Carr had revived it not all that long before Steinman arrived, so it would be odd if someone in Aztec didn't know about the story.

The next morning, Steinman and Harvey Melton met with someone identified only as B.L. who eventually gave them directions to the crash site, which was identified as Hart Canyon. They drove out and Melton pointed to the crash site, on top of a plateau and near an El Paso Gas Company installation. Steinman thought the chain-link fence was of significance.

Steinman learned of a man he identified only as W.M. and went to visit him the next day—or, as Steinman put it, "I went and confronted Mr. W.M...." and then asked him what he could tell him (Steinman) of the crash and recovery of the disk in Hart Canyon.

According to Steinman, "W.M. got down off his tractor and straightening himself up, stated, very belligerantly [sic], 'Nothing happened out in Hart Canyon in 1948!! Why do you people from so far away keep asking about that flying saucer crash?"

W.M.'s wife, according to Steinman, appeared on the scene to remind her husband that he had been away in April 1948. Steinman confirmed that with the Durango newspaper that carried a story about W.M. hitting a horse that wrecked his car and knocked out his teeth. W.M. bought a new car and continued his trip. I'm not sure of the significance of this, because the UFO crash took place in March, but Steinman reported it nonetheless.

Next, Steinman found H.D., who had actually owned the land on which the saucer had crashed. Steinman wrote:

> That same day [July 8]...I also contacted Mr. H.D., the 83 year-old owner of the ranch on which this UFO was allegedly recovered. I

confronted H.D. with questions pertaining to the alleged incident. He snapped back in very upset voice, "I don't know anything about what you are talking about—now leave me alone!!" I Sensed [sic] a tenseness and a nervousness in his voice, almost as if he were at one time coerced and coached into answering that way.

Of course, I'll point out that he might just have been annoyed at someone new showing up to ask the same questions he had answered in the past. He might not have known a thing about a crash, but people seemed to believe he did. The point is that he might not have been coerced and coached, but was just tired of the interruptions.

Next Steinman was off to interview F.G., who had been a youngster at the time. Steinman wrote, "F.G. admitted that she was a young girl at the time and did accompany her father into Heart [sic] Canyon on occasions.... She did hear the rumors about the saucer crash-recovery, but did not witness the event."

F.G. thought her father might know something, and by coincidence, her father showed up. When asked about the crash, he seemed not to hear. Asked again, he just changed the subject. Steinman wrote, "By that time both myself and F.G. got the hint. He simply did not want to talk about it."

Although Steinman tried to suggest that he was getting somewhere, basically all he had found were people who knew nothing firsthand and people who denied any involvement. He found people who knew the rumors, but these stories had gained national attention in 1950 with Scully's book, in 1952 with Cahn's exposé, and then again in 1974 when Carr reinvented the tale. He wasn't finding much that had any real value.

Steinman wrote, in his book:

> The next day, I decided to poke around the Bloomfield and Blanco area south of Aztec, to quizz [sic] old timers on the alleged incident. I lucked out on my first try! (Sinchronicity? [sic]) I noticed an oldtimer [sic] out watering a front yard there... after a few questions he referred me to a Mr. V.A., who claimed to have seen a flying saucer in trouble, up very close, during the time period I was referring to (early 1948).

Steinman went in search of V.A. and found him. V.A. said that one morning, somewhere between 1948 and 1950, he was out performing his usual chores...suddenly he heard a loud explosion, like a jet breaking the sound barrier. He looked...and saw a huge disc-shaped flying object with a dome on the top. This object appeared to be larger than his house, and was within 200 years of him. It appeared to be in trouble, skimming about 100 feet above the ground, and it wobbled as it flew.

V.A. said that it hit a rocky cliff, shot sparks and rocks in every direction, and headed straight north. Steinman, in a parenthetical statement, wrote, "Straight north was a beeline for the Heart [sic] Canyon crash site."

Later, he talked to V.A.'s daughter, who knew the rumors and talked about how the body count varied among four, 12, and 16. She then launched into tales of cattle mutilations, abductions, and sightings in the Aztec area, but then, she had seen nothing firsthand.

Steinman left the Aztec area after that and wrote his book about the crash, though it is filled with side issues and irrelevancies. All he succeeded in doing was finding a few additional rumors, no one who had actually seen the craft on the ground or seen the military response, and no evidence of the recovery.

Yes, I know that some of the same can be said of the Roswell UFO crash, which we've examined. However, there are firsthand witnesses to the Roswell crash debris, there are newspaper articles that do suggest something fell at Roswell, there are those who claim to have seen the military cordon, and there are former soldiers who say they were part of that cordon, which puts the Roswell case way in front of the others.

In 1991, William E. Jones and Rebecca D. Minshall, the two researchers living in Ohio, reported in their *IUR* article that they "decided to see what information could be independently found that would either support or disprove the Aztec story."

They identified Mr. W.M. as Wright G. McEwen, who was a deputy sheriff in March 1948 and had moved from Aztec to California. They wrote, "However, both he and his wife emphatically deny that a flying saucer crashed near Hart Canyon...as claimed by Steinman. Mr. McEwen admitted to having talked to Steinman and knew the general scope of the story. He denies that the story holds any truth."

That was the tone of what most of Jones and Minshall found. Steinman had believed the wild stories, discounted those who told him nothing happened, and leaped to conclusions not warranted by the information he had. They did find a woman who had heard that a farmer near Blanco saw a disk glance off a cliff on the supposed date of the crash. The farmer couldn't pin it down to a year.

All of this, from Scully to Carr to Steinman, seems to suggest that a saucer crashed somewhere in the Aztec area. Others, such as Cahn, McClelland, Jones, and Minshall, seem to suggest the story is a modern fable that might be traceable to a P-38 crash sometime in the mid-1940s. There is nothing to the story of dead aliens from a domed disk.

But there is one other factor that gives me pause: Carr would never identify his sources to the public, and he only revealed them once, that I know of, and that was to Len Stringfield, who, almost single-handedly, revived interest in UFO crashes and coined the term *crash-retrieval*. I visited Len at his home a year or two before he died. Don Schmitt and I were investigating Roswell, and Len had the leads to a couple of people with knowledge of that event. We did get off on other such crashes, and Len told us not to be too sure that the Aztec case was a complete hoax.

This surprised me, but then he said that he knew the five sources that Carr had used and that he (Stringfield) had talked to them as well. Len said that he believed them and this, in a way, put the Aztec story back on the map. Len wouldn't identify any of them for us, believing that he would be violating the agreement he had with Carr to protect those witnesses. And Len, if nothing else, was an honorable man.

There is one other thing to discuss. When McClelland said that there had been no crash at Aztec, Carr changed directions and said that he didn't know that it had been Aztec. It could have been some other New Mexico city, and that, of course, could mean that the sources Carr had were not from New Mexico, but had come into the story later. It could have been those involved at Wright Field near Dayton, or they could have been stationed somewhere else when they stumbled across the crashed saucer information.

It seems, based on the best information we currently have, that the crash at Aztec is actually a stand-in for Roswell. If that is true, then the comments made by some, that Scully's book frightened top brass at the Pentagon, was because they knew the truth and any discussion of a UFO crash in New Mexico could lead to Roswell.

## June 25, 1948

### DURANGO, COLORADO

While living in Colorado, and for years afterward, I had heard rumors of some kind of a crash near Durango. A quick check (in the early 1970s) with the local sheriff and with the newspaper showed that they knew nothing of the crash, but, of course, neither the sheriff nor the newspaper editor had been around in 1948. They did review their records and found nothing.

Given what I have learned in my investigation of the Roswell crash, and my searches of government records, I know that some of the cover-ups had been effective in the past, so I attempted a more thorough search. Again, I failed to turn up anything that would suggest a crash in that area. None of the long-time residents had a hint of what might have happened.

In today's world, I might have found an answer, or at least part of one. According to several writers, the recovery team for Aztec supposedly staged out of Durango. Durango isn't all that far from Aztec, and in 1948 had a larger airport. Rumors of this have been circulating for years.

The answer then, is that there was no crash in or around Durango, but was near Aztec. The staging for the retrieval was at Durango. Of course, if there was no crash at Aztec, then the rumors are just that, and searches of the records would produce nothing of interest.

## July 7, 1948

### THE LAREDO UFO CRASH AND THE "TOMATO MAN"

This report of a July 7, 1948 crash, struck a note with me as I was attempting to verify some of its components. I realized that some of the information I was seeking I had already researched. There were elements in it that I had seen elsewhere, and I found it all a little confusing, a little strange, and very disturbing.

The story is that about a year after the Roswell UFO crash, another object fell about 30 miles southwest of Laredo, Texas, across the Rio Grande in Mexico. Then–Secretary of State General George C. Marshall coordinated with the Mexican government so that American military forces could take charge of the wreckage, claiming it was an experimental craft that had gone out of control and crashed.

This part of the story wasn't all that far-fetched. A rocket launched from White Sands had gone out of control and crashed near Juarez, Mexico, across the border from El Paso, Texas, in 1947. Fortunately, no one was injured and the damage was minimal, but launches were suspended for a short time.

Colonel John W. Bowen, who was the provost marshal at Fort Worth, according to the story, was detailed to take charge of this new operation in Mexico, though there were military bases closer, including Fort Bliss in El Paso and Fort Hood near San Antonio. The crash area was quickly cordoned, and men were sent in to pick up the wreckage. It was hauled from Mexico to a location in San Antonio for processing, investigation, and eventual shipping to other facilities that could exploit the find.

However, before that was done, a special photographer was sent in—at least, according to a man who claimed to be that photographer. His job was to photograph everything as it was found as a way of documenting the case. This source surfaced in December 1978, and told researchers at Mutual Anomaly Research Center and Evaluation Network (MARCEN) that, as a young man, he had been detailed to take photographs of a flying saucer wreck (or more precisely, a UFO crash).

To prove it, he included an 8-by-10 glossy print showing the body of one of those killed before it had been removed from the wreckage. When they queried him, suggesting that to them this looked more like a human pilot killed in a light plane crash, they received a three-page reply with more detail.

According to the story told by this man (and here we need to pay attention to the details), at about 1322 hour (1:22 p.m.) on July 7th, the Distance Early Warning (DEW) line detected an object traveling at speeds of more than 2,000 miles an hours as it flew over Washington state and headed to the southeast. As it entered the airspace over Texas, two fighters were scrambled to intercept and identify the object.

As the two F-94 fighters approached, the UFO made a 90-degree turn without decreasing its speed. At 1410 hours (2:10 p.m.), other fighters, who had joined the pursuit, radioed that the object was slowing and now wobbling. At 1429 (2:29 p.m.), it disappeared from the radar, but, by using triangulation, the military realized that the object was down, in Mexico, but not all that far from Laredo. That is, unless it had flown under the radar coverage. Then it could be anywhere, but they did know where it had vanished.

At about 1830 (6:30 p.m.), an American detachment was on the scene of the crash, which had been located by others, and the detachment commander was notified that a special photographic unit was going to be dispatched to preserve the scene in pictures. This included the source who now lived in Tennessee and who had retained copies of some of the photographs he'd taken of this top-secret plane crash.

According to this guy, the photographic team was picked up in an L-19 at 2130 hours (9:30 p.m.). He said it was uncomfortable in the small airplane with the five team members and all their equipment on board. Yes, I know what you're thinking, but I want to do this in order.

He said that they arrived at 0210 hours (2:10 a.m.) and circled the area so they got an overview of the crash site. They saw a disk-shaped object that was still burning on a heavily vegetated hill. Apparently there were no Mexicans near the site, and it was in a remote area.

Once they landed, the man claimed that they had found one body in the craft and he and the others managed to take several pictures. When the craft cooled, the body was removed and they took additional photographs.

Although the craft and the debris were unusual, some of it looked as if it had come from Earth. There was, however, an absence of wiring, glass, wood, rubber, or paper. The whole thing looked to be held together by bolts, but they couldn't remove them and finally just used brute force to chisel them off. They used diamond drills and saws, and, on the lighter metals, used cutting torches so they could disassemble the craft.

A metallurgist who was unidentified by the photographer said that the structure was a honey-combed crystalline that was not like anything he had ever seen on Earth. He thought it might be silicon-based.

It sounds as if he was attempting to describe some of the composites now used in the aircraft industry—and remember: He was telling this story decades later, after those composites had been developed here and used in stealth aircraft.

The body was about 4 feet, 6 inches tall with a large head. There were no eyes, destroyed by either the crash or the fire, but there were eye sockets. There were no visible ears, noses, or lips, and there was just a slit for a mouth without either teeth or tongue. The arms were longer than a human's would be on that short of a frame and ended in a four-digit claw. The legs were of normal proportions with short feet, but no toes. Both the arms and legs seemed to have joints in about the same place as humans.

In fact, the source told MARCEN many details of the body and its structure, but none of it is important to us. The man, who claimed to be a Navy photographer, overheard the doctors talking as they conducted their preliminary autopsy on the site while he took pictures.

At 1300 hours (1:00 p.m.) the next day, a C-47 arrived and the body was then shipped out of Mexico, but the man didn't know where it might have gone. What was left of the wreckage was then loaded into trucks, and he didn't know their destination either.

The man said that he then returned to White Sands and began to develop the film and make the prints. He worked with a team of other photographic experts, and they all were watched by Marines. The team was disbanded when their task was completed and the commander, whoever he was, returned to Washington, never to be seen again.

A few years later, proving that no security system works—if we believe this man—he removed forty negatives from the file, made duplicates, and then put the original pictures back. That was why he had the pictures of the burned alien creature, or so he said.

William Steinman, who is largely responsible for the renewed interest in the Aztec crash, reported that, according to members of MARCEN, including Willard McIntyre and Dennis Pilichis of the UFO Information Network (UFOIN) and a booklet they wrote, they were able to get an original negative—that is, one of the copy negatives that the Navy man had made in the late 1940s or early 1950s. They sent it to Kodak for analysis. According to Kodak, at least as reported by

McIntyre and Pilichis, Kodak found the negative to be at least 30 years old, and they could detect no evidence of photographic trickery. Saying nothing about the image contained on the negative, they concluded that the negative showed no obvious signs of tampering.

Ron Schaffner of the old Ohio UFO Investigators League (OUFOIL) put together a private report on the photographs, based on research that he had conducted and that he circulated to researchers including the late Len Stringfield. He said that he, along with colleagues, wrote to Kodak, asking them about the tests they had conducted on the negatives. He wrote about the Kodak response, saying, "We were not surprised when the response came back that Kodak was not aware of any photo work done on the pictures enclosed. Furthermore, their representative said that Kodak would not perform any type of testing that we desired for authenticity."

This might have been the first time that Kodak was embroiled in a controversy about photographs of an alien body, but it wouldn't be the last as noted in the discussion about the alien autopsy and the Nogal Canyon case. Kodak would find itself corresponding in the mid-1990s with a man who claimed to have movie footage of the autopsy of an alien. This time Kodak would get involved, but only if certain conditions were met. As noted earlier, they were not.

However, this time, it seemed that Kodak had been quoted, but that no one had bothered to actually send them anything to evaluate. They didn't have any idea what was going on. That certainly didn't bode well for the authenticity of the report.

I wondered about this claim that they had all flown from White Sands Proving Grounds in an L-19. Here's what I learned about this from the Web. According to War Bird Alley (*www.warbirdalley. com/119.htm*):

> Structurally, the military version differed from its civilian progenitor, with the passenger capacity reduced by two [meaning only two people, pilot and passenger, the aft superstructure radically revised to provide a clear view rearward, and transparent panel being inserted in the wing above the seats....

So, we were being told that the L-19 was a modified civilian aircraft that had four places, but that was reduced to two—that is, a passenger and a pilot. It was further modified for its role in aerial reconnaissance, which would be ideal for artillery spotters, but not so great for long-distance travel with a pile of camera gear.

The real problem for the story is not that the aircraft couldn't have carried five people, plus their photographic equipment, but that the contract to build the aircraft wasn't finalized until 1950. In other words, the aircraft didn't exist in 1948.

The same can be said for the DEW Line. While distance early warning was probably discussed in 1948, and military planners realized that a Soviet missile attack would probably come over the north pole, the line hadn't been built yet. In fact, on February 15, 1954, the United States and Canada agreed to build the DEW Line, so the radars of the DEW Line were not in place in 1948.

The other radar defenses were discussed as early as 1946, but the money wasn't appropriated until much later. It wasn't until after the Soviets detonated their atomic bomb that this became a priority, but it wasn't until 1950 that work began. The point is that there were no radar fences in Canada in 1948 to track the intruder, though there might have been individual radars at bases in Alaska or Canada that could have, but their range would have been limited by the terrain and the curvature of the Earth.

So Steinman was wrong about that. And, it seems he was wrong about the activities at White Sands. This was an Army command and still is. It seems unlikely that there would be a large Navy contingent there, and, if there were Navy activities, the guards would probably be Army. So this idea that they were watched by Marines seems unlikely.

The same can be said for the fighters. The F-94 did not become operational until the 1950s. The first test flights of the prototype didn't take place until 1949. And the base he claimed that they had come from, called Dias in the reports, is in reality Dyess Air Force Base. It had been known as Abilene Army Air Field until deactivated in 1945, and it wasn't fully reactivated until 1956 as Dyess. There were units stationed there as early as 1954, as it was being recommissioned, however.

So, although you could argue, I suppose, that he simply got the nomenclature of the aircraft wrong after all these years, and that he wasn't familiar with the radar defenses in Canada, there really is no good explanation for Dyess. It didn't exist in 1948, and at that point, had never existed. This is a real stumbling block.

But let's get to the important point. The man supplied, eventually, two photographs of the bodies. Both are gruesome. Both show something that has been badly burned. According to some, those bodies are of alien creatures. To others, they are not.

Remember there was a claim that there were no wires in the craft, yet in one of the pictures, you can see the burned remains of those wires. There seems to be other terrestrially made debris around the body as well, including a six-sided bolt. Well, he did say that part of the craft had been bolted together, but what are the odds that an alien race would use bolts that looked so terrestrial?

The clincher, however, are the wire frames of a pair of standard aviator glasses without lenses, that can be seen off the left shoulder of the body. This certainly argues for terrestrial explanation.

Steinman, in his book, argues for the authenticity of this case by saying:

> All the public attention from other quarters of the ufological community who were pushed out of the limelight, and that came "in spades". The usual team of debunkers were roused by the various agensies [sic] of counterintelligence and disinformation, no difficult thing to do given the strong egos that predominate in this field, and sent in to do battle. Taking their cue from counterinformation [sic] slyly fed them the opposition took the form of condemnation, snubbing, outright lies, and character assassination of all involved. Ninety days later the hullabaloo still had not abated, and the wrath of the UFO heirarchy [sic] intensified as various tabloids publicized the photos and story. This old disinformation ploy has worked for 30 years and is still being used. As a matter of fact, the revelations you have read in this book [*UFO Crash at Aztec*] are expected to rouse the same kind of reaction. Please note who the heavies are. You will see them next time.

This provides a glimpse into the mindset of those who believe the photographs are of an alien visitor. In fact, Steinman wrote, "Universally condemned as hoaxes by skeptics and establishment alike, the photos remain unidentified. No other legitimate explanation has emerged, nor even any other plausible theory holds up. There has been no lack of attempts to explain them away as something else, but none has stood very long."

One of those explanations that Steinman attacks, and rightly so, comes from Ground Saucer Watch (GSW). According to their analysis, the arm versus leg lengths and a careful study of the extremities, hands, and feet, showed features that were common to a rhesus monkey. Steinman simply doesn't accept their analysis, asking questions that are, in the end, irrelevant.

Apparently GSW didn't notice the aviator's glasses in the picture, and if they missed this, which, it happens, is quite clear, then how good could their analysis have been?

In the end, it is quite clear that this photograph is of a human killed in an aircraft accident. The burns and the swelling of the head are consistent with exposure to high temperatures. Damage done to other areas of the body visible in the picture and damage done to the wreckage are consistent with a fire. The man who provided the pictures must have known what they showed, and then invented the story to go with it.

I suppose one additional comment should be made here, and I haven't seen anyone else address it: This is the picture of a human killed in an aircraft accident. It seems wrong that it should be exploited in this way. Family and friends of the pilot would be quite distressed to learn what has happened here, but in today's hardened society, no one seems worried about that.

This case should be removed from the Ufological records. It is a footnote, only because there is published information, both in book form and on the Internet, that suggests this might have been extraterrestrial. No matter what a few confirmed believers might think, this has nothing to do with alien visitation, and we need to remove it. To do otherwise would be to violate our own standards. This case is solved.

For those interested in following up, take a look at the Del Rio, Texas, case of December 6, 1950, as reported later. You should recognize many of the elements of that tale, though it is told from a different perspective. And there, rather than having an unidentified photographer, we have the name of the pilot who was still alive in 2009 as I completed the work on this book. I talked to him, and some of those who reported on what he had to say.

# Chapter 5

## March 15, 1949

FARMINGTON, NEW MEXICO

According to a report prepared by Chuck and Vicky Oldham, the information came not from a firsthand source who was there, but from a source who saw the relevant documents while assigned to a military base and had access to a classified document library. During his review of material in that library, he came across a report that mentioned the crash of a saucer-like object with a slight dome on top. It was tilted slightly and setting on the desert, though it didn't appear that it had created a crater or disturbed the desert's surface.

The problem with this report is that the source claimed that there was no damage to the craft except for a small hole in one of the portholes. Examination of the craft failed to reveal any way to open it or enter it. The scientists and military officials present then focused their attention on the hole in the porthole, but were unable to widen it. However, they eventually got a door to pop open. The supposition is that they pushed something through the hole and hit the right control to open the door. This

Pre-1947

1947
Pre-Roswell

July 1947

October
1947–1948

1949–1952

1953–1964

1965

1966–1978

1979–1999

2000–2009

smacks of the Aztec case, where similar events were described, down to the damaged porthole and the fortunate pushing of the right button.

That's not the only similarity, however. The bodies of the two beings inside had been badly charred. This too is a detail reported by Scully and others in the Aztec case.

The report by the Oldhams suggested that hundreds of alien craft had flown over Farmington on the anniversary of the crash. According to the newspapers and other documents of the time, that sighting, or series of sightings, took place on March 15 and 16, 1950.

I would note here that this is a report that comes not from a witness, but from someone who said he read classified documents and who is not identified. It could be that the source was making it up, but there is another alternative that does not make the story told true, but means the witness is not lying. He could have read a report that was sent through the normal message channels of the military, which might have classified it and then filed it away. The source came to that file, read it, and was accurately reporting what it said. But as we have seen, and will see again, these reports aren't always based on fact, but on tales told by others.

Without some better information, such as the name of the source, and without some additional details that would allow us to figure out if there is any substance to the case, we have to treat it as we would all other single-witness cases, and that means look at it, but don't attach a great deal of significance to it.

## August 9, 1949

### HEBGEN LAKE, MONTANA

According to documents in the Project Blue Book files, case number 514:

On 9 August 1949, the AGENT [John P. Brynildsen] received a telephone call from Mr. LANGEN, Assistant Supervisor, Federal Bureau of Investigation District Office, Butte, Montana, to the effect that a Mr [name redacted] of West Yellowstone, Montana, had advised the Butte Office, FBI, that an employee of his, and a number of guests at the Lodge had, on the morning of 9 August 1949, sighted a flight of nine flying discs, two of which had landed in the immediate surrounding area. Seven of them were reputed to have come across the Lake area at about 0930 hours, two of these falling in the immediate area on the opposite shore of the Lake and one in the Lake itself. Approximately one-half hour later another "flying disc" was observed to have flown across the Hebgen Lake area.

Brynildsen, on that same date, contacted a second man whose name was also redacted from the file and learned from an eyewitness, a guide employed by the first man, the approximate location where the disks had fallen. He thought that the guide knew, within a few hundred feet, where the disks had landed. Brynildsen questioned him closely to be sure that what he had seen wasn't an aircraft, balloon, or other mundane objects. Satisfied that he had seen something unusual, he continued the investigation.

The next day—that is, August 10—Brynildsen questioned another witness, again whose name was blacked out, and was told that he had seen the first flight at 0930 hours and then a single object about 30 minutes later. According to him, two of the objects had crashed near the lake.

According to the report:

...the objects were the approximate size and shape of an automobile tire, and at the time of the sighting were not flying in formation.

Mr. [name redacted] stated that they were definitely not balloons, having the appearance of being constructed of metal and were grayish white. At the time of the sighting, Mr. [name redacted] was standing on a boat siding at the edge of Hebgen Lake, the objects came across a ridge on the eastern shore of Hebgen Lake, just barely skimming the top of the ridge...and were proceeding rapidly in a southwesterly direction. Two of the objects in the first flight crashed, one which crashed in the lake threw up a geyser of water, and the one which crashed in the woods on the opposite shore (a distance of two miles from the point at which [name redacted] was standing) raised a large cloud of dust as it hit into the woods. No fire, explosion or smoke of any kind accompanied the crashes. The remaining five objects disappeared rapidly from view across the ridges which are two miles from the western shore of Hebgen Lake. Mr. [name redacted] could not estimate the speed of the objects, however, he stated that none of the objects were visible to him for more than five to ten seconds, and the objects that crashed were visible for about two (2) seconds....

Brynildsen reported that there were supposedly other witnesses, but he was unable to find them. One was a camper who moved on before he arrived on the scene, and the employees of the lounge and other guests saw nothing themselves. He also tried in the nearby town and at the Ranger Station, but found no one else who had seen anything.

There is an agent's note at the bottom of page three of his report that I found interesting. Brynildsen wrote:

There seemed to exist an apparent attempt by a number of individuals to convince this AGENT that [name redacted] was absolutely reliable, trustworthy and beyond question, that if he said this incident occurred, it did. The statement was made by the [name redacted], Mr. [name redacted] that if anything was found, the [name redacted] might become a "Mecca" for tourists, and it was this AGENT'S impression that whether anything was found or not, Mr. [name redacted] would have welcomed the attendant publicity. Frequent conversations with the [name redacted], Mr. [name redacted] clearly indicated that he had a decided tendency to exaggerate, and that his conversation was often made up of grossly exaggerated stories.

On August 11, Brynildsen and Special Agent Robert P. Spalding searched the wooded area for anything from the crashed disk. They found nothing at all. Brynildsen reported that they found no evidence that anything had crashed into the woods such as broken trees or some kind of crater. Two days later, they both searched the area of the lake where the witness had said the second object had hit and again found nothing.

There is an indication from the file that something was eventually found that had a disk shape, but that wasn't all that big. Several days after the FBI closed out their investigation, another of the special agents reported that he had "in his possession a 'plastic disc-like affair'" that had been found in the Hebgen Lake area.

The investigation seemed to suggest that this was an "astradome" that could be found in C-47 aircraft. Captain Edwin Sarr, who was a Supervisor of Maintenance at the Great Falls Air Force Base, was contacted and suggested that it was of no use to the Air Force and it should be destroyed.

On August 16th, a report was sent to the Commanding General of the Fourth Army at Fort Sam Houston about the case and directed to the Assistance Chief of Staff for Intelligence (G-2). Paragraph three said, "It is the considered opinion of the interviewer that the six (6) reports of 10 August and the attached report or 11 August can be explained as the <u>natural</u> phenomena of a shower of meteors from the vicinity of the star Perseids which reaches its maximum display at this time."

On August 17, a message was sent from the Great Falls AFB to Wright-Patterson AFB, Ohio, outlining the facts of the case, including the search of the woods and the dragging of the lake. He wanted to know if a detailed report was desired, which apparently it was. That report took up seven single-spaced pages, and I have quoted from it here.

## August 19, 1949

### DEATH VALLEY, CALIFORNIA

Two prospectors, Buck Fitzgerald and Mace Garney, reported that they had seen an object crash into the desert. They thought that it was flying at something just in excess of 300 miles an hour. The disk hit a sand dune and they thought the craft was about 24 feet in diameter. Two small creatures that looked human hopped out and ran off into the desert. The prospectors gave chase, but it was too hot for them, and the creatures were too fast. They returned to where the disk had crashed, but it was gone.

The story was reported in the Bakersfield newspaper on August 21 and later reported in *The Book of Knowledge* as a legitimate UFO sighting. Some have suggested that this story provided the inspiration for the Silas Newton tales about the Aztec crash.

In fact, in his original article in *Daily Variety*, Frank Scully wrote, "Weeks ago these sages informed me they had checked on two of the discs which had landed here from another planet and even told where the platters had landed. The Mojave Desert got one...."

Nothing more was learned about this event, and Scully eventually moved everything out of California and into Arizona and New Mexico. But many of the facts in his new tales matched those from this report.

## February 1950

### LAREDO, TEXAS

When a small flying saucer crashed at the Laredo airport, a National Guardsman rescued the pilot and tried to revive him with oxygen. The little man leaped up, punched his rescuer, and then collapsed, unconscious. Revived a second time, again with oxygen, the creature reacted in the same way, attacking the rescuer. After a third revival, the little man died.

## February 18, 1950

### COPENHAGEN, DENMARK

Farmer Christian Sanderson and his wife claimed to have seen two flying saucers over their farmhouse. One of them stayed airborne, and the other landed nearby. It then disintegrated into thousands of brightly glowing sparks. No evidence was recovered, no more information can be found, and there were no additional witnesses.

## May 10, 1950

### ARGENTINA

Dr. Enrique Caretenuto Botta, an "architectural engineer," reported that, while driving on a rural road in Argentina, he spotted a flying saucer on the ground. Curious about the craft, he stopped his car, got out, and then entered the craft through a side door. He examined various instruments and found the bodies of three small men. After touching one of them, he panicked and fled, returning the next day with two friends. The craft was gone. They found a pile of gray ash, and in the sky overhead were a cigar-shaped craft and two small disks. The three objects merged. The cigar then turned blood red and disappeared.

## July 30, 1950

### St. John's, Newfoundland, Canada

A number of people in and around St. John's and the Pepperrell Air Force Base reported that they had watched an object as it crossed the sky at a relatively ordinary rate of speed. The object seemed to break up, and it was believed that pieces of the debris hit the ground near the Air Force base, but there are no reports of a recovery.

Typical of these reports is that of a painter (whose name was redacted from the report in the Project Blue Book files) who said:

> I was sitting on the top of the hill at the ball park in St. John's with my eight year old son. He kept looking toward the buildings at Pepperrell and asked, "What's this building?" and so on. As we looked, I saw a strange object in the sky near the area of the towers on the far side of the base. It was a blunt headed object, perhaps two or three feet in diameter, and at least 10 feet long. It was moving fast and trailing a brilliant stream of flame. It was only in sight about three or four seconds, and was gone. It seemed to appear from behind the hills.

At the Pepperrell Air Force Base, another witness said:

> ...It was traveling at a rather high rate of speed and was in sight for approximately one full second. It was moving in a shallow downward arc and disappeared in the vicinity of the White Hills transmitter site. It looked as if it struck the ground. It appeared yellowish red in color, and was in appearance at that distance (one mile away) the size of a soft ball (5" in diameter). I could see no other details other than that it was round in appearance. No smoke that I recall. The object appeared to be spinning and it had a considerable flame and spark trail behind it... It was brightly aflame as long as I could see it.

A lieutenant colonel [name redacted] probably identified this correctly when he said that he had seen an aerial object shoot across the sky from southeast to northwest. He said that it traveled in an almost horizontal line, but had a definite arc. He said that he was positive it was a meteor, the most beautiful he had ever seen.

## December 6, 1950

### DEL RIO, TEXAS

Now we enter controversy, as if we haven't entered it time and again. Todd Zechel, a UFO researcher known for his annoying habits of showing up unannounced, long telephone calls charged to others, and a research technique that was often less-than-average, originally provided the lion's share of the work on this case. It was based on a couple of paragraphs in an old "shopper" type newspaper and concerned UFO reports by pilots who flew for the Civil Air Patrol (CAP), the official auxiliary of the Air Force.

But, as I say, this doesn't begin with the sighting, but with Todd Zechel, who claimed that, while he was in the military, he learned some UFO facts and that, once discharged, attempted to chase them down. He told others that he had learned some very disturbing things and wanted to find out more about them. To do that, he hounded one retired colonel until the man threatened legal action against him.

That man wasn't the only high-ranking officer that Zechel found and exploited. Another was Robert B. Willingham, who provided a signed affidavit about his involvement in a UFO crash for the National Investigations Committee on Aerial Phenomena (NICAP) that found its way to the Center for UFO Studies (CUFOS). Willingham's story was interesting and considered authentic because, according to the information released about it, Willingham was a retired Air Force colonel.

In 1967, a reporter learned of this UFO crash and did a short article about it for his newspaper. That is to say that the reporter was interviewing CAP pilots about their UFO sightings and Willingham told briefly of a crash near the Mexico–Texas border. That information was eventually sent on to NICAP, where, apparently, nothing was done with it. Then, 10 years later, Zechel found the report and started his own investigation.

Willingham's story then, as told to others, is this, according to a 1977 affidavit he made and housed at the Center for UFO Studies, among other locations:

Down in Dyess Air Force Base in Texas, we were testing what turned out to be the F-94. They reported on the [radar] scope that they had an unidentified flying object at a high speed to intercept our course. It came visible to us and we wanted to take off after it. Headquarters wouldn't let us go after it and it played around a little bit. We got to watching how it made 90 degree turns at this high speed and everything. We knew it wasn't a missile of any type. So then we confirmed it with the radar control station on the DEW Line (NORAD) and they kept following it and they claimed that it crashed somewhere off between Texas and the Mexican border. We got a light aircraft, me and my co-pilot, and we went down to the site. We landed out in the pasture right across from where it hit. We got over there. They told us to leave and everything else and then the armed guards came out and they started to form a line around the area. So, on the way back, I saw a little piece of metal so I picked it up and brought it back with me. There were two sand mounds that came down and it looked to me like this thing crashed right in between them. But it went into the ground, according to the way people were acting around it. But you could see for, oh I'd say, three to five hundred yards where it had went across the sand. It looked to me, I guess from the metal that we found, chunks of metal, that it either had a little explosion or it began to disintegrate. Something caused this metal to come apart.

It looked like it was something that was made because it was honeycombed. You know how you would make a metal that would cool faster. In a way it looked like a magnesium steel but it had a lot of carbon in it. I tried to heat it with a cutting torch. It just wouldn't melt. A cutting torch burns anywhere from 3200 to 3800 degrees Fahrenheit and it would make the metal hot but it wouldn't even start to melt.

Willingham said that he took the metal to a Marine Corps metallurgy lab in Hagerstown, Maryland, for analysis, which is strange, because he was flying the missions out of a Texas base. Hagerstown would be more conveniently located to someone living in Mechanicsburg, Pennsylvania, where Willingham lived at one time. This is a point that might be of value as we continue our search for answers.

Willingham said that when he tried to learn the results of the tests, he was told that the man he asked for had never worked there, and no one there knew anything about a piece of metal from a flying saucer. Willingham was later told never to discuss it and signed an oath of secrecy. Obviously, he decided against adhering to this oath.

Len Stringfield, in his privately published monograph *The Crash/ Retrieval Syndrome,* reported: "In September of 1979, Jim [Minton] called to relate that he had talked with a former Air Force friend, William Draeger of Austin, Texas, who had uncovered some information about a 1950 crash incident occurring in Mexico."

Len wrote:

I knew the incident well, and that it had been disputed by some researchers, however, I had not pursued the case beyond having referred to the alleged crash in my previous paper. At that time I had used information related by Todd Zechel to the *Midnight Globe.* Since, further research into the case by Zechel and others has revealed that not only the year of the incident was wrong, having changed from 1948 to 1950, but also the crash site had changed.

The connection here, then, is Zechel, and that is an important one. There are a number of stories about a UFO crash near the Texas–Mexico border. The 1948 incident seems to be the one that generated the "Tomato Man" photographs dicussed earlier. That case is linked to this one through Zechel, and, if that is true, then Stringfield has revealed a major flaw in both cases, which is the shifting date.

Draeger interviewed, or was present during the interview of, the retired colonel, who we now know as Willingham. Draeger reported to Stringfield for his *Crash/Retrieval Syndrome*:

The retired Colonel who witnessed the UFO in the air and later on the ground...reported the soldiers surrounding the crashed craft were Mexican troops. I contacted the Mexican Army General who had command of that specific area of the border and initially talked with him by telephone...and related that in 1950 a UFO was reported to have crashed 30 miles northwest of Del Rio, that we had along [with us] a pilot who had seen it in the air and later on the ground being guarded by Mexican troops until American Air

Forces arrived to retrieve the craft and the body that was found aboard. Without a pause, the General answered, "Yes, I now about that. I don't have any papers or documents to prove it, but due to my position, I know about this.

When I asked if he would consent to an interview he paused and said that he would be busy for 30 minutes but afterwards would be free for an interview in his home. When the 7-man-crew, the retired colonel and myself arrived and we talked to him, he totally denied any knowledge of the incident and on camera he denied and evaded any questions dealing with the incident and UFOs.

So we have two dates for the crash, and we have a witness, a high-ranking member of the Mexican military who, apparently said he knew of the event, but later denied that. We don't have the general's name, just that he was a general and very important. And, we have new locations and new facts that seem to be in conflict with one another, and that certainly doesn't bode well for this sighting.

I wanted to make sure that everything I knew had been updated as I worked on this story, so I decided to see what I could learn about it. According to various Websites, and the information in a book published in 2008, Willingham had again been interviewed, had been identified as at the center of the case and provided his extensive eyewitness testimony in great detail. Noe Torres and Ruben Uriarte, the authors of *The Other Roswell: UFO Crash on the Texas-Mexico Border,* were most gracious with their time and information as I tried to update the story. They reported:

A radio message warned Willingham and others about a fast moving UFO that was approaching Texas from the northwestern U.S. Suddenly it came into their view like an intensely bright light—like a bright star seen through a telescope. It blazed across the sky past them, and everyone in all the planes saw it. But because of the location of Willingham's jet, he was in the best position to see what happened after the object flew by.

Willingham estimated that the object was traveling at 2,000 miles per hour, and he saw it make a sudden 90-degree turn, without slowing down. As the UFO streaked toward the Texas-Mexican border, Willingham received permission to break from the formation and pursue the object in his F-86 fighter. Following the object's vapor trail, Willingham followed it down to near Del Rio, Texas, where he saw it suddenly begin to wobble and descend rapidly.

There were many additional details about this case available. According to the writers of the book, which is, of course, what was reported to them, Willingham was part of a group of F-86 fighters, and they were escorting a B-47 across West Texas when they received the message about the UFO. They watched the craft as it flashed across the landscape, eventually heading to the south of their position.

Willingham told Torres and Uriarte that the object hit the ground south of Langtry, Texas (which, by the way, is a little to the northwest of Del Rio), digging a 300-yard-long furrow before coming to rest alongside a sandy hill. Uriarte filled in more details when he said:

> The aviator [Willingham] returned to the scene of the crash a few hours later.... They landed the small plane right along side the crashed UFO and noticed that a large number of Mexican soldiers had already taken control of the crash site. They had cordoned off the area and would not allow Willingham or Perkins to approach the main part of the wreckage. However, what they were able to see and look at was so amazing that it forever changed their lives.
>
> Before being forced to leave the area by the Mexican military, Willinghan picked up a chunk of strange metal debris that was about the size of a man's hand. He later tried to burn it, cut it, and otherwise deform it, but was not able to.

Uriarte concluded that it was a piece of something not of this world—evidence of the crash that, if it could be analyzed today, might provide proof, but of course, we all know that Willingham lost it, as he had told others 20 or more years ago.

One of the major problems is that the story had now moved in time to the mid-1950s. Willingham told me he thought it might have been 1954, but he wasn't sure. Torres and Uriarte reported it was 1955. In other discussions with Willingham, it might have been as late as 1957. No matter how you looked at it, the date had been altered, again.

Here is where this takes us. A high-ranking officer, who claimed he was denied his pension (which, technically means he wasn't a retired officer) because he talked about his sighting, said that he had seen a

UFO crash, had witnessed some of the retrieval operation, and had even taken a piece of the wreckage that he had tried to have analyzed. Both Torres and Uriarte said that they accepted the story because of Willingham's credentials as a longtime military officer. He even provided them with some documentation to prove his case.

I, of course, having been burned in the past by accepting documentation given to me by the witness, wanted to pursue this further. I asked a number of UFO researchers who had been part of the investigations in earlier years what they knew about Willingham's background, and the answers were similar. Each assumed that Zechel had checked it out. One even told me he thought that Zechel was a careful researcher. Each assumed that Willingham's claims had been verified.

So I decided to check this out myself, and asked for help from both Torres and Uriarte. Torres sent me a picture of Willingham in an Air Force uniform, standing with a member of the Air Force Thunderbirds and a member of the Army's Golden Knights parachute team. That seemed to answer the question until I realized that Willingham was in a CAP uniform and not Air Force uniform. Close examination of the picture verified that.

I asked for additional information, and Torres sent me what they had, but it wasn't helpful. It proved a long association with the CAP, including documents dated in the 1960s showing that Willingham had changed CAP assignments, gave a CAP serial number, but again, did nothing to prove that he had been a member of the Air Force Reserve. Again I asked for more.

I received pictures of Willingham in uniform, one from the 1960s and one from 2004. There were problems here as well: The distinctive insignia on the lapels had been removed. On an Air Force uniform, it would have been U.S., and on the Civil Air Patrol uniform it would have been CAP. Clearly he is wearing his CAP ribbons on the uniform, along with CAP pilot's wings. He is wearing a number of Army ribbons as well, but on the CAP uniform, there is nothing wrong with that. On the Air Force uniform he would not be wearing his CAP ribbons or wings. That is simply not authorized, and that tells us this is a CAP uniform with the distinctive insignia removed.

So there is a problem with those pictures. They do not prove Willingham was in the Air Force Reserve and hints at his thinking, but it doesn't prove much. The changing nature of the tale, including dates, locations, and aircraft, is worrisome. The question becomes: What do we do with this story? Witnesses telling stories from memory often make small mistakes or alterations in the tale from telling to telling. Dates might shift as the witness consults notes or realizes that he or she has gotten the sequence wrong. We all expect these sorts of things, and a report made in the same way, perfectly each time, suggests hoax rather than authenticity.

But where do we draw the line? This report from Willingham moved from 1948 to 1950 and now to 1955, though Willingham has insisted that Zechel assigned the date. In his original affidavit, he said that he was flying F-94s, but now says it was F-86s. He originally said that he was denied permission to give intercept, but now claims he was ordered to do so. He mentions the DEW line, which wasn't established in 1950 and wasn't operational in 1955.

To try to get a handle on this, I consulted with the National Personal Records Center in St. Louis, asking about Robert B. Willingham. In a letter dated February 5, 2009, I was told that the only information they had, that was releasable under the Privacy Act of 1974, was that Robert B. Willingham had served in the Army from December 8, 1945 to January 4, 1947, and had been a Technician Fifth Grade, a low-ranking enlisted man. He had served in the European Theater of Operations, and his military education had been as an engineer, and he had gone to Welding School and had been a "Motor Vehicle Dispatchor [sic]."

They told me:

> If the records were here on July 12, 1973, it would have been in the area that suffered the most damage in the fire on that date and may have been destroyed. The fire destroyed the major portion of records of Army military personnel for the period 1912 through 1959, and records of the Air Force personnel with surnames Hubbard through Z from the period 1947 through 1963.

However, the record from St. Louis was for the right man. Willingham confirmed that it was his record and his Army service number. That would suggest that his files were not destroyed in the fire and that his claim of additional military service is in error. Also, Willingham's records wouldn't have been closed out until after 1973, if we believe his claims of military service, so they wouldn't have been there to be destroyed by the fire. But the records we can recover from a disinterested third party only document a short tour in the Army.

Both Torres and Uriarte finally received a number of documents from Willingham that seemed to prove his Air Force Reserve service. Here was something that we could check out in an attempt to verify his long military service.

I will note that he told me he had been originally commissioned in the Army, and I found nothing to support that. Having been commissioned in the late 1940s would have allowed him to go to flight school and serve as a pilot in Korea as he claimed, but that raised other concerns, given the documentation that he supplied.

To prove that he had been a commissioned officer, Willingham sent a copy of a listing of those in OCS from Shavetail, a yearbook for the OCS classes. This indicates he was in class 51 D, which graduated in December 1951, which means that he was not an officer in 1950 and he had not received a commission in the Army as he told me. If he was in that OCS class, then he couldn't have been a pilot in Korea. There is no way that a commissioned officer would be in an OCS class as a student. There is no way for an enlisted man to pilot Air Force aircraft, so he had to have been commissioned prior to 1950. This is a real problem for Willingham and, until he can supply some official documents verifying his military service, we are left with only his story about the UFO crash.

The final point to be made is that this is a single-witness story. There have been no others found to verify it, though there are suggestions that many would have been involved. Until additional and better information is offered, we must declare this as insufficient data.

# 1950

## Mexico City, Mexico

Ray L. Dimmick reported that a flying saucer had crashed, killing the pilot, who was only 23 inches tall. Dimmick said that Mexican authorities roped off the crash site and military officials removed the wreckage. At first, Dimmick claimed he had seen he craft crash, but later retracted that, saying that two friends had told him about it. All he had seen was a strip of metal about 6 feet long.

## November 2, 1951

### ARIZONA

A gigantic green fireball blazed over Arizona. Unlike some of the other green fireballs reported where there were only a few witnesses, more than 165 people reported having seen this one. Some claimed that it flew parallel to the ground, and some were lucky enough to see it explode. All the witnesses reported that there was no sound, either during the flight or during the explosion. The fireball just seemed to disintegrate.

## Late Summer 1952

### NORTH OF COLUMBUS, OHIO

Vivian Walton, who worked for the Army's Signal Corps, decoded a classified message that told of a crash near Columbus. Later, a co-worker showed Walton photographs of a saucer that she described as 30 feet in diameter with almost no damage. The retrieval team had trouble entering the craft, which was unoccupied. The saucer was taken to Wright-Patterson Air Force Base.

## September 12, 1952

### SPITSBERGEN ISLAND, NORWAY

The story that a UFO had crashed on Spitsbergen Island, north of Norway and situated between the Norwegian Sea and the Barents Sea, has been around since 1952 and is even responsible for a very credible report made to Dr. Steven Greer's CSETI organization. The Air Force received a number of classified communications about the crash, and those documents can be found in the Project Blue Book files. An officer who remembered seeing those reports shared that information with Greer, who did not realize that it referred to the Spitsbergen UFO.

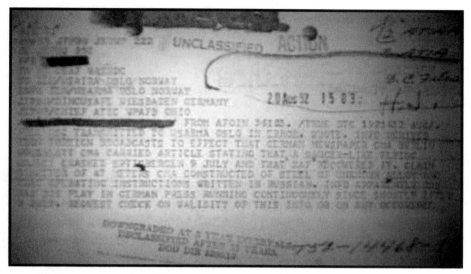

*5.1. Spitzenberg crash official report. Author's photo.*

The initial tale, as it appeared in the Project Blue Book files, reported that on July 9, 1952, a Berlin newspaper, *Saarbrucker Zeitung* reported that the Norwegian Air Force had recovered a flying saucer on Spitsbergen Island. According to the article, a translation of which is in the Air Force files, Norwegian Air Force Captain Olaf Larsen happened to look down, then entered a dive, and

> [o]n the white snowy landscape, the crusty surface of which had an icy glitter, there was a metallic, glittering circular disc of between 40 and 50 meters diameter, which was even brighter than the icy snow.... While circling for 60 minutes, the jet pilots could neither detect any sign of life nor determine the origin or type of vehicle.

Others, in five "flying boats" landed near the "bluish steel disc." According to the article, "'Undoubtedly one of the infamous flying saucers,' claimed Dr. Norsel, a Norwegian rocket specialist....'"

According to the report, the object had a diameter of 48.88 meters, with slanting sides, and was unmanned. It was made of an unknown metal compound. "After ignition, 46 automatic jets, located at equal distances on the outer ring, rotate around a plexiglass center ball that contains measuring and control devices for remote control, fired."

The real problem here is that the article reports that the "measuring instruments (gauges) have Russian symbols...[and it] has sufficient room for high explosive bombs and possibly nuclear bombs."

Finally, in what would make those who believe the Nazis had a flying saucer at the end of the Second World War happy, the report claimed, "After hearing of the description of the disc, the German V-weapon designer Riedel stated: 'That's a typical V-7 on whose serial production I have worked myself.'"

The article was signed only with the initials, J.M.M. Ole Jonny Braenne, a Scandinavian researcher, tried to find the writer, but was unable to do it. In an article published in the *International UFO Reporter*, Braenne wrote, "The author of the article...has proven untraceable. Newspaper archives have no useful information on the matter."

This seems, then, to be the first appearance of the story of the Spitzbergen crash. The important point here is that they—meaning either the journalists or the witnesses—weren't talking about an interplanetary or interstellar craft, but something that had been created by the Soviets using technology stolen from the Germans after the Second World War. This is more of a story of an experimental craft that went astray than something from outer space.

Air Force officers—meaning here, I suspect, the Air Attache in the United States embassy—sent a teletype message reporting on what the newspaper said and requested additional information. None appears in the Blue Book files, but the case is labeled as a hoax by them. According to other sources, however, the Norwegian Air Force told the attache that the story was definitely false.

Years later, an Air Force officer who was on duty in one of the Air Force communications centers told researchers that he'd seen a classified report about Spitsbergen Island come through the center. This was used to prove that the government was hiding something about UFOs in general and crashes in particular. The problem was that the Blue Book files have been declassified, and we have copies of those reports. The officer was right. There had been classified messages, but other additional information suggested the case was a hoax, some of it appearing not long after that Air Force officer had seen the initial report.

Some two years later, after the case was mentioned in a couple of books without much in the way of resolution, the story surfaced in another German newspaper, *Hessische Nachrichten*, on July 26, 1954. This time, the Norwegian General Staff was involved and was preparing a report based on their examination of the crashed flying saucer. The chairman of the board was identified as "Colonel Gernod Darnhyl."

Darnhyl was quoted as saying:

> *A misunderstanding developed, some time ago, when it was stated that the flying disc was probably of Soviet origin. It has—this we must state emphatically—not been built by any country on earth. The materials are completely unknown to all experts, either not to be found on Earth, or processed by physical or chemical processes unknown to us.*

Darnhyl said that they wouldn't release the report until they discussed some of what they had found with experts from the United States and from Great Britain. He did say that they "must tell the public what we know about the unknown flying objects. A misplaced secrecy may well one day lead to panic!"

That wasn't all Darnhyl said. He promised to release the information and then said that he thought that "within the next twelve months, a solution to these technical problems will be found, or, at least, science will be on the right track towards solving the UFO problem.... Scientific results will only be released subsequent to a UFO conference in London or Washington."

If nothing else, this provided some names, including the writer of the article, Swen Thygesen, and a time line for the release of information. We know, of course, that neither the information was released nor the UFO conferences held. It has been more than 50 years. Worse still, Braenne reported that he had been unable to find a trace of the writer.

The story then switched to South America, which means that South American newspapers began printing articles, and moved the crash to Heligoland. According to an article from *Verdens Gang* on December 19, 1954, a story from the Uruguayan newspaper *El National* reported that the famed (well, that's my comment—his fame is limited to these stories) Hans Larsen Loberg, who, it was claimed, had won a prize in physics in Hungary, was now involved. Loberg said that this concerned the same saucer that had been reported to have crashed on Spitsbergen but that it had crashed on a small island that had been a German submarine base during the Second World War.

Loberg said that there had been no Russian writing in the craft, and that it had a diameter of 91 feet and a thickness in the middle of 70 feet. Once inside, they found the food pills and heavy water reported in other crashes, books that they thought might be navigational aides, and seven bodies of the crew, burned beyond recognition. The bodies, according to Loberg, were between 25 and 30 years of age, were all just more than a meter and a half in height and all had perfect teeth. They did not explain how bodies burned beyond recognition would be determined to be so young. I will note that much of this description smacks of the Aztec tale.

Now we see that Frank Edwards, in his book, *Flying Saucers—Serious Business,* gets into this and reports the tale came from the *Stuttgarter Tageblatt.* Edwards commented: "The story vanished from the newswires as though it had been launched into space...until at last the silence was broken by a spokesman for the government of Norway... the account I quote is typical of the innumerable papers which carried the story:

Oslo, Norway, September 4, 1955:—Only now a board of inquiry of the Norwegian General Staff is preparing publication of a report on the examination of the remains of a U.F.O. crashed near Spitzbergen (sic), presumably early in 1952. Chairman of the Board, Colonel Gernod Darnbyl (sic), during an instruction for Air Force officers stated: "The crashing of the Spitzbergen disc was highly important. Although our present scientific knowledge does not permit us to solve all the riddles, I am confident that these remains from Spitzbergen will be of the utmost importance in this respect. Some time ago a misunderstanding was caused by saying the disc probably was of Soviet origin. It has—this we wish to state emphatically—not been built by any country on earth. The materials used in its construction are completely unknown to all experts who participated in the investigation."

This is basically the same article that had been circulating earlier, and still no one had confirmation of it. I wonder if Frank Edwards knew that quoting an article would make it seem as if he had checked it out to verify its authenticity. Edwards then hinted that the lack of follow-up information could be laid at the doorstep of the United States. He wrote:

> Therefore Norway, in 1955, was discussing with two of the leading exponents of UFO deception the proposed release of this information which would have exposed the falsity of both the U.S. and British official positions!... It is not difficult to conclude that the Norwegians never released the full report because of the advice they received from two of Norway's best customers.

In other words, both the United States and United Kingdom pressured the Norwegians through the threat of economic sanctions to keep their full report under wrap. Edwards never seemed to consider the possibility that the story isn't true. After all, he had the newspaper clipping about it. Or did he?

We go back to Braenne, who reported in his *IUR* article, "Several authors have used *Stuttgarter Tageblatt* as the source for their Spitsbergen story. It is, in fact, a nonexistent newspaper. [No researchers] have ever found any trace of either such a paper or such an article published on, or around, the date given...."

So where did this article come from? Braenne has an answer for that question. He wrote in his *International UFO Reporter* article that he had learned that a Dutch magazine *UFO-Gids* published, with minor changes, the article that had appeared in *Hessische Nachricten. UFO-Gids* lists *Stuttgarts Dagblad* as the September 5, 1955 source. According to Braenne, "Evidently someone tried to Germanize *Stuttsgarts Dagblad* and did not investigate his source."

Edwards apparently used a translation from one of those earlier sources without checking. Edwards did suggest he had tried to learn something more about this, reporting in his book, "In 1964 when I wrote to a member of the Norwegian Board of Inquiry which had investigated the Spitzbergen case, I received, after four months, a cryptic reply: 'I regret that it is impossible for me to respond to your questions at this time.'"

Edwards, caught up in the paranoia of the UFO field, believes that the reply is more of the cover-up. It might just be that there was no other reply that could be made if the case was not real. But Edwards doesn't identify his source on this, so we are left wondering about the legitimacy of this claim. If there was no Spitsbergen crash, then there was no Board of Inquiry and therefore no board member for Edwards to question.

Ryan Wood reported, in his *Majic Eyes Only*:

In 1985, the British researcher Philip Mantle looked into the case and was informed by the Norwegian Government that nothing even remotely resembling the Spitsbergen crash had ever occurred. "The whole story seems utterly unfounded," Mantle was told by Arild Isseg, the head of the Information Division, Norwegian Royal Ministry of Defense.

Furthermore, several of those people cited in both newspaper articles and official intelligence summaries of newspaper articles on the Spitsbergen story simply did not exist.

In 1986, the issue was confused again by William Steinman in his *UFO Crash at Aztec*. He got the Spitsbergen and Helgoland crashes confused. And he added that the pilot who first spotted the crash did not return from the mission.

William Moore, one of the authors of *The Roswell Incident,* reported in one issue of his *Focus* newsletter on December 31, 1990, that he had found a translation of a French article from 1954. This came from a Swiss report that suggested the crashed craft was the result of Nazi experiments with saucers and that it had been recovered by Canadian commandos. Moore thought this was the best account of the event and thought it the best explanation he'd heard for the Spitsbergen crash.

When all is said and done, there seems to be no evidence that the crash took place, and the origin of the story seems to be a newspaper that made up the details. I don't know if the editors of the newspaper trusted their reporters to get the story right, or maybe those editors just made it up to fill space and invented a name or added initials to give it a note of authenticity.

The problem here is the same one that has faced UFO research from the beginning: Each time a case is exposed as a hoax, another person comes along with inside knowledge that he claims will prove the case. No evidence is ever presented, but he still swears by the information, and five years from now, someone else will suggest the story is true.

## November 1, 1952

### HELGOLAND, GERMANY

Pat Bontempo, in 1995, provided me with a copy of his research into the Helgoland UFO crash of the mid-1950s. According to him, the first mention of this crash is in a men's magazine called *SIR!*, in an article written by E.W. Grenfell. Although it contained irrelevant information about the Mantell case, which Grenfell consistently misspells as Bandell, and about windshield pitting in Bellingham, Washington, it also contains information about the Helgoland crash, which all sounds suspiciously like the Aztec and Spitsbergen crashes recycled.

In this article, Grenfell told us that the UFO had been knocked down by atomic testing in the Pacific Ocean, which hardly makes sense. The object or craft crashed, or touched down, on the tiny island of Helgoland, in the North Sea and off the coast of Germany, which had been a German U-boat base during the Second World War. One of those investigating the crash in 1952, according to the article, told the tale to Dr. Hans Larsen Loberg, a retired Norwegian scientist who was described as a one-time winner of the Hungarian Physics Award and who popped up in the Spitzbergen case as well.

According to the story published in *SIR!*, this might not have been a crash but rather was a landing, because the instruments were in good condition. On the ground, outside the craft, however, were the bodies of seven men, all burned beyond recognition, but it wasn't clear if they were aliens killed in the crash or locals killed as they approached too close to the craft too soon.

Grenfell then went off on a tangent in his article, reporting on windshield pitting in the northwest, windshields that fell apart, and finally suggested that no one could come up with an answer for the mystery (though science actually explained it by saying that people had been looking through the windshields without noticing the pitting; now they were looking at them and seeing the normal wear and tear for the first time). The only motive for mentioning this mystery was to bring his article into the 1950s and to move it to the United States, though he did try to blame flying saucers for the windshield damage. Besides, magazine editors are always looking for the local angle to appeal to the readers.

Not satisfied with the mishmash of scientific fact, Grenfell then gave his inaccurate retelling of the Mantell crash, and in one short paragraph manages to misname the base, get Mantell's branch of service wrong, and even repeatedly misspell Mantell's name. Mantell was the National Guard officer killed in 1948 while chasing a UFO near Godman Army Air Field in Kentucky. I mention this only to point out that there isn't very much in his article that is reliable. The facts of the Mantell case are well-known and easily checked.

Finally, we move back to the Helgoland crashed saucer. According to Grenfell's story, Loberg thought the craft had landed, apparently under its own guidance systems and instruments. For some reason, the scientists called in to study the craft bombarded the area with cosmic rays, Geiger counters, and other protective devices before they approached. Yes, I know you can't bombard an area with a Geiger counter, but that is what was claimed in the article—and yes, I know that it makes no sense.

Loberg said the scientists on the site didn't know if the bodies found outside the craft were human or alien. Their clothing had been burned away. Although he couldn't identify them—or maybe those other, unnamed scientists couldn't identify them—they did suggest that all the victims were from 25 to 30 years old, all of the same height, and all had excellent teeth. The age and teeth sound like descriptions from the Aztec crash.

All the measurements of the craft—a diameter of 91 feet and a cabin of 70 feet—were divisible by seven. In fact, all the dimensions were divisible by seven. Loberg didn't explain why the aliens built a craft and used feet for a measurement, but this is reminiscent of the system of nines that Scully had reported concerning the Aztec crash.

Loberg claimed there were living quarters on the ship with enclosed bunks on one side of the main cabin. There was a liquid, like water but three times heavier, and a tube filled with pills, which might have been food.

The radio, according to Loberg, had no tubes or wires, was about 4 inches by 3 inches, and was about an inch or so thick. Found with it were pamphlets that he thought were for navigation, but no one could read the strange script, and Loberg didn't explain how he knew these might be navigation aids.

In fact, Bontempo, in his private report, including a copy he provided to me, said that he had counted 28 specific details that were lifted from the Scully book and were reminiscent of the Aztec crash. These included the bombardment with cosmic rays and a Geiger counter, the pamphlets that dealt with navigation, and that they studied the craft from a distance for two days before approaching.

Loberg, according to the article, believed that the craft might have traveled by using the magnetic lines of force around the Earth and that he believed encircled all the nine planets of the solar system. Of course, this was the 1950s when there were nine planets. He said nothing about the dwarf planets, nor those thought to be out beyond the Kuiper Belt, including some larger than Pluto.

With that, and some other later articles, a few of which confuse the Helgoland and Spitzbergen events, change the locations, and add some other detail, Helgoland basically disappears from the crashed saucer lore.

The one important exception appeared in Len Stringfield's *Status Report III,* in which he wrote:

> Some researchers speculate that the crash site may have been Helgeland, near Oslo, Norway. Stranges [meaning Frank Stranges, a contactee] writes about a Dr. Larsen Loberg from Oslo who investigated the case of a crashed UFO in 1946. But no man with that name lived in Oslo...a woman who visited Helgoland (German) in 1961 told a researcher many people in the island would speak about the UFO crash in the North Sea, east of Helgoland. There were many rumors. A business friend of the same researcher said that he heard about a UFO falling into the seas. The Administrator of Helgoland however, told him: "No fragments from outer space were found on the island." Note the cleverness of this statement about no fragments on our island. Nobody said anything about a UFO crash on Helgoland, only near the island.

Stringfield was, of course, reporting what he had been told about the case without explaining the shift in time and location from the island to a place in Norway with a similar name. The shifting nature of the data, the recycled nature of it, and the heavy borrowing from the Aztec case suggest that the report is nothing more than a hoax.

## 1952

### EDWARDS AIR FORCE BASE, CALIFORNIA

Len Stringfield reports that "a reliable person in a technical position" was on radar duty when he saw a UFO descending rapidly across his radar screen. When it was confirmed that the UFO was down, the captain on duty told him that he hadn't seen anything.

Later the radar operator learned that a flying saucer had crashed in the desert. It was more than 50 feet in diameter, with a row of windows or portholes around the center. He also heard that it had contained a flight crew who were approximately 4 1/2 feet tall. The ship, debris, and the bodies were shipped to Wright-Patterson Air Force Base.

## 1952–1955

### NEAR AURORA, OHIO

Jerold Johnson reported that he had interviewed a couple who had learned from the former chief engineer of the Kent office of Ohio Edison that he had gone out to investigate a power outage. The problem was cut lines, apparently caused by an object that had dropped from the sky, cutting through the lines. It created a crater 30 feet long and about 9 feet deep. The man, according to Len Stringfield in his *Crash/Retrieval* report, was able to approach the wreckage and saw a "small box of dense material with one knob on it, which continually emitted a tone or beep." The Army arrived and made sure the civilians left the area, telling them that there might be a danger of radiation. The military cleaned the site. It required two tractor-trailer trucks to remove the debris.

# Chapter 6

## 1953

### ONTARIO, CANADA

Police Constable Florian Giabowski watched an oval-shaped object in the evening sky. The object suddenly exploded, disappearing from sight. Moments later, a strange blue rain began to fall. Tests made by the Defence Research Board showed that the samples recovered were abnormally radioactive.

## 1953

### DUTTON, MONTANA

Cecil Tenny told Len Stringfield and reported in his *Crash/Retrieval Status Report* that, while on vacation, he saw an object at a low level that he believed to be in some kind of trouble. The cigar-shaped object was in sight for seven or eight minutes before it exploded, raining balls of fire down on the road.

Tenny stopped at the closest bar and told the patrons what he had seen. He was told later that a state police officer had been in and the patrons had given him Tenny's name as a witness.

Pre-1917

1947
Pre-Roswell

July 1947

October
1947—1948

1949—1952

1953—1964

1965

1966—1978

1979—1999

2000—2009

That evening, someone at the Great Falls Air Force Base called Tenny and told him to report to the base. For 30 minutes, he was interrogated in a colonel's office and then required to sign a statement.

As he was being escorted out, he saw two men carrying what he thought were laundry bags over their shoulders. When one of the men dropped his bag, it was obvious to Tenny that they contained bodies.

## 1953

### JOHANNESBURG, SOUTH AFRICA

One of Len Stringfield's contacts reported there had been a retrieval in South Africa in 1953. No other data is available.

## 1953

### ARIZONA

Len Stringfield, in his January 1980 *The UFO Crash/Retrieval Syndrome,* reported that he had spoken to a firsthand source, whom Stringfield did not identify other than to say that he had served as a warrant officer in the Army and then in the Air Guard until he left Ohio without leaving a forwarding address.

The man said that he had seen the bodies of aliens killed in a UFO crash that happened, as near as he could tell, in 1953 somewhere in Arizona.

Stringfield wrote that this was his first encounter with a firsthand witness and that he impressed Stringfield as a sincere and no-nonsense character. Stringfield wrote:

> ...he recalled that he had stood just inside a hangar at a distance of about 12 feet, peering at five crates on a forklift. In his judgement, the crates appeared to be hastily constructed and were made of wood. In three of these, little humanoids appearing 4 feet tall, were lying unshrouded on a fabric, which he explained prevented freeze burn from the dry ice packed beneath. As a number of Air Police stood silent guard nearby the crates, he managed to get a reasonably good but brief glimpse of the humanoid features. He recalls that their heads were hairless and narrow, and by human standards were disproportionately large, with skin that looked

brown under the hangar lights above. The eyes seemed to be open, the mouth small, and the nose, if any, was indistinct. The arms were positioned down alongside their bodies, but the hands and feet, he said, were indistinct. When asked about their attire, he said they appeared to be wearing tight-fitting dark suits, and, because of the tight-fitting suit, there was one revealing feature—a surprising feature. One of the humanoids appeared to him to be female. He said, "Either one of the aliens had an exceedingly muscular chest or the bumps were a female's breasts." Later he learned from one of the crew members, with whom he bunked at the barracks, that the body of one of the aliens was believed to be that of a female.

My informant also heard from the crew member that one of the entities was still alive aboard the craft when the U.S. military team arrived. Attempts were made to save its life with oxygen, but they were unsuccessful.

This might be the first of two reported cases in Arizona, as mentioned by a Stringfield source who appeared in support of the Kingman case which follows shortly. This could be a small corroboration for that source by providing some hints of the second crash... which means here, that I placed it first because all we had was a year and not a day or month. For more information, see May 21, 1953, Kingman, Arizona (page 160).

# 1953

## New Mexico

Len Stringfield reported that a letter dated April 8, 1964 was sent to the National Investigation Committee on Aerial Phenomena (NICAP), based in Washington, D.C., that described a possible UFO crash. According to the letter:

> Here at school [Bob Jones University] is an instructor, who during the Korean conflict was an adjutant to an Army Air Corps General at one of our New Mexico proving grounds. I got the following from him.
>
> In 1953 a flying saucer crash-landed near the proving grounds. Air Force personnel immediately rushed to the area and found the saucer, unharmed and unoccupied, with doors open. Upon searching the surrounding area they came upon the bodies of the saucer's four occupants, all dead.

Shortly after this, certain top level personnel were given the true saucer story by Air Force officials. In his capacity my source was included in this. They were shown the bodies of the four occupants of the ship, which he described as from three to four feet tall, hairless, and otherwise quite human in appearance. An autopsy had been performed on one of them to determine the cause of death. No cause for their deaths was ever found. Also at this time, they were shown three saucers which the Air Force has. He described them as ovoid, with a length of twenty-five feet and a width of thirteen feet. They were shown the interior as well and there were no visible means of control, no visible means of propulsion. He told me that since that time, the Air Force has been working intensely, though unsuccessfully, at trying to discover the means of propulsion.

Dick Hall, who has been involved in UFO research almost from the very beginning, said that he had met with a lieutenant colonel who claimed to know something about the case. According to Hall, the officer said he had seen four bodies of alien creatures at Langley Air Force Base, and he had been told they had been recovered from a crash near White Sands, New Mexico. Hall did not reveal the name of the lieutenant colonel.

## May 21, 1953

### KINGMAN, ARIZONA

Like so many of the crashed UFO tales, this one is basically a single witness—or rather, a single identified witness, and then some testimony from another source that suggests corroboration. That second witness is secondhand, having heard the story from her late husband. And then a hint of additional witnesses who seemed to have leaped on the Kingman bandwagon later. In other words, in the final analysis, it is not a strong case, but has the potential to be one.

When first reported by Raymond Fowler in the April 1976 issue of *Official UFO,* it seemed that it might be one of those reports that went nowhere. Without some corroboration and some documentation, it would be impossible to accept, and it is next to impossible to verify.

Fowler, however, accepted the report because he had interviewed the witness, and he had a signed affidavit and a few documents that seemed to support the story. The evidence was flimsy, but it did exist. That put Fowler, at least in the minds of some, ahead of most who had found other single-witness UFO crash cases.

*6.1. Kingman, Arizona. Author's photo.*

The first interview of the witness was conducted on February 3, 1971, by Jeff Young and Paul Chetham, two young men with an interest in UFOs. In fact, in a newspaper article published in the Framingham, Massachusetts, edition of the *Middlesex News,* Young was identified as a boy writing a book about UFOs for juveniles. The article mentioned that Young had interviewed a man who had claimed he worked with Project Blue Book, the Air Force's UFO study, and had made contact with a spaceship.

According to Young, the witness, later given the pseudonym "Fritz Werner" by Fowler to protect his identity (but known to us in today's world as Arthur Stancil; I will use the Werner name throughout to avoid later confusion), had been at the site of a flying saucer crash approximately 20 years earlier. Werner, according to the information provided, was a graduate engineer who had degrees in mathematics and physics and a master's degree in engineering. He graduated from Ohio University in 1949 and was first employed by the Air Materiel Command, which, according to UFO history, was responsible for the reverse engineering of the Roswell craft. There seems to be little evidence to tie Werner to any of that, though he was tied to Dr. Eric Wang, who has been identified in UFO circles as leading the team reverse engineering UFOs.

During the Young and Chetham interview, Werner first told of just seeing a UFO during one of the atomic tests in Nevada. He and his colleagues had been drinking beer when they heard a humming and whistling noise and ran outside. The object, coming toward them, hovered for a while, but they couldn't tell much about it because it was night.

During the initial interview Werner told Young that he had worked for Project Blue Book. He speculated that Blue Book was created because the Air Force "was getting too much publicity and there were too many people, other than official people seeing these things and reporting them."

I suppose here it should be mentioned that, in 1976, the Air Force declassified the Project Blue Book files and we were able to develop a history of the project. We know when it was created, the original name for it (Sign), and that its mission was to determine exactly what the UFOs were. Later, it evolved into something else, mainly a public relations effort, but Werner's analysis on this is in error. Of course, his mistake about the creation of Blue Book means very little. Many people are unaware of the histories of the organizations for which they work.

Anyway, Young and Chetham finally asked specifically about the UFO crash in Arizona, and Werner said:

> *The object was not built by anything, obviously, that we know about on Earth. This was in 1954 [actually, according to other information, 1953]. At that time I was out of the atomic testing, but I was still with the Air Force and this was the time I was on Blue Book. There was a report that there was a crash of an unexplained vehicle in the west and they organized a team of about forty of us. I was one of the forty.*

According to Werner, he had been alerted "through official channels and on a private phone line from the base commander at Wright Field [later Wright-Patterson AFB] saying that you're a member of Blue Book and we would like for you tomorrow to get on a plane, go to Chicago and from there to Phoenix." According to Werner, the object had crashed about 25 miles from Phoenix.

The object was 12 feet long and fairly intact, according to Werner: "It was more like a teardrop-shaped cigar...it was like a streamlined cigar." It was made of a material that Werner said he'd never seen before and it was dull.

Young mentioned that there had been stories of an object crashing in Arizona, and that one person had claimed to have photographed an occupant in a silver spacesuit. Werner responded, saying, "I saw the creature you're talking about. It was real and I would guess about four feet tall."

Werner described the creature as being dark brown and speculated that the skin might have darkened because of exposure to chemicals in the atmosphere. He saw two eyes, nostrils, and ears. The mouth looked as if it was used "strictly for feeding," though Werner didn't explain how he knew this. He hadn't gotten a good look at the body because, at the time he saw it, the military had already moved it into a tent.

Once he left the crash site, Werner wasn't through with UFOs. According to the second part of the interview, Werner claimed to have made contact with other beings from the saucers. It seemed that Werner had not only seen the body, but later conversed with the flying saucers. Werner told Young, "Now we're getting into things where you'll just have to take my word for it because I can't...prove it."

In subsequent interviews, Werner didn't mention his "contact" with UFOs. He would provide those later investigators with an excuse for this, but one that seems to hurt his credibility rather than help it.

Raymond Fowler, who later learned of the report though the newspaper, had figured it was just another tall UFO tale. He received a couple of telephone calls from friends interested in the case and then decided to look into it. Fowler contacted the witness and set up his own interview.

Werner told a slightly different version of the story to Fowler. None of the changes seemed significant at the time, and most could be explained as the normal shifts in the retelling of a tale. However, Werner also made some disturbing claims.

According to Werner, he was working in the Frenchman Flats area of Nevada when he was called by his boss, Dr. Ed Doll, and told he had a special assignment. Werner boarded an aircraft at Indian Springs Air

Force Base, north of Las Vegas, Nevada, and was flown to Phoenix. Once there, he was put on a bus with others who had already gathered. They were warned not to talk among themselves and then were driven into the desert to the northwest.

The windows of the bus were blacked out so that the passengers couldn't see where they were going. Werner believed they drove about four hours until they reached an area near Kingman, Arizona. Night had fallen before they reached their destination.

This is the first of the problems. Anyone who looks at a map realizes that it would have been quicker to take them from the Indian Springs Air Force Base to the Kingman area rather than travel first to Phoenix. I suppose you could suggest that they, meaning those running the operations, did that in an attempt to hide the real location. Or it could mean that Werner's guess about the location is in error. It might mean that the real site is somewhere in the Phoenix area rather than in the northwestern corner of the state.

When the bus stopped, they climbed out, one at a time, as their names were called. Although they had been told not to talk to one another, there was an officer supplying the names of all those on the bus, calling them out. It would provide those involved with a way of learning more about the assignment after they were returned to their regular duties, because they had the names of the others on the bus. That seemed to be a curious way to maintain security. It was a major breach. It also suggests the second of the problems with the Kingman report.

Werner was escorted from the bus by military police. Two spotlights illuminated an object that looked like two deep saucers pressed together at the rims. It was about 30 feet in diameter and had a dark band running around the center. The craft was dull, looking as if it was made of brushed aluminum. Werner estimated that the craft weighed about 5 tons.

There was no landing gear visible on the underside of the object and no sign of damage to it, although it had slammed into the ground. Werner could see no dents, scratches, or marks on the surface.

The only sign of impact was the evidence from the desert floor and the fact that a small hatch seemed to have sprung open. Werner said the hatch was curved and the interior of the ship was bright, but that could have been because of the lighting installed by the Air Force, rather than anything from the interior.

Werner made his examinations, including measurements of the trench the ship had gouged out of the sand, the compression factors involved, and estimated the weight of the ship. He believed that the craft had been traveling about 1,200 miles per hour when it struck the ground.

According to Werner, as each specialist finished his examination of the craft, he was interviewed in front of a tape recorder and then escorted back to the bus. None of the others was allowed to listen to his debriefing, and he was not allowed to listen to any of theirs.

Before he got to the bus, Werner saw a tent that had been erected on the site, guarded by armed military police. Inside the tent was a single body of a 4-foot-tall humanlike being. Werner said it was wearing a silver suit that had a "skullcap" that covered the back of the head but left the face visible and unprotected. The skin of the face was dark brown, but again Werner thought the coloration might be a result of exposure to the Earth's atmosphere or the effects of the crash. Allowing him a look at the creature is another breach of the tight security around the site.

It is interesting to note here that, in the descriptions of the aliens, one theme is mentioned again and again: The skin is a dark brown and it is believed that the color is the result of either something to do with the crash, or exposure to the atmosphere. I'm not sure if this detail is significant. It might be a coincidence born of thoughts of fire during the crash.

At any rate, on the way to the bus, Werner had the chance to talk to one of the others. The man had looked inside the craft. He'd seen two swivel-like seats, and instruments and displays, but that was about all. And here is still another breakdown of the security measures. Before Werner learned much more from the man, one of the guards saw them talking and separated them, warning them not to compare notes. He did nothing else, such as getting their names and reporting the security breach to his superiors.

On the bus, everyone was required to take an oath of secrecy. They were not to talk about what they had seen or done to anyone at any time. They were then returned to Phoenix and their regular assignments.

Werner supplied a long professional resume that listed not only his engineering status, but his educational background and a list of his professional publications. It suggests that Werner is a highly trained engineer, and it doesn't seem likely that he would jeopardize his professional standing with a hoax about a flying saucer. However, he didn't want his name used, so it could be argued that he was not jeopardizing anything.

In fact, Fowler, in his report to NICAP, documented a number of contradictions between what Werner had told him and what he had said to Young during that first interview. The major problem was that Werner originally reported that the object was 12 feet long and 5 feet high and looked like a teardrop with a flat bottom, not like two deep saucers fastened together at the rims.

Fowler pointed out that Werner told him that the object was disk-shaped, 30 feet in diameter, and about 20 feet from top to bottom. Fowler wrote in the April 1976 issue of *Official UFO*:

When confronted with this contradiction, the witness appeared flustered for the first time and said that he had described the object he had seen over Thule, Greenland, to the boys [Young and Chetham]. I reminded him that he had described the Thule sighting to me as having been a black disc seen at a distance. He started to insist until I produced the copy of the transcript, which clearly indicated that he had described the crashed object, not the Thule object, to the boys. At this point, he backed down and admitted that he had lied to the boys. He said that the description given to me was accurate because I was really conducting a serious investigation into the matter. In my opinion, this is the most significant and damaging contradiction without a completely adequate explanation.

There was a series of other discrepancies between what Werner told Fowler, and Young and Chetham. Most of them could be attributed to memory lapses, or, as Werner suggested, his exaggerations to the boys. It wasn't that he was intentionally trying to mislead them; he just wanted to tell them a good story. This, he suggested, was a result of the martinis he had consumed before the interview with the boys began.

For Fowler, he produced a page from his daily calendar dated May 20 and 21, 1953. It seemed to corroborate part of the story. The entries said, "May 20—Well, pen's out of ink. Spent most of the day on Frenchman's Flat surveying cubicles and supervising welding of plate girder bridge sensor which cracked after last shot. Drank brew in eve. Read. Got funny call from Dr. Doll at 10:00. I'm to go on a special job tomorrow."

The only interesting point was the reference to the special job given to him by Dr. Doll. But it doesn't tell us much, and it could refer to practically anything at all.

"May 21—Up at 7:00. Worked most of the day on Frenchman with cubicles. Letter from Bet. She's feeling better now—thank goodness. Got picked up at Indian Springs AFB at 4:30 p.m. for a job I can't talk about."

Again, nothing to suggest that Werner was involved in a crash retrieval—only that he had some kind of special assignment. And yes, it does seem strange that he would note in his unclassified desk calendar that he was involved in a special project that he can't talk about.

Fowler, to his credit, tried to verify as much of the story as he could. He tried to verify Werner's claim that he had worked with Blue Book. Fowler, in his report to NICAP, explained that he had spoken to Dewey Fournet, a former Pentagon monitor for Project Blue Book, and Fournet had said that he didn't recognize the witness's name, but then, he didn't know all the consultants assigned to Blue Book over the years.

Because that proved nothing one way or the other, Fowler talked to Max Futch, who had been a temporary chief of Blue Book. Futch said that he thought he had known all the consultants and didn't remember Werner, under his real name, being among them. Importantly, Futch was assigned to Blue Book during 1953, the time frame suggested by Werner.

On the other hand, Fowler called three friends of Werner's as character witnesses. Each of them said essentially the same thing. Werner was a good engineer and a trusted friend, and never lied or exaggerated.

However, noticing the differences between this interview and that conducted by Young and Chetham, Fowler had his doubts. Fowler said that he met Werner at his office on May 25, 1973, to discuss the problems with him. Werner claimed that the discrepancies were the result of mixing up dates, which he later corrected by checking his diary.

Werner also said that he had been under the influence of four martinis when he talked to the boys. When he drinks, he said, he exaggerates and stretches the truth. Fowler checked with Young and was told that Werner had only had one beer on the day that he was interviewed. Of course, Werner could have had his four martinis before the boys arrived. While they were there, he only consumed the one beer.

But what Werner had done was shoot down his own credibility. His friends said that they had never known him to exaggerate, but he told Fowler he did after he had been drinking.

It began to look as if his story was just like that told by Gerald Anderson about the Plains of San Agustin crash: No independent corroboration for it, and when the story was checked, those checks failed to produce results. Werner's explanations for the failure of the corroboration left a great deal to be desired.

William Moore, co-author of *The Roswell Incident,* in his 1982 presentation at the MUFON Symposium, reported:

> Fowler's source, the pseudonymous "Fritz Werner" (whose real first name and some of his background are known to me) claimed that on the evening of May 20, 1953, he received "a phone call from [his superior] Dr. Ed. Doll, informing [him] that [he] was to go on a special job the next day." When I asked Fowler if he had checked this part of the story with Dr. Doll, he responded that his efforts to locate Doll had been unsuccessful.

In fact, in his report, Fowler said that he had confirmed that Doll existed, and that Doll had been an employee of the Atomic Energy Commission and had been at the Stanford Research Institute. It seems unlikely that Werner would name a man for corroboration who could, if found, tear his story apart quickly, but that was what Gerald Anderson had done with his Dr. Buskirk.

Moore said that it took him just four days to locate Doll, and that he met with him on October 9, 1981. Moore asked him what he knew about the incident near Kingman, and Doll said that he knew nothing about it. Moore then asked him about Werner, using his real name, and wrote in his 1982 paper presented at the MUFON Symposium that year, "I was somewhat taken aback by his flat statement that no one of such a distinctive name and rather distinguished technological background had ever worked at the Nevada Test Site."

Moore then dismissed the Kingman story, writing, "I don't know quite what to make of this case...since my own investigations into the matter have produced nothing but dead ends...I am inclined to spend my time pursuing more productive matters."

The single glaring error in Moore's analysis is the claim that Fowler's source has a distinctive first name. In the past year, I have located a signed copy of the affidavit, along with the professional resume, and a full analysis of the case by Fowler. In other words, I have Fowler's source's name, Arthur Stancil, and there is nothing distinctive about his first name. Of course, knowing how Moore operates, it might be he said first name and actually meant last name, which is distinctive. It seems that Moore's claims about the case might be without foundation.

I have learned quite a bit about Moore in recent years, and, without something more definitive than his uncorroborated statements, I am inclined to reject Moore's analysis. It might be nothing more than an attempt to reject other tales of crashed saucers in an attempt to keep the Roswell case as the most important UFO crash case. This is similar to what he might have done with the Del Rio case told by Robert Willingham and reported by Todd Zechel. In fact, Moore's actions might be an attempt to return Roswell to unique status.

Remember, too, that in 1989, Moore claimed to have operated as an unpaid agent of disinformation. He told researchers that, in his role, he had spied on fellow researchers, supplying information about them to the Air Force. He engaged in a deception directed at another researcher to discredit him. And he said that he had supplied disinformation to researchers to divert them into areas that would provide nothing useful.

It doesn't really matter if Moore was telling the truth about these activities, because no matter how you slice it, he has killed his own credibility. If what he says is true, then we can't believe much of what he says because we don't know what is tainted by his association with these other agents of disinformation. If he is not telling the truth about this, then what else has he been less than candid about? It is the classic lose-lose situation. And the point is that Moore is the one who created it.

Len Stringfield, however, found another witness who corroborates part of the Kingman story. According to Stringfield's monograph, *Retrievals of the Third Kind,* Cincinnati researcher Charles Wilhelm said that a man identified only as Major Daly had told Wilhelm's father that in April 1953 he had been flown to an unknown destination to examine the remains of a crashed flying saucer. He had been blindfolded and driven to a point out in the desert where it was hot and sandy. Inside a tent, the blindfold was removed and he was taken to another location, where he saw a metallic ship, 25 to 30 feet in diameter. He saw no signs of damage. He spent two days analyzing the metal from the ship, which he claimed was not native to Earth.

Daly was not allowed to enter the ship, though he did note that the entrance, or hatch, was about 4 or 5 feet high, and 2 to 3 feet wide, and was open. When he finished his analysis, he was escorted from the area.

Daly's information didn't agree exactly with that given by Werner, but it was close enough. The discrepancies can be explained by the point of view of the teller. He saw things from a different angle, and his experiences were slightly different. It does seem to provide some corroboration for the Kingman crash story. The real problem is that it is secondhand, at best, and that moves us right back into the realm of Gerald Anderson. His story seemed to be corroborated by a series of secondhand sources, all of whom were unavailable for independent review. In fact, no one knows if Daly exists, or existed at all.

Stringfield also reported on a man who was in the National Guard (though I wonder if it wasn't actually the Air Guard, a distinction that those who haven't served in either might not make) who claimed that he saw the delivery of three bodies from a crash site in Arizona in 1953. He mentioned that the creatures had been packed in dry ice, and were about 4 feet tall with large heads and brownish skin, which does corroborate Werner to a limited extent.

Stringfield, in his 1994 self-published monograph, *UFO Crash/ Retrievals: A Search for Proof in a Hall of Mirrors,* reported still another claim of the Kingman crash.

According to him:

My new source JLD, a resident of Ohio, north of Cincinnati, in a surprising disclosure claimed that a close relative, the late Mr.

Holly, who had served in a top command (in a defense department capacity [whatever that might mean]) at Wright-Patterson in 1953, told him about one of two crashes in Arizona. He also told him three bodies, one severely burned, and parts of the wrecked craft, were delivered to the base.

Those two reports—Major Daly and JLD—are the classic "friend of a friend" stories. The information doesn't come from the source, but from someone else, and when you are that far removed, the chances for mistakes, misunderstandings, and confabulation increase. Yes, the information is interesting, and it does provide some corroboration, but the fact is that such reports are quite dubious. This is something we run into time and again when dealing with UFO crash reports.

There is more secondhand information about Kingman. A woman, June Kaba, who worked in the Parachute Branch (WCEEH-1) at Wright-Patterson Air Force Base, reported that a sergeant, who she didn't identify and who had a special clearance needed to enter the office, claimed that he had just come in on a flight from the Southwest. Thinking about it years later, she had believed he was talking about the Roswell crash, but an examination of her records, supplied to me, showed that she had not been working at Wright-Patterson until the early 1950s.

Further checking suggested that the incident she remembered took place in late 1952 or early 1953. The sergeant told all the people in that small office about bringing alien bodies to Wright-Patterson. Naturally, the people in the office didn't believe the story because it was so outrageous.

Within an hour, however, the base commander, Colonel (later Brigadier General) C. Pratt Brown, arrived at the office. He explained the story the sergeant told was just rumor and speculation, and that no one was to repeat these wild rumors anywhere. In fact, he brought an official form for them to sign, explaining that they were not to report what they had heard under penalty of a $20,000 fine and 20 years in jail.

I will note here that Brown was, in fact, assigned to Wright-Patterson at the time, first as the base commander and later as a special assistant to the commander of the AMC. This means, simply, that the information about Brown was accurate and lends a note of authenticity to the report. Please note that I suggest it is only a minor corroboration.

The problem is clearly that the secretary did not remember the exact time frame, location, or name of the sergeant. To suggest this was part of the Kingman case, we must resort to speculation based on the limited documentation of her employment experience at Wright-Patterson. The only crash that fits is the Kingman event, and the connection to it is extremely weak.

And the colonel coming around to tell them to forget it and that the story is rumor, and then demanding they sign statements, is another problem. The only thing the colonel did by those actions was tell them the story was true. He hadn't come around to stop other rumors, only this one. Then he underscored the importance of it by demanding they take an oath of secrecy.

The Kingman case has been blundering along on the periphery of legitimacy for a number of years. It would be easy to write off, especially with the problems of the Werner account, if not for another source, this one discovered by Don Schmitt, who reported it to me.

During research into the abduction phenomenon, he learned of a woman, Judie Woolcott, whose husband had written her a strange letter from Vietnam in 1965, believing that he wouldn't be coming back from overseas.

According to her memory of the letter, he had seen something strange 12 years earlier. Judie Woolcott thought that it had been August 1953, and, although she might be mistaken about the month, she was sure that it happened near Kingman. Her husband, a professional military officer, was on duty in an air base control tower. They were tracking something on radar. It began to lose altitude and disappeared from the screen, and then in the distance there was a bright flash of white light.

Woolcott wrote that the MPs began talking about something being down. Woolcott and most of the men in the tower left the base in jeeps. They drove in the general direction of the flash, searching. Eventually they came upon a domed disk that had struck the ground with some force, embedding itself in the sand. There didn't seem to be any exterior damage to the craft, and there was no wreckage on the ground.

Before they had a chance to advance, a military convoy appeared. Woolcott and those with him were stopped before they could get close to the disk. They were ordered away from it and then escorted from the site. They were taken back to their base, where they were told that the event had never happened and that they had never seen anything. Just as others have been, they were sworn to secrecy.

Woolcott didn't write much more in the way of detail. There didn't seem to be any external reason for the craft to have crashed, and he didn't see any bodies. But there was talk of them. Some of the military police said that there were casualties that were not human. Woolcott made it clear that he hadn't seen them; he'd just heard talk.

The letter indicated that he knew more, but didn't want to write it down. According to Judie Woolcott, about a week later, she learned that he had been killed.

Here was a source who knew nothing about the Kingman case who was able to provide a little more information about it. Although the time frame is off slightly, it is interesting that she was sure of the location. During his interview with her, Schmitt said that she brought up Kingman, and that stuck because he thought about calling Ray Fowler when the interview ended.

I need to note here something that I find curious about this end of the report, and that is that Judie Woolcott didn't have the letter. It would seem to me that one of the last communications with her husband would be of significant sentimental value. It would be something that she would want to keep, even if it took a trip into the unusual by mentioning a flying saucer crash. That document, dated in the mid-1960s, would be of value to researchers.

I will add here that after my mother died in 1995, I had the unhappy task of going through much of her personal property. I was surprised to find a stack of letters that I had sent to her from Vietnam. She kept them all, and I now have them. Of course, the difference here might be that I survived the tour in Vietnam. Still, I find it strange that Woolcott would not have saved the letters her husband sent to her during his tour.

There is a final chapter to this story. In today's world, all sorts of databases are available, and one of those lists every American who died during the Vietnam War. The only Woolcott listed is a PFC, Randall Woolcott, who was born in 1948 and died in Vietnam before his 20th birthday. He was unmarried.

But I have learned that Woolcott had been married a number of times and that her husband's name might not have been Woolcott. In her obituary, published online in July 2009, she was Judith Anne Woolcott (Miller, Fingal). Searches of the databases with the various combinations of names used by Woolcott have failed to produce any corroboration for the story of the crash.

This would suggest that the story told by Judie Woolcott is not accurate. Yes, I'm using a rather weasel-worded sentence here, because there is a remote chance that the Internet information is inaccurate in some way. I doubt that, and because of that I hesitate before calling someone a liar. But this information seriously compromises the veracity of the Woolcott tale.

Even with that, we can say that no longer is the Kingman case built completely on the testimony of a single witness of dubious reliability. Werner seems to be a solid citizen who, by his own admission, tells tales when he has been drinking. Given that, it would be easy to write off Kingman as nothing more than a delusion by someone who occasionally drinks and tells tall stories and slipped one about a UFO crash to a couple of teenagers.

The mere fact that nothing appears in the Kingman newspaper, as mentioned by Moore in his 1982 symposium paper, might not be completely relevant. A search I conducted of the Las Vegas newspapers also failed to supply a clue, but then, if the recovery was a military operation with no civilian participation or observation other than those brought in, the fact that the newspapers failed to report it might not be important. The military might have been able to keep the whole story bottled up.

And now, with two other independent, though admittedly strange sources that lead to Kingman, maybe it is time to reevaluate the case. It is interesting to note that Werner provided one date until he checked his desk calendar, finally providing researchers with a different date. Both Major Daly and Judie Woolcott provided different months, but they did get the location and the year right.

The testimony and documentation for the Kingman event are still quite thin. We had one firsthand source who might have been telling a story that mushroomed after it appeared in a local newspaper. We have two apparently independent sources who provide some corroboration, but both are secondhand. Woolcott, or whatever his name was, provides an interesting view of the event, but there was never a chance to interview him, whether Woolcott, Miller or Fingal, prior to his death in Vietnam.

Unlike some of the reports of crashed saucers, the Kingman story does have multiple witnesses, limited documentation, and a living firsthand source. For all its faults, it is still better than the majority of the UFO crash/retrieval cases. Without more information, more corroboration, and more firsthand sources, there is little that can be said for the Kingman case. Given what we now know, it seems that the report desires more attention. There are some names attached to the tale and there are some facts that we can attempt to verify, but with this case, the good, solid evidence seems to be just out of reach. The least we can do, however, is try to verify some of it, or prove it to be a hoax.

## Summer 1953

### FT. POLK, LOUISIANA

Len Stringfield, in his *Status Report III,* tells of a sergeant he identifies only as HJ who claimed personal knowledge of a UFO crash in Louisiana. He said that he was stationed at Ft. Polk and they were in the field training, when at dusk, an egg-shaped object crash-landed nearby. He said the object was large and had some kind of a fin-like protrusion around the center. He said that medics and high-ranking officers arrived, removed the bodies of three dead aliens, and assisted the single survivor. He said that it was about 4 feet tall and had a large head. He said that he heard it died soon after it was taken from the craft.

## 1954

### MATTYDALE, NEW YORK

Two people, an information specialist and his wife, claimed to have seen an object, about 20 feet in diameter, on the ground being examined by several men. Photographs of it were taken by officials. The next day, according to the source, the local police denied that anything had happened.

## Mid-1950s

### BIRMINGHAM, ALABAMA

The military cordoned an area around a crashed flying saucer. A helicopter transported the alien bodies of the flight crew to Maxwell Air Force Base.

## February 14, 1957

### CHILE

The Lima, Peru, newspaper *Las Prensa* claimed that authorities had discovered a 3,000-foot-long translucent object near the Bolivian border on the slopes of a volcanic peak. Although authorities were investigating, nothing more was ever reported.

## September 1957

### UBATUBA, BRAZIL

The skeptics are always asking for physical evidence, and frankly I don't see that as an unreasonable request. We are asking them to accept the idea that aliens are visiting Earth, and we should be prepared to offer some powerful evidence in return. Of course, coming up with piece of alien material isn't all that easy, though there is one case where it was claimed that pieces of metal came from an exploding flying saucer and some of those pieces were recovered by civilians. Eventually, two of the samples made their way to the United States, where they were tested several times.

The journey begins, or it might be said, ends (at least for the UFO), when Ibrahim Sued, a society columnist for *O Globo,* a Rio de Janeiro newspaper, received an anonymous letter. In his column, he wrote:

> Dear Mr. Ibrahim Sued. As a faithful reader of your column, and an admirer of yours, I wish to give you, as a newspaperman, a "scoop" concerning flying discs. If you believe that they are real, of course. I didn't believe anything said or published about them. But just a few days ago I was forced to change my mind. I was fishing together with various friends, at a place close to the town of Ubatuba, Sao Paulo, when I sighted a flying disc! It approached

the beach at unbelievable speed and an accident, i.e. a crash into the sea, seemed imminent. At the last moment, however, when it seemed it was almost striking the waters, it made a sharp turn upward and climbed rapidly on a fantastic impulse. Astonished, we followed the spectacle with our eyes, when we saw the disc explode in flames. It disintegrated into thousands of fiery fragments, which fell sparkling with magnificent brightness. They looked like fireworks, despite the time of the accident, at noon, i.e. at midday. Most of the fragments, almost all, fell into the sea. But a number of small pieces fell close to the beach and we picked up a large amount of this material—which was light as paper. I am enclosing a sample of it. I don't know anyone that could be trusted to whom I could send it for analysis. I never read about a flying disk being found, or about fragments or parts of a disk that had been picked up. Unless the finding was made by military authorities and the whole thing kept as a top-secret subject. I am certain the matter will be of great interest to the brilliant columnist and I am sending two copies of this letter—to the newspaper and to your home address. From the admirer (the signature was illegible), together with the above letter, I received fragments of a strange metal....

Dr. Olavo T. Fontes, a respected Brazilian physician and an investigator of UFOs, not to mention the Brazilian representative of the now defunct Aerial Phenomena Research Organization (APRO), saw the letter and contacted Sued. While in Sued's presence, Fontes was allowed to study the small samples. Fontes later wrote in his report to APRO that:

I saw the samples sent by the unidentified correspondent— three small pieces of a dull-gray solid substance that appeared to be a metal of some sort. Their surfaces were not smooth and polished, but quite irregular and apparently strongly oxidized.... The surface of one of the samples was shot through with almost microscopic cracks.... The surfaces of all samples was covered in scattered areas with a whitish material. These whitish smears of a powdered substance appeared as a thin layer. The fine, dry powder was adherent but could be displaced easily with the nail.... Mr. Sued said the material appeared to be lead at first sight—because of the gray color—but I could see that it could not be lead...the material was light...almost as light as paper.

Sued, who cared little about UFOs, gave the samples to Fontes for examination and analysis. There is no indication that Fontes took the letter, which was unsigned, but could have been of value to later investigators. He then took the material to the Mineral Production Laboratory, a division of the Brazilian Agricultural Ministry's National Department of Mineral Production. In other words, he found a competent lab to do the analysis that was not associated in any way with UFOs or APRO.

There, Dr. Feigl, the chief chemist, and Feigl's assistant, Dr. David Goldscheim, made an initial examination of a small chip from what Fontes had designated Sample 1. They determined that it was a metal. They then divided Sample 1 into several pieces. Two were left with the laboratory, and Fontes retained the rest (together with Sample 2 and Sample 3). Goldscheim sent one piece of Sample 1 to the Spectrographic Section of the Mineral Production Laboratory, where it was investigated by Dr. Luisa Maria A. Barbosa, a chemical technologist, using a Hilger mass spectrograph, model DMA 1-412 (a high-quality instrument). In her report, dated September 24, 1957, Barbosa reported, "The spectrographic analysis showed the presence of magnesium of a high degree of purity and an absence of any other metallic element."

So, using the best equipment available to them, they concluded that the first sample was made of magnesium and that there seemed to be no impurities in it. This led to the conclusion that it was 100-percent pure magnesium, which some investigators at the time said was unobtainable in any Earth-based process. That, of course, leads directly into the extraterrestrial, if those tests could be validated.

Fontes then requested a second spectrographic analysis of Sample 1, and this was done by Elson Texeira at the same lab using the same Hilger spectrograph. This yielded similar results to the earlier tests.

Fontes, in his report to APRO, wrote:

> The spectrographic analysis identified the unknown metal as magnesium and showed it to be absolutely pure—as it can be concluded from the study of the spectrographic plate taken with the Hilger spectrograph. No other metal or impurity was detected in the sample analyzed; even the so-called "trace elements," usually found with any metal, were not present.... A comparison... between the spectrum of the unknown metal and that of a chempur

magnesium salt...demonstrated the extreme purity of the metal in the sample.... Even impurities that might exist in the carbon rod used as electrode (i.e., traces of Mn, Fe, Si, and Ti), sometimes appearing as contaminants, were not detected in this case.

Details in his report do not support the claims of absolute purity. He wrote, "A comparison was made between the spectrum of the unknown metal and that of a chempur [sic] magnesium salt. It showed clearly that they were identical—in fact, all their spectrum lines corresponded with each other. This demonstrated the extreme purity of the metal in the sample."

Now we begin to get into the technical aspects of this, as one analysis argues with another and scientists attempt to interpret the results of the tests. If the magnesium is 100 percent pure, then the implication is that it is of extraterrestrial origin. If it is not, then the possibility of terrestrial manufacture is not excluded.

But the scientists who later reviewed the material, including Dr. Peter Sturrock and who noted in his paper, "Composition Analysis of the Brazil Magnesium," available from multiple sources on the Internet that

[o]ne would like to know why the Hilger spectrograph did not show the usual contaminants from the carbon rod. Clearly, there is the possibility that the Hilger spectrometer malfunctioned, but it would be surprising if a similar (presumably rare) malfunction had occurred for both the Barbosa and Texeira analyses.

The tests did not end there. The Brazilian Army requested a sample and Fontes sent one to Major Roberto Caminha, and a second fragment was sent to Commander J.G. Brando of the Brazilian Navy. The results of those tests were not given to Fontes, and I mention them only because it suggests an avenue to learn the truth about the purity of the samples before they left Brazil.

Fontes thought that X-ray diffraction might provide additional information. Although the samples had been declared "pure" in a spectroscopic sense, it didn't mean that there were no non-metallic contaminates. X-ray diffraction should detect those sorts of contaminates.

Dr. Elysiario Tavora Filho, a professor of mineralogy at the National Chemistry School and who was recognized as a pioneer for his work on crystallography, made these tests. His first test showed that the magnesium was of amazing purity and so surprised him that he ran the tests several times to be sure of the results. The magnesium was pure with no sign of contamination.

Throughout the tests there were hints of an impurity that couldn't be identified. The impurity seemed to be part of the gray dust, or ash, that covered the samples and might have been a result of the explosion or falling from the sky into the ocean. They were able to determine that the impurity was magnesium hydroxide $Mg(OH)2$, plus magnesium in its metallic form.

The end result of the testing was that the magnesium was pure and that the unidentified lines on the X-ray film were the result of contaminates on the surface of the sample but were not part of the internal structure. This sample was, according to these tests, purer than the ASTM standard for purity.

Fontes had more tests run, attempting to learn all that he could. In the report he sent on to Coral Lorenzen at APRO, he suggested that the sample he had was actually purer than the standard on which purity was based and that, according to Fontes, meant it represented something that was outside the range of the technological developments of science on Earth and that it was probably extraterrestrial in origin.

Fontes then sent the samples to APRO headquarters in the United States. APRO in turn submitted a small portion of one of the fragments to the Air Force for spectroscopic analysis. In what is probably just ineptitude, the Air Force technician accidently destroyed the sample without managing to obtain any results. The Air Force requested another sample, but because samples of possible extraterrestrial origin are difficult to obtain, APRO denied the request.

Now the story becomes confused because most of the testing had been done on the first sample, and it had been consumed by those tests. In some of them conducted in the United States, it was suggested that spectroscopic analysis had, in fact, detected some impurities, including aluminum, iron, silicon, calcium, and copper. These tests, conducted by the Atomic Energy Commission, seemed to indicate that the samples weren't all that unusual, and that would suggest they weren't extraterrestrial in origin.

But UFO research is nothing if not inconsistent. These latest tests might have been flawed. The impurities detected might have been contamination, not on the sample, but on the electrodes used to create the spectrum. Ironically, Texeira's opinion was that the American tests, to that point, were irrelevant and worthless from a scientific standpoint.

While all this was going on, Fontes was trying to find witnesses to the explosion. He spent time on the beach and the surrounding neighborhoods, but found no one who would admit to seeing anything... that is assuming there was anything for them to have seen. Fontes was of the opinion that Brazilian military officials had found them first and told them not to talk.

When the U.S. Air Force created the Condon Committee at the University of Colorado, APRO volunteered to loan a sample of the Ubatuba metal to researchers there. This might have been considered, at least by those in APRO, as the best evidence available to prove extraterrestrial visitation. After all, the labs in Brazil, and some of the work done in the United States, suggested that the technology that produced the samples was not available on Earth at the time the debris was recovered. It was only 10 years later that technology existed to prove the case.

Analysis of the Brazilian sample was given to Dr. Roy Craig, who has given a narrative account of his experiences with the Colorado Project. The results of his investigations into the Brazil magnesium are summarized in the Condon Report (pages 94–97 of the paperback edition).

According to the information published by Sturrock, Craig said he contacted and early in 1968 visited Dr. Busk, who informed him that Dow Chemical Company had, for about 25 years, produced a number of batches of very pure magnesium by the process of repeated sublimation, and provided him with a specimen of triply sublimed magnesium. Craig was advised that the most sensitive tests for impurities would be neutron activation analysis. He therefore arranged to take a specimen of the Brazil magnesium and (for comparison) a specimen of the Dow triply sublimed magnesium, to the Alcohol, Tobacco, and Firearms Laboratory, in Washington, D.C. This visit took place on February 5, 1968, and the specimen was analyzed by Mr. Maynard J. Pro, whose report on the analysis was mailed to Craig on February 29, 1968.

The results of Pro's analysis of the Brazil specimen and of the Dow specimen are included in the Condon Report. Clearly, this specimen of the Brazil magnesium was not "100% pure." In fact, it was not as pure as the triply sublimed Dow specimen.

Condon then commented: "...the magnesium metal was found to be much less pure than the regular commercial metal produced in 1957 by the Dow Chemical Company at Midland, Michigan. Therefore it need not have come from an extraterrestrial source, leaving us with no basis for rational belief that it did."

But this wasn't quite accurate. First is the point that the magnesium created at Dow was not a commercial grade, but a piece of triply sublimed magnesium. It was, you might say, magnesium created to see how pure they could make it, but not something they created for any commercial application.

The analysis also reported on a high content of both strontium and barium in the Ubatuba sample. Neither is an expected impurity in samples made under normal circumstances, but Dow, in their experimentation with ways to improve the "hardness" of the magnesium, had used the strontium as an alloy.

Because of the negative results, APRO decided to submit the remaining samples for non-destructive analysis. Dr. Walter W. Walker, working with Dr. Robert W. Johnson, made several additional tests. They concluded that the fragments were directionally solidified castings. That technique was not being studied in 1957. Dr. Walker, according to Coral Lorenzen and reported in Ron Story's *Encyclopedia of UFOs,* concluded, "This might be interpreted as meaning that the samples are from a more advanced culture."

The Condon Committee had also dismissed the Ubatuba sample by saying that its general low hardness made it the equivalent of the Dow sample. Dr. Walker determined that the Ubatuba sample had a better high-temperature property than the Dow samples of equal purity and that Dow had not produced the Ubatuba sample. That left the source of the metal open to speculation.

The APRO scientists also expressed surprise that the Condon scientists did not believe the Ubatuba sample came from a fabricated object.

Their conclusions appeared in the *ARPO BULLETIN*, where they said that the Condon Committee did not accept castings as fabricated metal objects.

So, what part of this discussion boiled down to was a matter of semantics; One group of scientists saying one thing and another group saying something else. Each came down on the side they had been on before the testing, and this added little to our overall understanding of what had been found in Brazil and how important it was.

Dr. Peter Sturrock, however, was not happy about letting it remain there. He began to work with the Lorenzens, attempting to locate the samples and subject them to more rigorous scientific scrutiny. He hoped to be able to resolve the matter and add an important piece of evidence to the debate about the origin of the UFOs.

Sturrock, writing in "Composition Analysis of the Brazilian Magnesium," said:

> The Lorenzens kindly transferred ownership of the remaining specimens to me in 1987. It should be noted that, by that time, the association of the remaining specimens with the original three specimens (A, B and C), had been completely lost. The specimens had not been carefully protected and tracked. In my discussions with the Lorenzens, I learned that two specimens were out on loan. One was in the possession of Mr. Robert Achzehnov of Costa Mesa, California; I subsequently retrieved this specimen from Mr. Achzehnov in 1986. The other has a more interesting history.

Sturrock wrote, writing in "Composition Analysis of the Brazilian Magnesium," said:

> Mr. Harold Lebelson, a journalist, had expressed an interest in the Brazil magnesium in 1978. As a result, a specimen (the same specimen that had been analyzed by the Colorado project) was given into his care by the Lorenzens. He took this specimen to Professor Robert E. Ogilvie of the Metallurgy Department at MIT. The results of Ogilvie's analysis were reported by Lebelson in an article in *OMNI* magazine [1979] which read in part:
>
> > The specimen was examined by metallographic analysis to determine its mechanical and thermal history.

Electron probe microanalysis was employed to determine the chemical composition and the distribution of elements within the specimen. Results of these tests showed the metal to be pure magnesium. No impurities or alloying elements, such as aluminum, zinc, manganese, or tin, were found. An oxygen x-ray map picked up magnesium and oxygen x-ray signals, thus confirming the network to be magnesium oxide.

"My conclusion," says Ogilvie, "is that the specimen from Brazil has a composition that would be found in magnesium weld material. However the structure is indeed unusual. In my opinion it could only have been formed by heating the magnesium very close to its melting point in air. It would be necessary to hold the temperature for only a minute or so. This would produce an oxide coating on the material, which is clearly visible. Also, oxygen would diffuse down the grain boundaries, thereby producing the oxide network. It is therefore quite possible that the specimen from Brazil was a piece of weld material from an exploding aircraft or a reentering satellite."

Sturrock then wrote: "The first part of this report is not accurate. I visited Ogilvie and discussed his analysis with him in June 1982, when he informed me that he had in fact detected impurities in the Brazil specimen, including calcium at a few thousand ppm, and strontium, iron and zinc at lower concentrations."

So now we seem to learn that the Ubatuba metal isn't nearly as pure as everyone had thought, and that even some óf the impurities, if not artifacts created in the testing, suggested nothing about an extraterrestrial origin for the metal.

Sturrock asked the Lorenzens in 1986 if he could contact Ogilvie so that he could take possession of the specimen that he had been analyzing, but Ogilvie had given the sample to another man. He didn't remember who or where the man worked, but did remember that Lebelson had called him to tell him to give up the sample. Lebelson denied this so that, in the end, another of the Brazilian samples had disappeared.

But Ogilvie had one other piece of information. He reminded Sturrock that he had had a conversation with Dr. Donald Beaman of Dow, who told him that in the late 1950s an Air Force officer had brought a sample of magnesium to the lab for analysis. Once the analysis was completed, the officer took all the records and the sample, putting them into a briefcase chained to his wrist. Beaman, according to Sturrock, denied that it had happened.

Not everything with Ogilvie slipped off the track. Sturrock reported that Ogilvie had suggested that the Brazilian magnesium was found in September 1957 and that was only a month before the Soviets announced the launch of Sputnik One. Ogilvie thought there might have been a Sputnik Zero, launched a month earlier, but it failed. What was picked up in Brazil, though part of a spacecraft, was not part of an extraterrestrial craft. It was the theoretical failed Soviet satellite.

Although an interesting theory, Sturrock didn't think it was right. In 1999, after the collapse of the Soviet Union, he obtained a sample of the materials used to built those first artificial satellites and learned that they didn't match. Clearly there had been no Sputnik Zero—or if there had, it hadn't fallen back to earth in Brazil.

This was, of course, interesting, but tells us nothing useful about the Ubatuba sample. It does tell us where it didn't come from, but not where it did.

Sturrock continued his attempts to find the samples and to have them analyzed in an arena that was completely transparent. About this, he wrote, in his "Composition Analysis":

> We have finally completed our look at the Brazil magnesium sample. The SEM [Scanning Electron Microscope] with EDAX [Energy Dispersive Analysis of X-rays] has proved to be the best way to examine the sample.... The metal...is essentially pure magnesium. I have also enclosed a copy of the mass spectrum obtained on our ion microprobe mass analyzer (IMMA).... When we drilled deeper into the sample than 1 micron, we saw only Mg and various interferences. The spectra, with the exception of the Fe and Ti near the surface, is the same as we obtain from commercial, high-purity magnesium wire which we use as a standard.
>
> Our EDAX analysis should be sensitive at about the 0.1% (1,000 ppm) level; our IMMA analysis at the 100–1 ppm level depending on the mass. Our essential conclusion is that the specimen behaves like commercial, high-purity magnesium which

has had its surface contaminated by handling, and which has been exposed to a "plastic" potting compound which appears to be the source of the Ti, Si, and possibly the Fe.

All this was becoming, for the lay person, increasingly difficult to understand. It would seem that the metal wasn't as pure as the original investigations had suggested, and that the impurities were not the result of contamination of the electrodes used in the various processes. The origin of the metal, other than from somewhere in Brazil, was still an open question, but it seems that the answer is on Earth rather than in outer space.

Skeptics, among others, have suggested that one way of determining the origin of a sample is isotopic ratios. The presumption is that metal created on another planet would not have the same isotopic ratios as metal created (or maybe refined would be a better term) here on Earth. If those isotopic ratios differed significantly, then it would be evidence of the extraterrestrial nature of the metal.

Sturrock, aware of this, did attempt to analyze the various existing samples of the Ubatuba metal. He wrote in his report:

There has been sustained interest in the isotopic composition of the Brazil magnesium. An anomalous isotopic composition would be the strong evidence for an extraterrestrial origin. This possibility was of interest to Dr. Craig, who arranged for the neutron activation analysis carried out at the National Office Laboratory, Alcohol and Tobacco Tax Division, Bureau of Internal Revenue, on behalf of the Colorado Project. The neutron activation analysis could be used to make an estimate of the percentage composition of 26Mg and it was found that the abundance of this isotope did not differ significantly from other magnesium specimens.

As mentioned in Section 1, in December 1975 I arranged to have a specimen of the Brazil magnesium analyzed at the Meteoritic Laboratory of Professor Gerald Wasserberg of the California Institute of Technology. I received a report from Dr. Typhoon Lee and Dr. D.A. Papanastassiou in October 1976. Lee and Papanastassiou did not provide me with their raw data, nor with separate estimates of the abundances of the three isotopes (24Mg, 25Mg, and 26Mg), but they did present an analysis of their data indicating that the measurements were consistent with fractionation of normal magnesium. When magnesium is heated, it tends to lose the lighter isotopes preferentially: the change in the abundance ratio 26Mg/24Mg should be twice the change in 25Mg/24Mg. Lee and Papanastassiou informed me that their measurements were a close fit to this expectation[.]

More recently, I have attempted to obtain precise measurements of the isotopic composition of the Brazil magnesium, but this has not been easy. The first laboratory that I approached led me to believe that they could make accurate measurements by means of secondary ion mass spectrometry (SIMS) analysis, but they did not deliver on this promise.

I next turned to Charles Evans and Associates in Redwood City. They first attempted to measure the isotopic ratio using an unmounted specimen, but the results were very erratic, and they decided that it would be essential to mount the specimen, polish it, and then gold-coat it. Charles Evans and Associates also advised me that it is essential to have comparison specimens. Accordingly, I supplied their analyst, Dr. Jack Cheng, with one specimen of the Brazil magnesium (SU-A); two specimens of triply sublimed Dow magnesium that had been provided to me in the 1970s (Dow A and Dow E); a specimen that had been used at Johnson Space Center for comparison, derived originally from the Baker Company (Baker A); and part of the triply-sublimed magnesium that the Dow Chemical Company had provided to the Colorado Project in the 1960s (Dow CP). The Baker specimen was kindly provided by Dr. Williams of Johnson Space Center, and the Dow CP specimen was kindly provided by Dr. Craig of Durango, Colorado (formerly at the University of Colorado).

Charles Evans and Associates took great care in the mounting, polishing and coating of the specimens and they made a number of runs with SIMS instrumentation.... The measured isotopic ratio for Dow CP is very close to that expected of normal magnesium, for which 25Mg/24Mg = 0.127 and 26Mg/24Mg = 0.139. The solid line...is the track to be expected if fractionation occurs due to heating. We see that all specimens lie on that track. It is curious that the isotopic ratios for the Dow CP specimen are quite close to the values for normal magnesium, since this specimen and also the specimens Dow A and Dow E were all produced by triple sublimation. The mechanism for the production of the Baker specimen is unknown, but it may well have been sublimation since that is the normal procedure used to purify magnesium.

We see that the Brazil specimen SU-A is the furthest from normal composition. However, it is on the same track as the other specimens. One may therefore infer that a specimen with the same isotopic composition as SU-A could be produced from normal magnesium by multiple sublimation. Hence this analysis does not point towards a non-terrestrial origin for the specimen SU-A.

However, these results are somewhat surprising. Sublimation (or any other form of fractionation) moves the isotopic composition away from the normal ratios ($25Mg/24Mg = 0.127$ and $26Mg/24Mg = 0.139 = 0.139$), along the track shown in Figure 1. However, it also tends to purify the magnesium, although this tendency is contingent upon the sublimation thermodynamics of the ensemble of elements. One therefore tends to expect that the specimen with the most deviant isotopic composition will also be the purest specimen. However, we see that SU-A is the furthest from normal composition, but it is less pure than the DOW-CP specimen, for example. The former has high abundance of Ca, Sr and Ba, whereas the latter is almost free of these three impurities.

In addition to the abundance analyses reported in Sections 2 and 3, Elemental Research also analyzed certain specimens with greatly increased mass-to-charge resolution in the neighborhood of the values appropriate for the magnesium isotopes. The results are shown in the four panels of Figure 2. Panels (a) and (b) show the scans obtained for two specimens of the Brazil magnesium, SU-Ia and SU-H. Panel (c) shows the scan obtained for specimen ALFA-a, one of the standards used in this work. Panel (d) shows the scan obtained for specimen Iso-A, part of the magnesium isotopic standard obtained from the National Institute of Standards and Technology. We see that the isotopic compositions of these four specimens are indistinguishable: the isotopic composition of the Brazil magnesium is clearly compatible with terrestrial origin.

So, where does that leave us in this case? The very first problem is that the samples of the metal cannot be traced to the beach in Brazil. Instead, they can be traced to the columnist in Brazil. No one has ever come forward, nor has anyone been located, who can corroborate the tale told in the letter to the columnist. The metal appears in his hands and from there goes to Fontes, then to APRO, and then to various others. The chain of evidence is severed before we reach the beach in Brazil, and that is a real problem.

Secondly, the claims of purity have not held up to scrutiny. When the early lab reports suggested no sign of contaminates, Fontes inferred this to mean that the metal was 100 percent pure, which is not quite the same thing. It meant that the labs conducting the tests had not found anything other than magnesium, not that there weren't other compounds present. It would seem that subsequent tests have shown that the metal, though extremely pure, was not 100 percent pure.

Yes, I'm aware that the sample tested in Brazil was lost during the testing, so it could be argued that this sample was that pure, but it seems a more logical conclusion is that it suffered from the same contaminates as those other samples. The problem was in the technology available in 1958 as opposed to that even eight or nine years later.

Third, the samples have been handled in a fairly cavalier fashion. Once they arrived in the United States, no one had kept track of them, and it could be argued that the chain of custody was broken here as well. The Air Force destroyed a small sample given them for testing without obtaining any results. The Lorenzens loaned various samples and pieces of samples to any number of people, and some of those samples have been lost. In the end, it might be nearly impossible to say that the samples as they exist today are in any way related to those that were first sent to APRO. Dr. Fontes died decades ago, as did the Lorenzens. That is another stumbling block.

Then we come to the final problem. Although magnesium of a purity equivalent to the Ubatuba metal was available at the time, we don't know the source of that sample. The testing done to date, regardless of the quality of the equipment or competency of the researchers, has not provided a clue to the source of the original samples. It is unlikely that it is of extraterrestrial origin, but no one can rule that out.

We are left with several samples of magnesium that are unique. There is nothing in them to suggest the extraterrestrial, yet there is a hint that these samples might not have been made on Earth. This, I think, would be the classic definition of "unidentified." But even with that, it is not proof that some UFOs are from other planets. In the very end, we are only left with questions that might have no answers.

## 1959

### FRDYNIA, POLAND

Witnesses reported that an object fell into the harbor. Divers were able to retrieve a shiny piece of metal, which was examined by the Polytechnic Institute and the Polish Navy. Several days later, a small humanoid was reported to have washed up on a nearby beach. It was recovered and supposedly sent to the Soviet Union for examination.

## July 18, 1962

### LAS VEGAS, NEVADA

In the Project Blue Book files there are few cases that offer multiple chains of evidence. That is, few cases offer multiple eyewitness testimony over a large region, radar confirmation of the object's passing, interaction with the environment, and even the possibility of physical evidence. Such a complex case, if properly researched and analyzed, could go a long way in demonstrating the reality of alien spacecraft in our atmosphere.

On April 18, 1962, there was a case that offered all these research elements. Unfortunately, at that time, the Air Force wasn't all that interested in furthering belief in UFOs and the investigations conducted by the officers and NCOs left a great deal to be desired. Investigators were later sent to Utah twice, where there was a possible landing and dozens of witnesses, and spent "one full day" investigating, according to the Project Blue Book files. They failed to interview all but a few of the witnesses, and they failed to find any trace of an extraterrestrial object, though they seemed to believe they were searching for a meteorite and not an alien spacecraft.

On the other hand, I spent more than "one full day" in the area, and talked to dozens who had seen something and many who had a close up view. As we've seen in other cases, the motivation of the Air Force investigators seemed more geared to explanation than investigation.

And, as we've seen, if the Air Force investigators didn't talk to the witnesses then, to their way of thinking, those witnesses simply did not exist.

The Air Force split the sightings into two separate cases: one on April 18 in and around Las Vegas, and the other on April 19 in the Nephi-Eureka area of Utah. They investigated them as if they were two separate events. This made it easier to explain the sightings because if the events were linked, many of the possible mundane explanations were eliminated.

According to Project Blue Book files, the April 18 case was a radar sighting from Nellis Air Force Base just outside of Las Vegas, Nevada. The project card, a brief summary of the case in those files, gave this brief summary of the sighting: "Radar sighting. Blip. Speed of object varied. Initial observation at 060 [degrees] no elevation. Disappearance at 105 degrees az[imuth] 10,000 feet altitude. Heading tentively [sic] NE, however disappeared instantly to S. Observed by search and height radars. No. Visual."

In the comments section of the project card, it said: "There is insufficient data in the report to form a valid conclusion. Speed, changes in course, and altitude not included. Appearance on both search and height finder confirms that some object was there. Track characteristics indicate possible balloon as the source." It is not explained why the investigators, who offered some intriguing information, didn't attempt to answer the questions they posed. They just noted the information was not readily available and let it go at that, but also suggested that the information had been available. They just didn't bother to follow up on it.

Let's take a quick look at another aspect of that report. The Air Force claimed that there were no visual sightings. The *Las Vegas Sun,* however, reported on April 19th, the day after the radar sighting, in a banner headline, "Brilliant Red Explosion Flares in Las Vegas Sky." That article suggested dozens of witnesses had seen something and even named some of them. In the lead paragraph, Jim Stalmaker, a reporter for the newspaper, wrote that a "tremendous flaming sword flashed across the Las Vegas skies last night and heralded the start of a search for a weird unidentified flying object that apparently had America's Air Force on alert."

Stalmaker reported that Frank Maggio, a staff photographer, had seen the object. According to the newspaper, Maggio said that a series of bright explosions broke up its trail across the sky.

I talked to Maggio in the early 1990s as I was originally investigating this story. He couldn't tell me anything more than what had been published in the newspaper. It had been a long time ago and the sighting, at least from his point of view, was of nothing truly extraordinary. It was just a visual sighting of a bright light that seemed to be related to the radar tracks recorded out at Nellis, but he couldn't add anything. At least I have been able to verify that he did see something.

That same article mentioned Sheriff's Deputy Walter Butt, who was in charge of the department's search and rescue team. The consensus seemed to be that the object was heading out toward the east and there had been a final explosion near Mesquite, Nevada, on the Utah border. Butt took his team into an area between Spring Mountain and Mesquite, but nothing else had been reported to the newspaper.

Butt told me, in a telephone interview, that they had searched the area in jeeps and, when the sun came up, used airplanes. They didn't find anything of importance, except some ashes that he thought were probably part of a campfire started by a hunter some weeks earlier. When no one reported any missing aircraft, and they had run up against the fences of part of a Nellis firing range, they called off the search.

At the AEC's Nevada Test Site was a man who also saw the object in the air. He said that it looked like a nuclear explosion, but added quickly that it came from the wrong direction for that answer to work. And those explosions were high-altitude air bursts.

In Colorado Springs, where the North American Air Defense Command (NORAD) is located, the information officer, Lt. Col. Herbert Rolph, said they had one report of a sighting as far away as New York.

A NORAD astronomer said that the object could have been a "Lyrid meteor," which are often seen between April 19 and 22. But he had seen nothing himself, had heard none of the eyewitness reports, and was merely pointing to a possible solution. The Air Force, in the years following this, and probably in the years preceding it, had often trotted out a scientist who made an off-the-cuff analysis without benefit of all the information available. Often, the press grabbed the explanation and ran with it, assuming it was the final solution.

Interestingly, a Nellis Air Force Base spokesman, as reported in the Project Blue Book files and in contradiction to the astronomer, said, "There's only one thing wrong with that: a meteor cannot be tracked on radar. And this object was." So it seems that the Air Force hadn't handed out the script, or some of the officers were not on the same page as everyone else.

There is a handwritten note in the Project Blue Book files impacting on all this. Lt. Col. H.C. Showers at the NORAD command post called "FTD [Foreign Technology Division in Dayton, Ohio] of the following event reported to the war room at the Pentagon."

Here's where that gets interesting. The command post log entry said:

General [Laurence S.] Kuter (NORAD) took off and was climbing through 10,000 [feet] when he saw a "meteor" [quotes in original document] come out of orbit as 0319Z 19 April. He described the object as cherry red, clear green, with a long white and red tail. He estimated object near Colorado Springs and [the] AF Academy. USAF indicated reports coming in from Idaho, Utah, Arizona, "OCD" 28th and 29th (??) Regions, Navy Aircraft, B-52 crew and DC-8 pilots. All reported alike in shape, color, and general direction of travel...south to north. An "Air Force Colonel" [quotes in original] reported that object [over] the western range—but there was no noise. Denver center [FAA flight center] reported at 0332Z that after 10–15 minutes after the first reports the trail could still be seen. No radar pick up reported as yet. Visual sightings only.

6.2. *General Kuter, Las Vegas. Photo courtesy of the U.S. Air Force.*

About 50 minutes later, just after midnight, the command post got another report, this time from Lt. Col. James Howell, who wanted to report

numerous reports to the FAA and AFLC [command post] on the above sighting. It was observed in Los Angeles, Col. [Colorado],

Montana; Kansas; Utah. A Captain Shields [more on him later] of the 733 Troop Carrier Squadron, Ogden, Utah, reported to AFLC that the object appeared around 0300Z and was extremely bright—like burning magnesium. He happed to be in a procedure turn [meaning he was airborne] and thus estimated the life to be 10 seconds. He further stated it was traveling from the southwest to the northeast.

The notes were signed by Howell A. Dennis, an Air Force captain, and appear in the Project Blue Book files.

During the Air Force investigation, Captain Shields was identified as Captain Herman Gordon Shields, an Air Force pilot. In a report created by Douglas M. Crouch, the Chief of the Criminal Investigation Sections, Shields said:

I was flying a C-119 aircraft from the left seat (captain's seat). We were approximately two miles west of La Van, Utah flying at 8500 feet MSL.... We were making a right turn.... We were approximately 25 degrees of bank...when it began to get very bright in the cockpit. The illumination was from above. It built up slowly. My first impression while the intensity was low was that it was the landing lights of another aircraft. Of course when the intensity increased this was ruled out automatically. The cockpit was illuminated from above.... The light source was coming from this area that was blanked out, in other words, straight behind this instrument panel because neither Lieutenant Larson, who was in the right seat not [sic] I saw the source of the illumination.... The light intensity increased until we could see objects (on the ground) as bright as day for a radius of five to ten miles from the aircraft.... The intensity of the light diminished faster than it had increased. After the light had decreased in intensity we were still looking for the light source, and I noticed an object to my left between the wing and the lower part of the fuselage of the aircraft against the hills. By this time the light had decreased so that the hills were dark. It was night again. And this object which I saw was illuminated. It had a long slender appearance comparable to a cigarette in size, that is, the diameter with respect to the length of the object. The fore part, or the lower part of the object was very bright, intense white such as a magnesium fire. The second half, the aft section was a clearly distinguishable yellowish color. I would say the object was just about divided in half, the forepart being intensely white, the aft section having a more yellow color to it.

Later in that same report, Shields said, "I saw only a slender object. I don't know what shape it was. It was only a slender object.... There was no exhaust, no trail following after it. It was clearly defined. I saw it for a period of maybe one or two seconds."

What all this has done is connect these sightings in Las Vegas and in Colorado with those over the rest of the United States. The best of them came from Utah, where there were dozens of witnesses, talk of the craft interacting with the environment, and the possibility of a landing near the small town of Eureka.

The Blue Book project card for the Eureka sighting originally gave the date as April 19 but that was using Greenwich Mean Time. When corrected to local time the sightings were made within 15 minutes of those in Las Vegas and were therefore on the same day.

The project card noted: "Obj[ect] came in over Cuba & apparently landed in rough terrain West of Eureka Utah. Bright enough to trip photo electric cell which controlled city street lights. Multiple rpts. Attempted recovery by Col Friend & Dr. Hynek. See case file."

The investigation conducted by Dr. J. Allen Hynek and Lt. Col. Robert Friend lasted less than 48 hours and consisted of interviews with local residents and an aborted attempt to find the object that everyone was sure had fallen not far from Eureka. Or maybe landed would be a better word for it, depending on who was providing the information.

On May 8, 1962, Hynek and Friend, accompanied by Douglas Crouch, who had interviewed Shields, and who had interviewed other Utah residents, arrived in the Eureka area. Friend, writing to "Hq USAF, SAFOI-3b (Major Hart)," reported:

> The number of reports generated by the 18 April 1962 sighting, and the fact that the Air Force investigation came to a negative conclusion regarding the UFO, they indicated it couldn't have been a meteor (Attachment #1), prompted further investigation by FTD [Foreign Technology Division at Wright-Patterson Air

Force Base].... This investigation was completed in one full day and it was concluded that the object was a bolide [meaning an extremely bright meteor also called a fireball]. An attempt was made to locate the object but this effort failed due to the general nature of the data. Further study of this sighting indicates that the meteor probably struck in the area of the Wasatch National Forest; however, the Air Force has made no effort to recover it.

That statement, written by Friend, that Hynek and Friend actually went into the area to conduct the investigation, and that they found no conflicting data, suggests that Friend might be right. In fact, Dr. Robert Kadesch, who was an associate professor of physics at the University of Utah, confirmed this in an interview I conducted. Kadesch said, simply, "[It]...probably was a bolide."

There is, however, more to this case. I visited the area in 1991 and interviewed a number of the witnesses. Among the first to sight the object was Sheriff Raymond Jackson of Nephi, Utah. According to newspapers, the photoelectric cells on the streetlights were tripped by the bright object. Jackson told me that he had "heard a kind of a roar." He glanced up and saw a yellow-white flame going west, heard a series of loud booms, and saw that the lights went out, all consistent with a bolide that tripped the photoelectric cells on the streetlights.

Jackson also told me that he noticed, specifically, that the lights in a doctor's office near where he was standing that night had gone out. He said, "All the lights went out temporarily." He meant that not only had the streetlights gone out, but other lights in the town that weren't controlled by photoelectric cells had gone out as well.

The local newspaper, the *Nephi Times-News,* reported that Maurice Memmott and Dan Johnson were south of town, working their farms, when the object flashed overhead. Memmott told me that he remembered very little about the incident. It was just a bright light in the sky that lit the ground like the noontime sun. He said that he believes it was a meteor.

Johnson told me that he remembered the event quite well. He said, "The two of us were out in the fields.... There were no lights so we were in total darkness." According to him, it came over the southeastern horizon and passed directly over them. "It was a very bright light."

Unlike many of the others, Johnson remembered no sound associated with the object. He did believe that it had landed somewhere to the northwest. He didn't think it was more than 5 or 6 miles away. Distances and sizes of objects in the sky are hard to judge, and Johnson's estimate of the distance to the landing site, if there was one, was probably wrong.

What is interesting is that Johnson told me that several men had come out to talk to him about the sighting not long after it happened. This wasn't Hynek and Friend, but apparently soldiers from the Army's Dugway Proving grounds not all that far from Eureka.

Tracking the times and dates as they appeared in the newspaper, Johnson's conclusion seems to be correct. There were two separate teams of investigators, and there is no indication that any of the information gathered by the soldiers from Dugway ever found its way into the Air Force files. If Hynek and Friend ever learned of the earlier investigation, they mentioned nothing about it and didn't record the information for inclusion in the file.

I also interviewed Sergeant E.C. Sherwood of the Utah Highway Patrol. He said that he looked up in time to see a ball of fire and thought that it was something from the White Sands Missile Range in southern New Mexico. He said that it was mostly a blue light that seemed to explode right over him, throwing off a cloud of white sparks.

Sherwood's wife heard the explosion and ran outside to see what had happened. She told me that most of the neighbors were outside, too. All were looking up into the sky.

I talked to others in the area who told me that there was a series of explosions—20 to 30 of them strung together. Their descriptions ran from a rocket's engine to an artillery shell flying over. There was nothing in these descriptions to rule out a bolide. They are often associated with a roaring sound or a series of detonations.

As the object traveled from Nephi toward Eureka, it flew over Bob Robinson and Floyd Evans. According to what Robinson told me, they were traveling south of Eureka when they stopped for a moment and both men got out of the truck. Robinson saw the light in the southeast and pointed it out. Evans thought it was some kind of a jet aircraft. This is a description that had been made in other, similar sightings over the years.

The object approached them rapidly and then passed directly overhead. Robinson told me he thought it was no more than 500 feet above them but, again, they were looking up into the sky and had no real frame of reference. His estimate could have been way off. He said it was a flaming object and he thought he could see a series of square windows on the craft almost hidden in the glow. This, too, was a description that would surface in other UFO sightings in many other places.

Robinson told me that both he and Evans were frightened by the experience. As they had dived under the truck for protection, the engine began to sputter and run roughly, and the headlights dimmed, but the engine didn't stall and the lights didn't go out completely. And once again, we run into a description that has been made many times, but this interaction with the environment suggests the object was low enough to cause the trouble so that Robinson's estimate of the altitude might have been close to accurate.

Robinson thought as the object reached them it slowed, as if taking a look at them. Robinson thought the object, or at least the light from it, was visible for about two minutes. As it disappeared in the west, the engine of his truck smoothed out and the headlights brightened.

Robinson's wife, Betty, told me that when he returned home, he looked as if he had seen a ghost. His face was white and he was so excited that it was hard for him to speak. While she had been sitting in the house waiting for his return, she had heard the roar of the object as it flew over. The interior of the house lit up with a strobing effect.

Joseph Bernini, the police chief, told me he was at the city council meeting when they all heard the roar. Bernini said that it sounded like an artillery shell flying over. He said that he only saw a bright light, but he didn't see any object.

Bernini also told me that, as the object flew over, the lights outside went out, but these streetlights were on photoelectric cells and no one else reported any other power failures in the town. The object, according to many of the witnesses, was certainly bright enough to affect the photoelectric cells.

Both Bernini's wife and his son saw the light, and his son said that he also saw an object. He said that it was moving from the southeast to the northwest.

Kadesh, the astronomer, when I asked, said that he believed the object to be a bolide that exploded 60 to 70 miles high. The flash was so bright that people in Kansas saw it. There were those in Reno, Nevada, who also said they saw the flash.

Kadesh thought that people on the ground, looking up into the night sky with no real points of reference, would be unable to accurately judge distances and speeds. There have been a number of UFO reports in which this problem has been demonstrated time and again. Add the complication of the unidentified nature of a bright object, and most people would inaccurately describe size, speed, and altitude.

But, naturally, they would be able to judge direction. In Utah it was heading to the northwest. In Reno, Dan Dyer and the controllers in the local FAA control tower saw the flash and told reporters that it was a brilliant white with a long tail, changing to green, orange, and red.

According to officers at Stead Air Force Base (near Reno), a Bonanza Air Lines pilot said that the light passed beneath his aircraft, which was flying at 11,000 feet. That made two different flight crews, Shields in Utah and the Bonanza crew in Nevada, who reported the object below their aircraft. That alone should have ruled out the bolide theory.

I also checked the local Nevada newspapers. The newspapers create a problem because, according to the Reno newspaper, the path of the object, as it passed overhead, was traveling from the north to the south, and then suggested that it had crashed somewhere in Utah. The *Los Angeles Times* reported that the object seen over Reno was traveling to the east. Had the object been a fireball as Dr. Hynek and Lt. Col. Friend suggested, there wouldn't have been such a substantial change in direction, or a discrepancy in the reported direction.

The real question here is if we have a single sighting or if we have two. Project Blue Book created two separate files and suggested that one had taken place on April 18 and the second on April 19. If this case was of two sightings, then natural phenomenon, including bolides, make sense. True, it would be unusual to have two bolides on two separate nights but it wouldn't be impossible, especially given the time of the year. It would mean that something had fallen near Eureka, Utah, and something different was tracked on radar near Las Vegas.

I have talked to a man who wishes to remain anonymous, who told me on audiotape that he had been traveling through Utah on the night the object flashed over. He said it was a glowing, orange ball that approached the ground and knocked out all the lights in Eureka, not just the photoelectric cell streetlights.

When he got close enough, he saw that it had an oval shape, and, as it took off, heard a quiet whirring noise. He said that it headed to the west, toward Nevada. He watched it until it faded from sight.

At one time, I would have given great weight to an eyewitness sighting, even if the witness didn't want his name associated with UFOs. I could understand that, given public reaction and perception. In fact, not all that long ago, I heard a cable network news anchor say that she thought there was something to stories of flying saucers and she said that she wasn't even a little crazy. And days later, a candidate running for president was tarred with the brush that he was crazy when he acknowledged a UFO sighting. That reinforces, in today's world, that those who see UFOs are a little unhinged. Or they are perceived that way by society.

But, the man's tale is shaky because he won't allow his name to be used. If he is telling the truth, and this would be an important truth, then he should let me report who he is. Because he won't, there is no way for others to evaluate his stability, education, qualifications, or truthfulness. His is just another report that fits into the stream near Eureka, but that the skeptics can claim is irrelevant because they don't know who it was. I have to agree with them on that particular point.

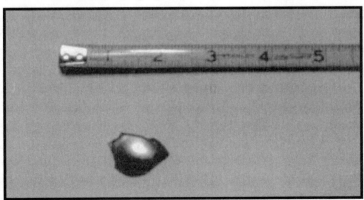

*6.3. Vegas debris. Author's photo.*

This fits into another piece of the puzzle that, in the past, I would have given great weight to. Not so much today. I received a letter, the writer of which claimed that he had been a young lieutenant at Nellis Air Force Base on the night the object was seen there. He didn't identify himself, but did provide a picture of a piece of debris.

This man claimed that he had been awakened in the night and taken out into the desert, where he and about 30 others were put to work picking up debris. When the sun came up, they were all loaded onto a bus that had the windows blacked out with large pieces of paper. Through a hole, or a place where the paper didn't fully cover the window, he could see out. According to his letter, he saw a disk-shaped craft that had been smashed.

At Nellis, they were all debriefed, and told that this was a classified event and not to talk to anyone about it. They were told only that they had helped recover debris from an experimental aircraft that had crashed, and anything that leaked about the event could help the Soviets who were always trying to steal American scientific information.

I have never heard from this man again, and he didn't sign the letter. It is an anonymous tale with a hint of physical evidence in the form of the picture. But then, in today's world, without a name so that we can verify his claim to having been an Air Force officer and stationed at Nellis at the right time, there is no reason to accept this story as authentic. I mention it here only because someone else might have heard the story or someone else who was there is willing to talk about it now. Without additional corroboration, this is little more than rumor.

When we look at all these sightings, it begins to look as if a single object was responsible for all the reports. It may have landed in Utah, but we also have witnesses to it taking off again, heading to the west. Then over Nevada, we have additional reports of the object moving to the southeast, apparently making the turn over Reno, flying near Las Vegas, and disappearing in a blinding flash east of Las Vegas over Mesquite, near the Utah border. All this suggests a single object was responsible for the sightings.

The Air Force, which had received most of the sighting reports, initially thought the same thing. One object was responsible for everything. Officers at Stead Air Force Base, Nellis Air Force Base, and at NORAD all drew the same conclusion. The reports from Utah and Reno show the sightings were made within 15 minutes of each other when corrected for the time zones and the fact that some of the sighting reports were filed using Greenwich Mean Time.

The Air Force file for the Nellis Radar sighting puts the incidence some 16 minutes after the sightings in Utah, but the official spokesman at Nellis said the Air Defense Command was alerted by the fire trail seen at approximately 7:20 p.m., or within a few minutes of the Utah sightings.

In these files, which I believe were never meant to be seen by anyone other than project officers and those making UFO policy, we see that a spokesman for the 28th Air Division at Stead Air Force Base admitted the power in Eureka was knocked out and that fighters had been scrambled from Nellis as a result of the radar sightings there.

But, on September 21, 1962, Major C.R. Hart of the Public Information Office, in a letter responding to a letter from a New York resident, claimed:

> The official records of the Air Force list the 18 April 1962 Nevada sighting to which you refer as "unidentified, insufficient data." There is an additional note to the effect that "the reported track is characteristic of that registered by a U-2 or a high balloon but there is insufficient data reported to fully support such an evaluation." The phenomena reported was not intercepted or fired upon.

Reports in the Project Blue Book files clearly show that fighters had been launched and intercepts had been attempted. I suppose it could be argued that Major Hart did not have access to these reports and he had written only what he had been told.

His explanation also left something to be desired. He wrote that "track is characteristic of that registered by a U-2 or a high balloon...." Well, which was it? A balloon track would be made at the whim of the wind, and a U-2 would have a track that showed intelligent control. Surely the radar operator would have been able to tell if he was tracking a balloon or a jet.

Why didn't they know this for certain? The answer is simple. They could find no record of a U-2 flight or balloon launch that would have put one or the other over Las Vegas at the proper time. So, it might have been a balloon. It could have been a high-flying U-2 spy plane. In reality, it wasn't either.

So, in the end, what do we have here?

We have an object seen by thousands. In Utah, it was near the ground and it interacted with the environment, stalling a car engine and dimming the lights, and putting out the lights in Eureka. It maneuvered while close to the ground so that dozens saw it and provided descriptions that do not match a bolide. One witness, who remains anonymous claims the object landed and took off again. The object continued its journey, reaching Reno, where it turned to the southeast and flew on toward Las Vegas, where there were more witnesses and it was tracked on radar. Then east of Las Vegas, near the Utah border, it apparently blew up.

There is a variety of documentation from the newspapers including the *Las Vegas Sun, Los Angeles Times, Deseret News and Telegram, The Salt Lake Tribune, The Eureka Reporter,* and the *Nephi News-Leader.* Additional documentation, including the reports created at the time came from the Project Blue Book files now available online, at the Center for UFO Studies, and at the National Archives in Washington, D.C.

This case was connected in the Air Force files even though they created two separate files and treated it as two separate events. When put together, the bolide explanation fails, but separated they are spectacular events that can be explained in the mundane.

On a page in the file that appears prior to the Intelligence Report prepared by Douglas Crouch, an unknown officer wrote:

> On April 18, 1962, the Air Force Defense Command was puzzled by an aerial object that exploded and seemed to be a meteor, but had the unique distinction of being tracked by radar 70 miles northwest of Las Vegas, Nevada in a blinding flash. An Air Force Defense Command alert reported the object was tracked and traced over New York, Kansas, Utah, Idaho, Montana, New Mexico, Wyoming, Arizona and California, so that its light covered almost as much area as that created by the big hydrogen space bomb test held later in the Pacific hundreds of miles high.

The thing about this is that the note is not in the Las Vegas file but in the Utah file. And it suggests radar tracks in other parts of the country as well as that from Nellis. The flight time, according to the files, was 32 minutes, much too long for a meteor.

With the cases separated, the Air Force was able to deal with the cases piecemeal. The Utah case becomes a bolide and Robert Kadesch, a scientist not involved with the UFO project or the Foreign Technology Division, made a plausible expert. His statement, reported throughout the country, sounded reasonable when the testimony of the witnesses is ignored.

This reveals that the Air Force was not interested in investigation or solving riddles. They were interested in clearing cases, slapping a label on them, and letting it go at that. We know it because they interviewed the Utah witnesses such as Bob Robinson and Floyd Evans. They interviewed a dozen witnesses, some of whom described the object and who said it was close to the ground. They knew the power had been knocked out in Nephi, but reported only the light was so bright it affected the photoelectric cells in Eureka. I was told that lights in offices went out, and they weren't on photoelectric cells. They ignored the information that didn't fit with the bolide theory.

Something extraordinary happened on the night of April 18, 1962. The Air Force offered, as it so often did, a series of explanations, and ignored those facts that didn't fit with their explanation. But the witnesses who were there know the truth. They saw something from outer space, and it was not a meteor. It was a craft from another world. There is no doubt about it.

## Summer 1962

### NORTHERN NEW MEXICO

The craft, looking like two saucers end on end, was a dull aluminum in color. It had apparently skidded on impact, digging a shallow trench when it crashed.

Two bodies, small and dressed in skintight silver flight suits, were put into a van and taken from the scene. The craft and bodies were both taken to Holloman Air Force Base near Alamogordo, and then sections of the craft were sent to Los Alamos National Laboratory, Los Alamos, New Mexico, and other, unidentified research centers.

The major problem with this scenario is that, if the craft had crashed in northern New Mexico and authorities wanted to keep it secret, why take it through the state to the south-central area and then take it back to the north? Why not take it straight to Kirtland Air Force Base, Albuquerque—or better yet, take it straight to Los Alamos?

## October 31, 1963

### Sao Paulo, Brazil

A number of witnesses, including Ruth de Souza, heard a roaring that drew their attention to a shiny disk-shaped object. It was moving slowly at treetop level, clipped a tall palm tree, rocked violently, and then plunged into a river.

The disk was reported to be about 3 feet thick and just more than 15 feet in diameter. It was very bright and might have been internally lighted. It was described as an "aluminum basin."

The object dived beneath the surface of the river, which erupted, and the water seemed to boil. It disappeared into the thick silt at the bottom of the river.

Divers arrived shortly after the event but were unable to locate the object. A second attempt failed, and the use of metal detectors and other probes produced no results. Whatever fell into the river was not recovered.

## December 10, 1964

### Fort Riley, Kansas

Aaron Kaback claimed that, as a soldier stationed at Fort Riley, Kansas, in the mid-1960s, he had been on guard duty when the duty officer drove up and ordered him to climb into the jeep. They drove for about 10 minutes and hiked for another 10. Kaback was given a loaded magazine for his M-14 rifle and told never to mention to anyone what he was guarding.

The object, according to Kaback, was 35 to 48 feet in diameter and had a fin at one end, an exhaust port or hole of some kind below the fin, and a row of squares around the rim. The object never moved in the two and a half hours that Kaback guarded it.

Under pressure from various researchers, including Citizens Against UFO Secrecy (CAUS), Kaback provided copies of his various military records. They showed that the incident could not have happened on the date Kaback originally claimed, because he had already been discharged from the Army. He said that he had forgotten the date. He later produced a letter written to his fiancé that mentioned a duty he couldn't talk about with a December 10th date.

Kaback also said that he had been handed the magazine for his rifle by General Jonathan O. Seaman, a retired officer who had commanded Ft. Riley in 1964 and 1965. However, when contacted, Seaman told researchers that he knew nothing about the incident. Researchers were inclined to believe the general. When they confronted Kaback with the information, according to what Len Stringfield wrote in his *Crash/Retrieval Status Report*, he admitted that the general sounded sincere, but Kaback also said, "All I know is it happened."

This is another case where there is no corroboration for the tale of a single witness. The problem is that he was confronted with data, denied it, and then proceeded to grant interviews with various radio and television stations, always with the condition that his name not be used.

# Chapter 7

## December 9, 1965 ———————————————

### KECKSBERG, PENNSYLVANIA

It was late in the day, just before 5 in the afternoon, Eastern Standard Time, when a fireball flashed overhead. It was first seen in Canada, then by thousands in Michigan and Ohio, and over the northern edge of Ohio, near Cleveland, it was reported to have made a slight turn, headed to the southeast and Pennsylvania. At 4:47 p.m., it hit the ground southeast of Pittsburgh, near the small town known as Kecksburg.

Thousands of people saw the object in the air, hundreds reported or saw some debris that appeared to be associated with the object, and dozens were at the impact site outside of Kecksburg. Fires were started near Elyria, Ohio. Near Lapeer, Michigan, bits of metal rained down. Phone lines to sheriff's offices, police departments, and the news media were jammed, as callers reported their sightings.

Sometime after 6:30 p.m., Frances Kalp called radio station WHJB in Greensburg, Pennsylvania, where she talked to news director John Murphy. He was in the middle of a nightly news digest, but he interviewed her for the

Pre-1947

1947
Pre-Roswell

July 1947

October
1947–1948

1949–1952

1953–1964

1965

1966–1978

1979–1999

2000–2009

breaking story of the object. She told him that the object or fireball had crashed into the woods near her home. Her children wanted to walk down to where her son said he'd seen "a star on fire." At first she gave permission, but then decided it might not be a good idea. She walked after the children to call them back.

Kalp caught the children about a half mile from the crash site. There was smoke climbing out of the trees, and there was a bright object off to one side. Kalp said that it was like "a four pointed star."

Murphy thanked her for the information and then called Troop A of the Pennsylvania State Police, giving them the information. Within minutes, the state police tried to call Kalp, but her telephone was busy. The operator broke in and advised Kalp that she had an emergency telephone call from the state police.

Kalp agreed to meet the police in nearby Kecksburg and lead them to the crash site. While she was driving into Kecksburg, the County Emergency Center was activated, and about that time, the volunteer firefighters were searching the nearby woods.

Kalp wasn't the only one to see the object in the air. Bob Blystone, Jr., who was 15 in 1965, saw what he describes as an orange jet trail at low altitude. Mary Keto, another local witness, saw a hovering fireball just above the tree line with blue smoke coming up. Blystone said he saw the round object glide slowly toward the treetops in what he thought of as a controlled landing into the trees.

*7.1. Kecksburg UFO mock up. Photo courtesy of Stan Gordon.*

John Murphy, sensing a good story, drove down to the Kecksburg area. He was there when two state police cars and Kalp arrived. He also saw the state police fire marshal, in the company of a state investigator, walk into the woods carrying a yellow Geiger counter and flashlights. Murphy then interviewed Kalp and her sons in person.

The two men who walked into the woods, Carl Metz and Paul Shipco, returned 15 minutes later. Murphy sent one of the photographers with him to question the fire marshal. According to Murphy, in his radio documentary "Object in the Woods," Metz told the photographer, "You'll have to talk to my lawyer." Metz and Shipco then continued walked to their car.

Murphy ran toward them and asked Metz, "Did you find anything down there?"

Metz, according to Murphy, looked puzzled and then said, "I'm not sure."

"Well," said Murphy, "let me ask you a different way. After you make your report to the captain [Josephy Dussia of the Pennsylvania State Police], do you think that you or the captain may have something to tell me?"

"You better get your information from the Army," responded Metz.

Murphy, during a later radio broadcast, said, "Now this was the first time the name Army was brought into the conversation. This was the first time anyone made mention of the military. Now to me the significance of this was that the State Police Fire Marshal [Metz] examining the fire or the possibility of a fire, almost out of the clear blue sky is turning me over to the Army. This was very unusual."

Murphy was confused. He didn't know if there was anything going on in the woods, if it was all some kind of mistake, or if there was a reason to pursue the story. He had about convinced himself to wrap it all up, but then decided to call the state police in Greensburg. He spoke to Captain Dussia and asked if he should pack it in or stay on the scene a little while longer.

According to Murphy:

He advised me that maybe I'd be interested in coming to the barrack. By the time I get to the barracks perhaps he and the United States Army would have a joint statement to make. I questioned him about the Army and he said that he understood members of the 662d Radar Squadron would be there. [It must be noted that the radar squadron is, in fact, an Air Force unit.]

Murphy then drove to the State Police Troop A barracks in nearby Greensburg. Murphy reported that when he arrived, there were "not only members of the United States Army there but I also saw two men in Air Force uniforms, one of them wearing lieutenant's bars." The lieutenant, who was on the telephone, told Murphy he didn't know much. He was only a first lieutenant.

The significance here is that we have already identified more than three military people in the Greensburg area. Murphy reported that there were members—plural—of the Army there, and two Air Force people. Skeptics would later claim that only three military people arrived, but Murphy's statement seems to confirm that early on, more than three military personnel were on hand and they represented two of the armed services (the Army and the Air Force).

Before he talked to the military, Murphy, according to his radio broadcast, found Captain Dussia and asked if Dussia could tell him anything "off the record."

Dussia replied, "Well, I'll give you something for the records. I have something official to tell you."

Murphy asked, "What's that?"

Dussia said, "The Pennsylvania State Police have made a thorough search of the woods. We are convinced there is nothing whatsoever in the woods."

Murphy thanked him and went in search of a telephone to report the statement when he heard Metz and several others talk about going back out into the woods. While Murphy was telling the radio station how he wanted the story handled, Metz came back into the office and said that he was going back out with members of the military. When Murphy hung up, he asked if he could go with them, and Metz said, "Sure, if it's all right with the captain."

Murphy said, "I looked promptly to the captain and asked, 'Is it okay if I go with these people.'"

Dussia said, "Of course."

As Murphy was leaving, he ran into a state police trooper who had just come from the woods. Although Murphy had been told officially just minutes earlier that there was nothing out there, the state police trooper told him of a pulsating blue light seen in the woods. According to Murphy, "[T]he military wanted to see this pulsating light...."

Back out near the reported crash site, Murphy walked over to the car driven by Metz and asked again, "Are you going down into the woods?"

When Metz nodded, Murphy said, "Me too."

Metz said, "No."

"I'm going too," repeated Murphy.

"No, I'm sorry, " said Metz.

Murphy said, "Please. You have to let me go."

Metz was now "very firm. Very definite." He said no.

"But the understanding before we left the barracks was that I was going to come out, that I was going into the woods. What do you mean I can't go into the woods?"

Again, according to Murphy, Metz looked very firm and said, very slowly but very definitely, "I'm sorry. No."

"That," according to Murphy, "was the last time I saw the military. This was the last time, to my knowledge, that any civilian had anything to do with the search. I was told not to go into the woods."

What this means is that somewhere along the road between Greensburg and Kecksburg, Metz received new instructions. They could have come over the radio from Dussia, or they could have been issued by the military men in the car with Metz. Whatever the source, the result was the same. Murphy, on orders from the state police fire marshal, was denied access to the woods.

With the radio and television reporting that something had landed in the woods, the few dirt roads leading toward the crash site were soon choked with traffic. A few managed to drive close to the impact area and saw that the state police had cordoned off a section of the woods. New media, both radio and television, were broadcasting from close to the site. A number of them were talking about an unidentified flying object crash in Westmoreland County. Like Murphy, none of the other reporters was allowed to enter the woods.

There were, however, other civilians who did. Stan Gordon, of the Pennsylvania Association for the Study of the Unexplained (PASU), said that he'd interviewed a volunteer firefighter, Jim Romansky, who had gotten deep into the woods before the military sealed off the area.

In fact, according to Gordon, Romansky got down to the streambed where the object, not a meteorite according to his source, had first touched down. It cut a furrow in the streambed and came to rest in a hollow where it was partially concealed. From the roads leading into the area, it would be impossible to see anything in the streambed.

7.2. Stan Gordon, Kecksburg. Photo courtesy of Stan Gordon.

Romanski approached it and saw that it was acorn shaped, and speculated that it was 9 to 12 feet in diameter, and had a gold band around the bottom of it with writing on it. "There were no wings, motors, or a fuselage, as we know them," according to what Romanski told David Templeton in the *Pittsburgh Press*. The writing was described as like "ancient Egyptian hieroglyphics." But then, more importantly, he said that there were characters of broken and straight lines, dots, rectangles, and circles. He noticed there was a dent in the metal, but no rivets, seams, or welds visible.

But this man wasn't the only witness that Gordon managed to locate. In September 1988, he, working with other members of PASU, including John Micklow and George Lutz, found a man named Bill Bulebush who had been nearly as close to the Kecksburg object as was Romansky.

Bulebush told investigators that he was working on his car and looked up in time to see an object in the sky making a series of S turns or maybe a figure-eight before disappearing into the trees. He then drove out to the area using Meteor Road (as it's now called). At the high point, he looked down into the wooded area and saw lights in the distance. He parked his car and worked his way down the steep bank toward the area where "arc-welding flames were bluish sparklers" were shining, according to what he told Templeton. The trees had been knocked down in the area, and about 20 feet away was an object partially buried in the ground.

By this time it was nearly dark, and Bulebush used his flashlight to examine the object. He was about 15 feet from it. Like the first witness, Romansky, he said it was an acorn-shaped device with a gold band around the bottom. The object, according to Bulebush, was about 12 feet long and maybe 6 or 7 feet in diameter. He thought the color was a "burnt orange." He could still see "bright blue sparks" coming from it, but there was no sound associated with the object, and the sparking slowed and had nearly stopped by the time he left the area.

Before Bulebush left, he saw lights appear in the area from a different direction than that taken by the first witness or the military and the state police. According to Gordon, the lights bobbing in the woods could have been the military party.

*7.3. Kecksburg woods. Photo courtesy of Stan Gordon.*

There are still others who saw the object before the military retrieval. Bill Weaver turned onto a farm road and found several people standing near a cow path, studying the woods. He too saw an object that he said was glowing. He didn't approach it, however, saying later than he was too scared to go down toward it.

Weaver told Templeton he was there long enough to see four men dressed in white "moon suits," like those worn by astronauts, carrying a huge white box down into the woods on a stretcher. Not long after that, he was ordered from the area by a man in a business suit who threatened to take his car if he didn't move it.

Romanski also mentioned to several investigators and reporters including Stan Gordon that men in business suits whom he thought were military men in civilian clothes. They began to infiltrate and ordered the firefighters out of the area. One of them said that the woods were now a "restricted area to all civilian personnel." Armed men moved in to secure the hollow where the object had landed. No civilians were allowed to approach. At least the military was trying to keep them from the area, but they were having little luck doing it.

Meteor Road, however, had become a tourist attraction. Dozens of cars were lined up along it, while the drivers and passengers milled around outside, trying to see something interesting.

Those who had gotten close to the crash site saw a military flatbed truck arrive. Several hours later, others reported it leaving the area at a high rate of speed. One man even commented that if he had been in front of that truck, it would have run him down.

The truck carried something that was covered by a tarp, and it was escorted front and rear by other military vehicles. Robert L. Bitner, a firefighter who saw the events, said that one of the military trucks left after 10 or 10:30 p.m.

Bitner was not alone in the observation of the truck and its tarp-covered cargo. John Hays was 10 years old when the object fell in the woods. His house was the closest to the impact sight. According to Hays, military officers moved in, commandeering the house. They ordered his parents to send the children to bed, but Hays kept returning to the first floor for a drink of water or to use the bathroom.

When Hays was not on the first floor, he was at his bedroom window, trying to see what was happening outside. He saw a loaded flatbed truck coming from the woods with a tarp-covered cargo that reminded him of a Volkswagen Beetle under a huge piece of canvas. Hays thought this happened sometime after 1:00 in the morning.

There is a problem with this testimony, and it has nothing to do with the youth of the witness. Robert Gatty, a reporter from Greensburg, interviewed Hays's father for a report that appeared in the *Greensburg Tribune* (late edition) on December 10, 1965. Gatty said that Hays was outside working on his car when the object supposedly crashed. He said that he hadn't seen or heard anything.

Shortly after the truck disappeared, the military men who had been in the woods began to leave. Word circulated that the suspected plane crash was nothing more than a meteorite. The object that came down was extraterrestrial, but of natural origin.

*7.4. Hays family house, Kecksburg. Photo courtesy of Stan Gordon.*

The next day, the newspapers were filled with the story of the fireball that had caused so much trouble in the eastern United States. There were pictures of two teenaged boys displaying rocks they had recovered. The newspaper identified the rocks as part of the meteorite.

From Michigan came pictures of police officers holding up bits of metal that looked like thin, short strips of aluminum foil. Air Force spokesmen wrote that off as chaff from Air Force planes participating in one of the many training exercises they conducted.

Lanny Tolly, a deputy in the Lapeer (Michigan) County sheriff's office, said that he found several handfuls of a foil-like substance in the woods where witnesses had reported something had come down. Analysis revealed that it was a common variety of household aluminum foil.

Project Blue Book records show that someone called the Air Force to report the material. Rather than being silver, that report claimed the material was gold in color, about 1 inch long, and a 16th of an inch wide.

On December 28, 1965, Eric T. Jonchkhiere, the Air Force deputy for technology and subsystems at Wright-Patterson Air Force Base, wrote to Lapeer sheriff Kenneth A. Parks, telling him that the material submitted was nothing more than radar chaff. According to the letter, "This material is dropped by aircraft to confuse radar complexes when participating in interdiction exercises. 'Chaff' can travel for many miles, depending on wind currents and wind velocities."

The Air Force officers also made it clear they believed that it was a coincidence that the chaff began raining on Lapeer County about the time the fireball passed overhead. That seems to be a reasonable explanation. There certainly is no observed data to suggest that the chaff was related to the fireball other than that the two events happened at about the same time on the same day.

Near Elyria, 20 miles west of Cleveland, Ohio, firefighters were called to extinguish fires started as debris of some sort, possibly from the fireball, hit the ground. Mrs. Ralph Richards said she saw a fiery object about the size of a volleyball fall among some trees just before the small fires started.

Firefighters who responded to her calls said they had no trouble with the 10 or 12 grass fires that were burning. They reported finding nothing that could have caused the fires.

According to documents and newspaper reports contained in the Project Blue Book files, neear Livonia, Michigan, two boys discovered what they believed were "chunks of the meteor." Larry Jones and Brian Parent, both 11, saw the object. "I looked up and saw a streak of red shoot through the air," said Parent.

Parent thought the object landed in a vacant field. Searching with Jones, he found a slightly smoking rock embedded in the ground. Parent was wearing leather gloves and was able to pick up several stones.

Both boys were also photographed by the newspaper holding a stone on a piece of paper. They were quoted as saying, "If anyone asks us for them for testing, they can have them." Apparently neither the Air Force nor any other governmental agency believed that any other tests were necessary because no one asked for samples of the stones.

Project Blue Book files also show that a picture of the object had been taken. In one of the "memos for the record," it is claimed that a photographer from Royal Oak, Michigan, "was able to get a picture.... He also told Dr. [?] that a search was made in [an] attempt to recover the object." The Blue Book file does not explain what happened to the photograph or if it was ever submitted to Blue Book for analysis.

The photograph referred to, however, seems to be one taken by Richard P. Champine and published only a couple of months later (February 1966) in *Sky & Telescope*. It confirms the eyewitness accounts of the passing of the object or fireball. Because there was a "train" associated with the fireball—that is, "ionized air" caused by the passing of the object—it is believed that this could account for the descriptions of the object that say it was hovering or landing. The evidence shown in the photograph and the eyewitness testimony are not inconsistent with a fireball.

Coast Guard officials in Windsor, Ontario, Canada, reported that a flying object had exploded over Detroit. Pilots in the area reported the flash and shock waves, which could be consistent with a bolide, a very bright meteor that is sometimes associated with a roaring sound or multiple detonations.

The *Boston Record American* reported: "ARMY, POLICE SEAL OFF WOODS IN UFO PROBE." A spokesman said that a "team of radar experts from the 662 Radar Squadron here said, 'We don't know what we have yet.'"

Other newspapers carried nothing other than the reports of the fireball seen by thousands. Dr. William P. Bidelman, an astronomer at the University of Michigan, was quoted in dozens of newspapers. "It was undoubtedly a fireball," he said.

Bidelman, who didn't see it, was joined by other astronomers who didn't see it. In New York, Dr. Fred C. Hess, associate astronomer at the Hayden Planetarium, said that it was undoubtedly a large meteor that blew up, scattering fragments.

Dr. Nicholas Wagman, an astronomer at the Allegheny Observatory, said that the object was not part of the Geminid meteor shower visible at that time of year because the Geminid meteors are not very bright. That didn't mean it wasn't a meteor, just not one associated with a specific shower.

And the Air Force said that it was not an aircraft or missile, and that all space debris was accounted for. To the Air Force, it meant that whatever it was, it had to be a meteorite. No other explanation seemed to fit.

Other witnesses to the event began to come forward. Some of them described the flight of the object; others described the scene in Kecksburg. Both groups added to the data being circulated about the events.

One witness said that the object, as it came down, was engulfed in flames. Although there was very little smoke, the flames were bright orange, yellow, and white. A few heard a rumbling sound that the astronomers explained was a common occurrence with a large, bright meteor.

Ivan T. Sanderson, a naturalist interested in UFOs, in a report to the National Investigations Committee on Aerial Phenomenon (NICAP) that he marked confidential (though he submitted it for publication elsewhere), said that he had spoken to a number of officers on various police desks and tried to get additional information from the UPI and the Associated Press. According to Sanderson, he calculated the speed of the object at a little more than 1,000 miles an hour, much too slow for even the slowest of meteors. And even if Sanderson's calculations were off by a factor of 10, the object would still be flying at only 10,000 miles an hour, slower than the slowest speed ever recorded for a meteor. All this is if Sanderson's calculations of the speed are accurate, and there is some evidence that his calculations were based on faulty assumptions.

The military, however, had found an answer that worked and continued to push it. The official explanation in the Project Blue Book files was "Astro (meteor)." In a dozen or so memos for the record, the Blue Book staff repeated that the state police had searched the area but found nothing during their search.

Part of the state police's failure to locate anything was confirmed by Dr. Robert Murray and a couple of his students interested in UFOs. When they heard the reports on the radio, they left their eastern Ohio college about 10 p.m., driving into the Kecksburg area. According to them, when they arrived, at about 4 in the morning, there was nothing to see: no military around the Kecksburg fire department, no sightseers along the roads, and no evidence of a crash of anything anywhere. They finally gave up at about 7 or 8 a.m. and returned to their college.

But there were hints of something going on behind the scenes. Even if the eyewitness accounts of a military presence were discounted and the report of a flatbed truck under escort leaving at high speed was ignored, some kind of an event still could be documented.

The original teletype message of the news services proves that. The search, according to documents, got under way after seven Kecksburg residents reported the smoldering object crashed to Earth.

"There's definitely something down there," said a state trooper who, according to the documentation in the Project Blue Book files, saw a light partially hidden by the trees.

The most interesting report came from Lieutenant Steven Paquette, who, according to the notes and memos in the Project Blue Book files, said that he had been ordered to participate in the search even though he was stationed in New Hampton, Massachusetts. Paquette said, "From what I've heard, the Air Force Department in Washington is supposed to release something in the morning."

There is no evidence that Paquette ever traveled to Pennsylvania, and it seems unlikely that an officer in Massachusetts would be ordered in, unless he was part of a special unit or had some sort of special training or expertise. That seems to be the case here.

There were others who reported armed military men. Stan Gordon interviewed a family who said their home was invaded by Air Force officers who were armed and who were wearing rubber gloves. The family reported they had seen a large truck close to the crash site and that something was loaded onto it. That, of course, confirmed the stories told by the sightseers who had rushed into the area after the news reports on the radio.

Project Blue Book files do confirm that military men were in the area. According to a handwritten log found in the Blue Book files, Major Livers, Detroit Air Defense Sector, received reports from Ohio, Indiana, Michigan, and Pennsylvania. Livers called

Major Hector Quitanilla [chief of Project Blue Book] for his advice and assistance. He came to the base and called Major Livers. A further call was made to the Oakdale Radar Site in Pennsylvania. A three man team has been dispatched to Acme [Kecksburg] to investigate and pick up an object that started a fire.

Other records from Blue Book say that "Lieutenant Cashman said that the search ended about 0200. They searched with the State Police. They could not find anything. They do not plan on going out again. The news media, etc. stopped calling about 1 o'clock."

All this meant that the people who claimed to have seen military men at the site were correct. Although Blue Book talks about a three-man team being dispatched, which was assumed by others to have come from the Oakdale Radar Site, there were apparently others from other areas and other military organizations involved. Lieutenant Paquette, for example, was in Massachusetts when he was alerted.

That three-man team, however, is the one of the interesting aspects of this case. In the mid-1960s, and into the 1980s, the U.S. government operated a secret project known as Moon Dust. This, according to documents recovered through the Freedom of Information ACT (FOIA) by Robert Todd, a researcher in Pennsylvania, was an official government project known as Moon Dust that was "used in cases involving the examination of non-US space objects or objects of unknown origin."

According to the official Department of the Air Force document, dated November 3, 1961, Moon Dust "teams are comprised of three men each, to include a lingist, a tech man, and an ops man. All are airborne qualified..."

The document also says:

Peacetime employment of AFCIN intelligence team capability is provided for in UFO investigation (AFR 200-2) and in support of Air Force Systems Command (AFSC), Foreign Technology Division (FTD), Projects Moon Dust and Blue Fly. These three peacetime projects all involved a potential for employment of a qualified field intelligence personnel on a quick reaction basis to recover or perform field exploitation of unidentified flying objects, or known Soviet/Bloc aerospace vehicles, weapons systems and/or components of such equipment....

The document, although four years old by the time of the Kecksburg event, said:

Manning of the intelligence teams from those sources has not reached the point of diminishing returns. Only 21 qualified intelligence team personnel are now assigned, and of those approximately half are scheduled for PCS [permanent change of station] departure from the organization during the next 12 months. There is no forecast input of previously qualified personnel.

What this means is that there were only seven qualified teams throughout the entire Air Force. They could all have been deployed to bases inside the United States, or they could have been split among the bases inside the United States to other Air Force bases around the world. Either way there were not many of them, which might explain why Paquette was alerted in Massachusetts. He could have been a member of a Moon Dust team and been the closest one to Kecksburg.

The obvious conclusion is that Moon Dust was activated for the Kecksburg event. It means that the military, with its sophisticated radar and sky surveillance, believed that something was down in the Kecksburg area, it is reasonable to believe that the object, whatever it was, ended its journey there.

Although the documents recovered by Todd under the Freedom of Information Act suggest that Moon Dust and Blue Fly no longer exist, it is only because the names were changed once those names were compromised. According to an Air Force letter received by Todd, "The nickname 'Project Moon Dust' no longer exists officially. *It has been replaced by another name which is not releasable* [emphasis added]."

Controversy about the Kecksburg event wasn't limited to the military role or what had fallen into the woods. The town, it seems, was split by those who believed that the whole story of an object in the woods was a hoax and those who had seen something they considered mysterious. Robert Young, a researcher living in the area, has spent years studying the events and believes the official statements that the object seen in the sky was a bolide, and that no object was found on the ground. He has said, repeatedly, that the Kecksburg event—that is, a flying saucer crash—"appears never to have happened." In a 1991 paper privately published, he wrote that "the sole witnesses to the saucer crash apparently were two eight-year-old children who were among the thousands in nine states and Canada to witness a bolide (exploding) meteor."

The controversy heated when *Unsolved Mysteries* decided to air a segment about Kecksburg. The trouble began in 1990 when the TV crews descended on the tiny community to begin filming. According to an article by David Templeton in the *Pittsburgh Press* called "The Uninvited," "The show, which accurately detailed eyewitness accounts, turned quiet opinions into political philosophies, pitting true believers against certified skeptics. Feuds broke out between relatives, neighbors and community leaders."

Robert Bitner, who claimed to have witnessed some of the military activity, is convinced, according to the article, that something happened. His brother-in-law, Carl Porch, hasn't spoken to him since the film crews arrived and was one of those who tried to block the *Unsolved Mysteries* broadcast with a petition. Porch insists that it's all a hoax.

Porch is joined by Charles Hilland, who lives near the crash site. Hillard said that nothing happened. Hilland was another of those who tried to stop the broadcast.

In fact, the petition was signed by 45 residents of the area who either owned land near the crash site or had been out along Meteor Road on December 9, 1965. The petition said:

> We the concerned citizens and friends of the small community of KECKSBURG, in southwest PENNSYLVANIA are asking you not to air the segment that you filmed in our area. Since Mr. Stan Gordon has been doing interviews in this area it has caused the landowners much harassment and endangered the health and welfare of our residents. The curiosity seekers wanting to see the landing site, are leaving empty cans, bottles and other debris, also using private buildings as restrooms. If this show goes nationwide many more people will want to see this so called site and cause more confusion. Many people saw something in the sky, but no one has evidence of it landing. We beg of you to please talk to our property owners in the questioned landing site, who have no knowledge of any type of object landing. We fell that the story has been blown our of reasonable explanation. The authorities of 1965 insisted that they found nothing and we concur.

The main thrust of the petition seemed to be to keep people out of the area. They were concerned about damage to their property and rightly so. A secondary consideration, though one that couldn't be overlooked, was their belief that nothing was recovered. The authorities said nothing was recovered and they hadn't seen anything recovered. In fact, many of the newspaper articles published in 1965 said that a search of the woods had found nothing.

It should be made clear that many of those who signed the petition have no firsthand knowledge of the events. They talked to friends or family, but were not physically present when anything happened. Don Scott, for example, told me in 1993 that he wasn't in Kecksburg and had heard about it from his mother. He signed the petition because he was concerned about outsiders trespassing on private property.

One man, who wished to remain anonymous, told me in 1993 that he knew many of the fire fighters, but on the night of the crash, he wasn't in Kecksburg. Two days later, he arrived at the firehouse, but the events were over. He did acknowledge that military officials had been present the Thursday before. But he also said that the story was nothing more than "bull****."

To counter that point is other eyewitness testimony that tells of something found and taken out on a flatbed truck, covered with a tarp. It is eyewitness testimony that the skeptics are quick to reject simply because it does not fit into their view of the events of December 9, 1965.

Young, in his report, wrote that the official and scientific explanation is a meteor. He reported that astronomers from Michigan, Ohio, Pennsylvania, the American Meteor Society, and the National Research Council of Canada have concluded the object was a bright meteor. In his report, Young wrote:

> The late astronomer Von Del Chamberlin, then of the Abrams Planetarium, East Lansing, Michigan, concluded after analyzing more than one hundred written reports that the fireball occurred about 4:44 p.m., lasted about four seconds and appeared brighter (about visual magnitude -15) than the full moon.

Robert Young reported in "Old-Solved Mysteries," in *Skeptical Inquirer,* that G.W. Wetherill, a geophysics and geology professor at UCLA in Los Angeles,

> ...reported that he had personally located and interviewed many witnesses and studied twenty-three reports received by the Federal Aviation Administration (FAA) from pilots, many of whom thought an airliner was down. He concluded from witnesses on the south shore of Lake Erie who saw the object to the north that no impact occurred south of the lake, and that the object burst apart and disappeared some miles over the western end of the lake. He

decided that the steep trajectory reported by the witnesses indicated that the fireball had an extraterrestrial (meaning meteoric) origin and was not a returning orbital spacecraft.

There had been discussions that the object that fell at Kecksburg was, in fact, the returning Russian Kosmos 96, a malfunctioning Soviet Venus probe. The Foreign Technology Division of the Air Force at Wright-Patterson Air Force Base denied there was a record of such a retrieval. The Soviet Embassy, according to Templeton, said that the crash was not part of the Kosmos 96. And Stan Gordon said that the U.S. Space Command showed that the Kosmos 96 reentered about 13 hours before the events at Kecksburg. Though it is true that Moon Dust would be activated to retrieve the craft if it was of Soviet design and manufacture, there is no evidence that whatever fell was the Soviet spacecraft. The evidence available suggests that Kosmos 96 crashed in Canada at 3:18 a.m.

James Oberg wrote an article in *Omni* in 1993, re-evaluating the Kosmos 96 explanation. According to Oberg, "By going on a hunch and tapping my own expertise in space operation and satellite sleuthing," he changed his mind. Oberg said that what had reentered earlier was not the Kosmos 96 itself, but could have been a jettisoned rocket stage or a large piece of space junk. "The probe itself," according to Oberg, "could have been headed off toward Kecksburg."

Other reports suggest that a misfire of a missile launched on that day from Vandenberg Air Force Base in California might have been responsible. In fact, some had said it was the reentry of a Mark Six Reentry Vehicle (MK-6 RV) that was manufactured by General Electric. If that was true, then small pieces of debris that didn't burn up might have struck the ground near Kecksburg. But there has been no evidence to suggest that this is correct, and the trajectory of the object suggests something else.

That returned the area of speculation to a bolide. Frank Drake, an astronomer and quoted by Young in his "Old-Solved Mysteries," said that eyewitness reports of bolides are typically inaccurate. He pointed out that, in his experience, the percentage of witnesses who are wrong about something is one-half after a day, three-quarters after two days, and about 90 percent after four days. Beyond that, Drake believed that the reports were more fantasy than fact. According to

Drake, witnesses often grossly underestimate the distance of fireballs, which may be dozens of miles high. When meteors disappear over the horizon, witnesses sometimes believe that the event was nearby.

Robert Kadesch, an astronomer in Utah, pointed out that people looking up into the sky often had no points of reference. Because of that, it was difficult for them to properly judge height and distance. That was for an object high in the sky and at great distance. For those who saw it closer to the ground, with points of reference, their ability to judge the size and distance improved markedly.

Young, in his analysis of the case in *Skeptical Inquirer* in 1991, reported that there were published accounts that the object, whatever it was, had crashed or landed in seventeen widely scattered areas. He wrote:

> Over Lake Erie a pilot reported watching as it "plummeted" into the lake. At Midland, PA., west of Pittsburgh, falling debris were reported but police found nothing. Nearby, other "falls" were reported in Patterson and Chippewa Townships, near Beaver Falls, PA. In one, a boy saw a "big ball of fire fall into the woods and the woods are smoking"; in the other two boys thought the object landed and was smoking in a field. Nothing was reported found except some broken tree limbs, one of which appeared to have been cut with a saw.

Young continued:

> At Elyria, Lorain County, Ohio, a woman reported a "volley ball" sized fireball fell into a wooded lot. Firemen reported ten small grass fires...at Elyria, boys found slag-like fragments but there was nothing to link them to the meteor...near Cleveland, a boy reported a flaming object fell out of the sky into some woods.... Two 11-year-old boys at Livonia, Michigan, reported picking up a piece of light-weight, grayish, fused metal the size of a baseball which they said had fallen into a field.... At Lapeer, Michigan, 40 miles north of Detroit, Sheriff's officers investigating the report of a "fireball crashing" found only pieces of foil...he said he did not know whether the foil had any connection to the fireball....

The suggestion being made is that all these other cases are based on the false impressions of the various witnesses. If such is the case, then isn't it reasonable to assume that those near Kecksburg made similar mistakes when they claimed the fireball had landed in the woods near Kecksburg?

But more importantly, it was at Kecksburg that the only recovery operation was mounted. The state police, the state police fire marshal, unidentified civilian officials, and military officers appeared, apparently interested in something in the woods. At all those other locations, there was no real response by the government, or you might say by governmental agencies whether local, county, state, or national. That, in and of itself, is significant, and underscores the difference between what happened at those other locations and what was happening at Kecksburg. Those other reports might be considered irrelevant.

Young wrote about the photograph taken by Champine and published in December 1965 in *Sky & Telescope*:

> This quarter century-old published photograph provides dramatic and *irrefutable* [emphasis added] support for the accounts of eyewitnesses. It also provides a clear-cut, prosaic explanation for the "hovering" and "landing" now alleged to be reported by "new" unnamed [in fairness it must be pointed out that Young's statement was written before many of these witnesses had consented to making their names public].... [It] is necessary to explain this photograph and the eyewitness accounts that supports it—including Kecksburg witnesses.

And, although Young might not like it, there is an alternative explanation for the bolide. Northrop Aircraft began experimenting in the mid-1960s with electrostatic shock. They wanted to charge the air around an aircraft with a positive charge, and the airplane itself with a negative charge. Their experimentation suggested that this could reduce or eliminate the sonic boom. It would also, according to the experimental data, make the craft flying through air look like a comet. In other words, a fiery craft with a long, ionized trail strung out behind it.

Although it is true that Young raises a number of fair questions and proposes a number of good points in his counter-arguments, he also falls into the same trap as many believers. He is so enthusiastic for his own position that he ignores, in some cases, the evidence that doesn't support him, or draws conclusions not warranted by the established facts.

In an article published in the *Skeptical Inquirer* in 1991, Young claimed:

> According to all original published accounts, the sole witnesses to the saucer crash apparently were two eight-year-old children among the thousands in nine states and Canada to view a bolide.... Add to this a gullible local flying-saucer buff who has finally found "his own" thrilling flying-saucer crash to investigate.

But the truth, as developed through the documentation, is that Young hasn't reviewed all the evidence. Murphy's radio broadcast reveals that there was more than just the story of two 8-year-old boys. Testimony recorded by Murphy showed that others were talking of something tangible in the woods within hours of the reports of the crash. The UFO buff—probably Stan Gordon—had little to do with the story. It was the testimony of those involved and the contradictory statements of the state police, military, and other officials that kept the story alive. To suggest otherwise is not a fair statement.

Gordon, in his research, managed to obtain the records for the 662d Radar Squadron through the Freedom of Information Act. For the crucial December 9 date there was no entry. In a 1993 interview with me, Gordon asked, "How could so much equipment and personnel be activated, yet the log showed that they were not involved in any activity on the date of the incident?"

According to what Gordon told me in the 1993 interview, Captain Dussia said in his statements that nothing was found and "[r]eports of something carried from the area only referred to equipment used in the search."

So, Gordon is right that equipment was involved in the search. He is right that military personnel were activated, based on official records, and he is right that the area of the woods was searched.

Young, however, disagrees that there is anything significant about the lack of a record for the 662d Radar Squadron on the night of December 9. He wrote in his "Old-Solved Mysteries" article, "It is unlikely that Air Force units listed each and every wild goose chase due to a mistaken UFO report in their unit histories."

But Young is wrong. It wasn't a unit history, but the command post log. And this is precisely the sort of event that would be listed in the log simply because it is out of the ordinary. That is the purpose of the logs. Other unit logs, available through the National Archives, show that events on December 9 were noted. Young's assumption about the logs is without merit.

What we are left with is an enigma. It seems there is very good evidence to suggest that the object observed was a bolide. The characteristics it exhibited are consistent with that belief. Suggestions by Ivan Sanderson, for example, that the object made a turn, seem to be the result of the false assumption that the debris picked up in various locations came from the object. There is no evidence connecting the flight of the object (or fall of the object) with the debris from Lapeer, Michigan, or from the area near Livonia, Michigan. The path of the object, as best described by the eyewitnesses, is a straight line, consistent with a meteor.

The problem arises when the Kecksburg end is plugged into the equation. Young, in his article, dismisses the testimony of the eye-witnesses to an object on the ground in the woods by citing them as "24-year-old recollections of local citizens, and the recent materialization of 'new' witnesses."

Young accepts the testimony of those calling it a hoax, and rejects that of those who say that something was recovered from the woods, suggesting in his 1991 report: "Some residents have blamed two local men whose story of a copper-colored, 12 by 7 foot 'acorn-shaped' object with 'hieroglyphic' markings surfaced only a couple of months before [the *Unsolved Mysteries* program], almost a quarter of a century after the original publicity."

The truth is that Gordon had presented the testimony of one man in the fourth quarter 1987 issue of *Pursuit*. Although having it printed in a magazine does nothing to validate the testimony, it shows that the data were circulating years before the *Unsolved Mysteries* filming and broadcast and not only for the months claimed by Young.

To be fair to Young, it is also necessary to point out that the testimony of Jim Romansky is, in fact, highly questionable. According to the July 28, 1966 Kecksburg *Tribune-Review*, "James R. Romansky, the 20-year-old Latrobe man convicted of robbing Latrobe's Mellon National Bank...earlier this year, was sentenced to serve from four to six years in prison."

That certainly hurt Romansky's credibility. However, his troubles with the law weren't over. The March 1, 1994 *Tribune-Review* reported that "following yesterday's preliminary hearing, [Derry area district justice Mark] Bilik ruled there was sufficient evidence to hold [James R.] Romansky for trial on charges of rape, aggravated indecent assault, indecent assault and terrorist threats." Although none of this proves that Romansky lied about his involvement in the Kecksburg crash/retrieval, it ruins his credibility, and his testimony must be considered in the light of these revelations.

There is good evidence that the discussion of an object in the woods had been going on since December 1965. Murphy, in the radio program he aired just days after the events, reported that there were those who had seen an object in the woods. He found that some people were afraid to talk about it in 1965.

Young, on the other hand, showed that some people, in their support of the Kecksburg crash, have misinterpreted the information as well. During the TV program *Sightings,* Romansky said, "The Freedom of Information Act states there was 212 military personnel here that night." Young points out that the act itself governs the procedures for the release of government data and does not reflect what is contained in those data. And, although the records show that the 662d Radar Squadron had 212 people assigned on December 9, 1965, it is doubtful that all of them would have been deployed to the Kecksburg area, even if the unit had been activated.

There is evidence that three military people, assigned as part of Project Moon Dust, were activated for the retrieval. We could say that the military is not in the habit of activating highly trained intelligence personnel to recover what might be the remains of a meteorite, but that would be speculation. The activation suggests—only suggests—that something was known to be down and a team was sent to recover it. This doesn't mean that only three military people were there, just that this is documentation for those three. (Murphy's statements on the radio just days after the event confirm more than three military people, from both the Army and Air Force, were in the Kecksburg area.) Even if no other orders went out, there would be support people—pilots, for example—who would accompany them.

Oberg's theory of the reentry of the Kosmos 96 is also at odds with Young's report. Young has suggested repeatedly that nothing fell into the woods. Oberg claims that it was Kosmos 96, not a spacecraft from another world, but a spacecraft nonetheless. Oberg believes that something did fall at Kecksburg, and Kosmos 96 would have required the activation of a Project Moon Dust team.

Young also disputes the claim that there were armed military personnel in the Kecksburg area. He wrote, "None of the many articles published in 1965 described armed troops at Keckburg. Proponents of the *Unsolved Mysteries* version of events must show that Army or Navy National Guard [there are no Navy National Guard units but are Naval Reserve units] military police were present."

Although he is correct that none of the newspaper articles mentioned armed military personnel, it could be that various reporters didn't bother with the detail simply because it seemed to be redundant. There are no mentions of armed state troopers, but those men were armed.

Documentation available through the Freedom of Information Act removes this complaint of no armed men from the realm of speculation. One of the documents uncovered in the search for Moon Dust and Blue Fly material addresses the problems of armed soldiers. Discovered on Micro Film #31,641 from the Air Force Historical Research Center (USAFHRC) at Maxwell Air Force Base was a report that discussed "Financing the Operation." According to it, "In the Cuban crisis no effort was spared in supplying the BLUE FLY team with normal supply items (e.g. B-4 bags and .45 calibre automatics)." In other words, a historic precedence for armed teams for the Moon Dust/Blue Fly had been established. It means that similarly armed teams might have been sent into Kecksburg.

What we know is that both the skeptic and the believer have resorted to overstating the case. There are questions that both sides must answer before a final and definite conclusion can be drawn.

Here is what we know. Something entered the atmosphere about 4:44 p.m. on December 9. Some eyewitness testimony and a photograph suggest the object was nothing more complicated than a bolide. Because bolides are a rare phenomenon, and because it was early evening, thousands saw it, but were unable to identify it correctly.

Meteors enter the atmosphere on a daily basis. Few of them are large enough to light up the sky, and fewer still reach the ground before they burn up. Air Force spokesmen often claim meteors don't show up on radar, though the ionized trail they leave behind can. With recently developed radars that can be set to discriminate between natural and manufactured objects, that can be set to detect rain showers, thunderstorms, or the turbulence in them, or to see and track objects in orbit, it is likely that NORAD in Colorado Springs, as well as the operators in Oakdale, knew what they were tracking.

Within two hours of the impact, according to some witnesses, the military had arrived in sufficient force to take over the fire department. They had brought in radios, telephones, and other equipment. And they were making preparations to enter the woods, though the state police claimed there was nothing to be seen, and Dussia made statements to the newspapers the next day that nothing had been found.

Within eight hours, around one o'clock, according to some of the witnesses, a flatbed truck with a tarp covering its cargo was seen leaving the area at high speed. Ten-year-old Hays, among others, claimed to have witnessed this.

Within eleven hours of the impact, the military presence was no longer easily visible and, in fact, almost all activity had ended. By the time Murray and his students arrived, the town was quiet and everyone had gone home. Although they drove some of the back roads, searching for anything out of the ordinary, they saw no sightseers, military, or state police.

*7.5. Broken trees near Kecksburg crash site. Photo courtesy of Stan Gordon.*

Within 24 hours, almost all military presence was gone, but their orders were still being obeyed. Kalp and her children were under bombardment by the news media for interviews, but military officers had already talked to her. Although the military was telling most people that a meteorite had hit the ground, one man—possibly military—supposedly told Kalp it was one of our Gemini spacecraft that had somehow "been expelled in the area."

But, like everything else in UFO research, there are problems with this, some of which were pointed out by Tom Printy on his skeptical Website (*home.comcast.net/~tprinty?UFO/kecksburg.htm*). He wondered about the rapid deployment of the military forces into the Kecksburg area on the night of the crash. We just saw, based on the time lines established by various witnesses, that the military arrived there quickly.

Though it is not difficult to get several men, who are on duty at the time, into an area quickly, it is not a simple task to move a military unit and its equipment. This means that the three men that have been documented as going into Kecksburg—that is the three man team from the 662d Radar Squadron—could have arrived, and apparently did arrive within an hour or two, but a larger military presence would be difficult.

Although Printy makes the case that military personnel in garrison work normal hours, the truth of the matter is that the military is on a 24-hours-a-day schedule and the men could be kept on duty until the close of business, which means when the work is done. So, the personnel would have been available.

There is another problem, and that is the concept of *Posse Comitatus,* which prohibits the use of active duty military personnel in a law enforcement role. Simply stated, they are not authorized. They certainly could go out to recover equipment, as is alleged here, but when we begin to talk of them commandeering private homes, we run into trouble. They had no authority to do that, and it might have been even worse than a violation of *Posse Comitatus*; it is in violation of the U.S. Constitution.

Even when acting with local law enforcement, such as the Pennsylvania State Police, there are problems. Had the homeowners protested, or the civilians on what became Meteor Road objected, the military had no authority to require compliance. Only the local law enforcement could have done that.

When we move beyond the few members of the 662d we run into more trouble. According to some of the witnesses, there were quite a few armed men brought into Kecksburg, and they had some heavy equipment with them. That includes a flatbed truck and other military vehicles, but no one ever talked about any kind of a convoy. To move military vehicles on the civilian highways does take some preparation and coordination. There are no reports in the newspapers about any of that, and had the military moved equipment and soldiers into the area, something should have been mentioned at some point in the local newspapers.

There are mentions of the military in the newspapers, but it almost always refers to the airmen who came from the 662d, and there is no evidence that the Army responded. A likely explanation here is that reporters, seeing men in uniform, assumed they were Army when they were, in fact, Air Force.

And remember that, when Dr. Robert Murray and his students arrived at 4 the next morning, they saw no evidence of the military presence. This is quite disturbing. Had something been found in the woods, it would seem that it would have taken more than eight or 10 hours to clean the site. The military would certainly have wanted to survey the scene in the daylight to make sure they had recovered all the evidence. That they were gone already suggests that their involvement was limited in scope.

Few of those who served with the 662d Radar Squadron have been located and interviewed. One of the officers, James Cashman, called Project Blue Book at Wright-Patterson Air Force Base and said that nothing had been found, according to the records. Cashman had not been one of those sent into the field. However, if he was making the official report to Blue Book, he would have known what had been found.

Leslie Kean, writing for the *International UFO Reporter (Volume 30, Number 1)* suggested:

> Our private investigator was able to locate Cashman and three other key personnel from the 662nd, and Gordon interviewed a fifth in 1991. Only one of these, a lieutenant whom I will not name to respect his privacy, said he actually went out to search for the object that night. This officer said he did not observe any Army presence in the area, any excess civilian activity, or the large spotlights in the woods observed by witnesses and reporter John Murphy. This seems impossible if he was anywhere near the correct location and directly contradicts press reports about the large military presence and civilian crowds. He said he and three other members of the 662nd searched the woods with flashlights and found nothing.

It is revealing that puzzling discrepancies exist among key points of the various accounts, as well as between aspects of the statements of these officers and reports from both the media and Project Blue Book. For example, the lieutenant who searched the woods said there were four in his search team; another officer told us that he had driven with the team to a nearby barrack while two from Oakdale conducted the search with a state trooper. (This could have been the three man team referred to by Blue Book, although Blue Book said that the three were all from Oakdale.)

Another officer told me there was no search at all, and that the reports coming in to the Oakdale base concerned only an object in the sky and not an object on the ground. He remembers very well the high volume of calls from the local area and speaking to some of the callers, and says that if there had been a search, he definitely would have known. He was adamant that there wasn't one. And yet another told me that the object was a Russian satellite, but insisted that he made that determination only from newspaper and television reports.

According to Project Blue Book records, Cashman called Blue Book headquarters at Wright-Patterson Air Force Base twice from the Oakdale base, including a final call at 2 a.m., to report that nothing was found. Oddly, Cashman says he has no memory of any event, phone calls, or heightened activity at that time. He stated that he was the Blue Book liaison officer (as stated in the Blue Book files), as opposed to the lieutenant who told me he was the Blue Book officer.

We are not certain whether these contradictory and sometimes confusing reports are simply a question of jumbled memories after all these years, or if other factors are at play. Is it possible that this small group was taken to a different location from the one that was cordoned off by the Army, and that they searched the wrong site? If this did occur, was the state trooper who took the Air Force team to the wrong site instructed by someone to do so? If so, the officers are honestly reporting that nothing was found. Would it therefore have been possible since Project Blue Book did not have access to cases higher than a secret clearance that Blue Book actually never knew about an object retrieved from another location by the Army?

On the other hand, Murphy reports seeing what appeared to be members of the 662nd Radar Squadron at the edge of the woods after leaving the police barracks where he had first encountered them. If the lieutenant was one of these men, he could not possibly have missed the surrounding military and civilian activity. Were these officers perhaps sworn not to reveal what happened for national security reasons, and thus their cover stories have differences? We don't know, and we won't know until the government releases the records.

The real point seems to be that there are contradictions, but these can be resolved by looking at the record as it was produced in 1965. The reporters on the scene, who produced articles for their newspapers, fail to mention this heavy military involvement. When Kean suggests that, "We are not certain whether these contradictory and sometimes confusing reports are simply a question of jumbled memories after all these years, or if other factors are at play," we can deduce the answer. The memories appear to be jumbled.

John Murphy, news director of WHJB radio and one of the first civilians on the scene, put together a news special containing interviews with a number of witnesses, including Kalp. Just before the program was to be aired, some of the witnesses called and told Murphy they didn't want their names or their voices broadcast. They told him that they feared reprisals from either the military or the state police. Murphy was forced to air a watered-down version of the broadcast. Without the authentication of his report the interviews would have provided, the program was less believable. Murphy hinted that someone had put pressure on the witnesses not to talk about what they had seen or done.

Newspaper reporter Templeton took it further in his 1991 *Pittsburgh Press* article, reporting that "whole sections were edited out after eyewitnesses withdrew their stories in fear of police or military retaliations. Murphy did report that people saw flashing lights, and the military placed an object into a 'cement-lined drum.'"

Bonnie Millslagle, Murphy's wife in 1965 (Murphy was killed years later in an unrelated automobile accident), said that he was convinced that the object that fell was not a meteor and was not something from Earth. In fact, she said that he had gotten down into the crash area before anyone else, with a camera. After photographing the object and making taped notes, he climbed out of the impact site, where he was met by military officers. The military officers or the state police confiscated the film in his camera and the tape in his recorder. It was clear to her that Murphy had seen something in the crater and had taken pictures of it.

In the weeks that followed, she said that his attitude changed. At first he had been convinced that this was a big story that the government was attempting to suppress. Later, he talked about it less frequently. She thought that someone had said something to him in the days after the event. She was sure that it was the military, though Murphy said nothing to her about that.

This is secondhand testimony that doesn't seem to be corroborated by the reports made in 1965. It also seems strange that, had this happened, Murphy didn't protest it then, take pictures of the military and its equipment on the public roads, and then mention that his recordings and film had been confiscated by the military. He was, after all, telling the world on his broadcast that something extraordinary happened. Why leave out the details of the military trying to prevent the story from getting out?

Adam Lynch, working for KDKA-TV in 1965, on the other hand, saw nothing except the military and the people. He returned to the station after the announcement that it was nothing more than a meteorite. This is not to mention Robert Gatty's reports that suggest nothing extraordinary had been found.

There is another point that Tom Printy makes, and it is a good one. It is a suggestion that we should have more information about this based on the newspaper reports of the time. On his Website, he wrote:

> According to Gatty's article, he states photographer Jim Downs was with him and also states that, at one point, they went into the field to look for the lights in the woods but did not see any. Why didn't the massive military cordon prevent him from going into the field? One would think that if a massive military involvement was there, we would have some evidence from their reporting. Where are the photographs of heavy military vehicles arriving or leaving the area? Where are the photographs of soldiers armed with orders to shoot? Exactly why didn't the news media

personnel go down into the gully and take pictures of what had happened on the day after? Surely, they could have found some evidence of trees being knocked down as described by John Hays and, possibly, of the trench described by Bulebush (or at least the covered up trench). The tracks left by the flatbed truck would have been fresh and easily seen the next day. Surely photographs would have been taken of this. For that matter, why didn't the Hays family take out the "old brownie" and get a couple of snaps showing where the Army had tore up their land? The lack of this evidence makes one seriously question the new Kecksburg legend. Of course, UFOlogists will state that the media would have been prevented from getting these critical pieces of evidence by the vast cover-up that had been established and the military would never allow such photographs to be taken. I find this to be a ridiculous excuse. All this implies is that these reporters were extremely inept at doing their job. Even in 1965, a newsman couldn't resist a good story like this. Recall these two reporters were supporting a small rural area. This was big news and it was putting them on the map! Robert Gatty stated recently that he wished that he had heard these extraordinary stories back in 1965 and also claims that there were army soldiers blocking him off from the area. Apparently, he was an inept reporter and did not accurately report what really happened that night in his 1965 news reports! His photographer was also inept because he did not capture one photograph of the military units blocking off the area. Were Gatty and Downs just incompetent or is Gatty now making stories up to cement his place in Kecksburg lore?

We do have a record of this event from the newspapers at the time and they do not suggest a massive military involvement. There are no photographs to confirm it and, whereas in Roswell you could argue that there simply weren't that many cameras, in 1965, almost every home had some kind of camera and many had 8mm movie cameras. Yet, no one has ever produced a picture of the military in the town, the military and police cordon, or anything else that would suggest a large-scale recovery.

Gordon and Kean did sue NASA over their lack of cooperation in their search for documents. The courts ruled in their favor, but it might not have been something to make them happy. In December 2005,

NASA, according to Kean's *IUR* article, said that they had examined metallic fragments from the object and that they had determined it was a reentering Soviet satellite.

The Associated Press report said, "The object appeared to be a Russian satellite that re-entered the atmosphere and broke up. NASA experts studied fragments from the object, but records of what they found were lost in the 1990s."

But here is the problem now. We have spent all this time saying that nothing was recovered in the woods. The military was there, but in small numbers, certainly no more than a dozen and probably half of that. They searched the woods, as did some of the state police troopers, maybe some members of the fire department, and everyone who voiced an opinion said nothing was found.

Now we're being told that something was found and that it was analyzed by NASA. I won't bother to speculate why, if this is true, they would have hidden that information, though there could be some very real national security issues. However, they are saying that something was recovered and that they not only analyzed it in 1965, but they identified it as Soviet, and then they lost the records. Is it any wonder that some in the Ufological community suggest a conspiracy to keep information out of the hands of the public?

This explanation, of course, contradicts what the Air Force said in 1965, and what various astronomers suggested back then, and that many have held onto since then. It also contradicts what Nicholas L. Johnson, NASA's Chief Scientist for Orbital Debris, told Kean in 2003. He told Kean that the orbital mechanics made it impossible for any part of the Kosmos 96 to account for either the fireball or any other object that might have been picked up near Kecksburg.

So what we have here might seem a rather schizophrenic presentation of the Kecksburg crash. The eyewitness testimony seems to be, at best, contradictory and, at worst, a series of lies designed to bring that person into the spotlight. There is no doubt that people will invent their involvement in almost any event and say almost anything to get their 15 minutes of fame, which explains, I suppose, one man's claim in 1997 that he was the reincarnation of Andrews, one of the primary architects of *Titanic*. In other words, people will often say what they have to so that they will get a chance to be on television.

But then we run into the lost records and the claim that NASA did analyze debris from Kecksburg. They claimed it was the remains of a Soviet satellite that had reentered, which, of course, means that what fell at Kecksburg was a spacecraft; it just wasn't extraterrestrial. But it also proves that one part of the government has no idea what another is doing, that something was found contrary to the reports, and that this is another case filled with government lies.

I confess that at this point I'm so confused, I'm not sure what to believe. The fireball answer seems logical, and the photographic evidence seems to support that. The satellite answer does not seem logical based on everything that everyone said until NASA changed direction and said it was. The UFO answer seems logical because there are too many other answers.

Like so many of the UFO crash reports, nothing concrete can be said. It seems reasonable to accept the military and official answer that the sighting was the result of a bolide, but, to do that, too much eyewitness testimony has to be discarded. If it weren't for the number of people who claim to have seen something on the ground, and who witnessed part of the retrieval; if not for the use of Moon Dust, it could be said this was a case of mistaken identity. However, a post of the case can't be thrown out because it is difficult to explain. Until all the facts are known, the case must remain open.

# Chapter 8

Pre-1947

1947
Pre-Roswell

July 1947

October
1947–1948

1949–1952

1953–1964

1965

## January 1967 ————————————————

### SOUTHWEST MISSOURI

A small object, 40 inches in diameter, was found by a man identified only as Loftin. He gave it to the U.S. Testing Company for analysis. No other details are available.

However, this case surfaced during a time of great UFO activity in the area with four days of reports being made from police offices, civil servants, and civilians. The object in those reports was described by some as blue-green with flashing lights. Some said that what they saw was as big as two houses and others said that it remained stationary for a time, giving them a good look at it. Others thought that the UFO was as low as 1,000 feet above the ground.

A report about these sightings made to the Condon Committee, and they sent a team into the area to investigate. The case was labeled as "Case 14, South-Central, Winter 1967." That report concluded: "Of the six [UFO sightings], three were promptly identified, two as astronomical objects and one as a chemical release-rocket. The other three remain unidentified."

Of those three unidentified sightings, they wrote: "In only one case [of the three they failed to identify] of an unidentified object was the evidence strong for both its reality and its strangeness. That was the first, which involved a slowly drifting sphere, metallic in color."

So, although there isn't much information available about the crash, there was a series of sightings in that area at that time, one of them of sufficient strangeness that even the Condon Committee, which tended to identify everything they looked at even if they had to invent the answers, that they mentioned it specifically.

That wasn't the only period of UFO sightings in that area. Ten years later, in 1977, the same area was flooded with more reports that included landings and occupants, but no other crashes. The sightings were again made by police officials with the radio dispatcher coordinating the efforts to identify the craft. There were multiple civilian sightings, and there were even a couple of photographs offered as proof that something was going on. The one picture that did surface during my investigation was identified as a triple exposure of the moon. It seemed that the photographer had a shaky hand and wasn't attempting to fool anyone. He thought he had something truly unusual in the picture, not realizing what he had done.

Of all the sightings in 1977, most were identified and many times by the people in the area. But there was a core of reports that weren't easily resolved, meaning that it was a hot bed of activity for several weeks.

## August 17, 1967

### SUDAN

A cube-shaped satellite weighing about 3 tons was found 50 miles from Kutum. There were no markings visible on the surface. Authorities took photographs of it and cut samples from it with difficulty. There is no reason to believe this was anything other than a terrestrially manufactured satellite. It was retrieved under the Project Moon Dust program.

## October 4, 1967

### SHAG HARBOUR, CANADA

Although the Condon Committee had been commissioned to review the UFO evidence, and although they had received a report that

*8.1. Shag harbor by air. Photo courtesy of Don Ledger.*

something had crashed into Shag Harbour, Nova Scotia, their entire investigation of the incident was a telephone call or two to the Royal Canadian Mounted Police. They were alerted to the event by Jim Lorenzen, then the International Director of APRO. Given that information, they launched their "investigation" using the telephone.

Dr. Norman E. Levine provided the information for the Condon Committee and it was reported on pages 351 and 352 as Case No. 34, labeled as "North Atlantic," and dated as "Fall 1967." Levine wrote:

> He [Jim Lorenzen] stated that the original report had come from two teenagers and that the Navy was searching for wreckage. No aircraft were reported missing in the area.... A corporal of the RCMP [apparently Victor Werbieki] stated that the first report had come from five young people, 15–20 yr. old, who while driving near the shore had seen three or four yellow lights in a horizontal pattern comparable in size to a "fair-sized" aircraft.... They observed the light while they drove about .25 mi., then reported the incident to the RCMP detachment.

Chris Styles and Don Ledger, two Canadian researchers who have between them decades of experience in UFO investigations, provided me with a thick file on the case. Just a quick reading of that information certainly suggested that something quite unusual had happened. According to them, the events began on the night of October 4, 1967, near the small fishing village of Shag Harbour. Something, estimated to be about 60 feet in diameter, descended to the surface of the water about a half-mile from shore. On it were four bright lights that flashed in sequence.

Newpaper articles, one of them published in the *Halifax Herald,* reported that Laurie Wickens, with four others, spotted something above and in front of them at about 11 p.m. that night. It was a large object that had four flashing amber-colored lights that was descending, as opposed to falling, toward the harbor.

As it hit the water, there seemed to be a bright flash and explosion. Wickens decided to contact the police and drove through one village and into another, trying to keep the object in sight so that he could provide precise information. They entered the parking lot of the Irish Moss Plant. All five of them, Wickens included, ran to the water's edge when they could see what they would later describe as a dark object floating or hovering just about the water. The flashing lights were gone, and only a single, pale yellow light that seemed to be on top of the object could be seen.

Wickens decided that he would report the sighting to the Royal Canadian Mounted Police (RCMP), but rather than driving back to the detachment outpost, he would drive west to Wood's Harbour in search of a telephone. There he contacted Corporal Victor Werbicki, who wasn't very impressed with the report. Instead of asking him anything about the crash, Werbicki asked him if he had been drinking. Werbicki then told Wickens to hang up but to wait by the telephone.

Several others witnesses, some of them thinking that some sort of aircraft had crashed, called the same RCMP detachment at Barrington Passage. Mary Banks, who was on Maggie Garron's Point, which is near the harbor, told Werbicki that she had seen an airplane crash into the sound. A third call came in from two women who were about 13 miles away and who had seen the same thing. A man, in a fourth call, said that he had also heard a whistle and a bang. Although they all talked in terms of an aircraft accident, and others mentioned only bright flashing lights, no one suggested that this was a UFO.

It was now apparent to Werbicki that something had happened out there. He called Wickens back and told him to meet him at the Moss Plant. Three of the RCMP officers made it to the shoreline and one of them, Constable Ron Pond, said that he had seen the lights from his car and that he'd seen the object, or the lights, or whatever, dive toward the water. He thought he saw a shape behind the lights, which certainly changed the dynamic of the sighting. In other words, Pond saw not only the lights, but he believed those lights had been attached to something solid.

Standing on the shore with the Mounties were a number of other witnesses. These included Wickens and his four friends, and the occupants of a pickup truck that pulled into the lot. Norm and Wilfred Smith had seen the object in the air before stopping for a better look. Although Werbicki didn't see anything until Wickens pointed it out to him, all could see the pale yellow light that floated about a half mile from shore. Through binoculars, they could see that whatever floated on the surface was creating a foaming, yellow wake as it moved. Because the object was in the water off shore, the Coast Guard was notified and fishing boats were called in to look around. Although the cause of the yellow foam disappeared before the boats arrived, they could still see some evidence of its passing. The Coast Guard cutter arrived too late to see anything, and by 3 in the morning, the search was suspended but would resume the next day.

This is the situation as it stood when Jim Lorenzen notified the members of the Condon Committee. Levine, in his preliminary statement, suggests that the first reports were made by teenagers, and he seems to be suggesting that others saw lights on the water, but nothing in the sky. Levine went on to write in his report to the committee:

> Two officers [RCMP constables Ron O'Brien and Ron Pond ] and the corporal [Werbicki] had arrived about 15 min. later, in time to see the light on the water. It persisted about five minutes longer. Ten minutes after it went out the two officers were at the site in a rowboat; a Coast Guard boat and six fishing boats were on the scene. They found only patches of foam 30–40 yd. wide that the fishermen though was not normal tide foam....
>
> The site of the presumed impact was in between an island and the mainland, about 200–300 yd. off shore. Apparently no one actually saw anything enter the water [though I must point out that a number of people saw the object descend to the water, which is, essentially, the same thing]. However two young women driving on the island reported that a horizontal pattern of three yellow lights had tilted and descended, and then a yellow light had appeared....

The RCMP corporal stated that the light on the water was not on any boat, that Air Search and Rescue had no reports of missing aircraft in the area, and an RCAF radar station nearby reported no Canadian of U.S. air operations in the area at the time, nor any unusual radar object.... A search by Navy divers during the days immediately following the sighting disclosed nothing relevant.

Five days later the Naval Maritime Command advised the project [that is, the Condon Committee] that the search had been terminated. The watch officer read a report from the RCMP indicating that at the time in question a 60 ft. object had been seen to explode upon impact with the water.... A captain of a fishing boat that had been about 16 mi. from the site of the earlier reports, reported to the project that he and his crew had seen three stationary bright red flashing lights on the water, from sundown until about 11 p.m. The ship's radar showed four objects forming a six mile square; the three lights were associated with one of these objects [so now we see that Levine is contradicting himself with radar reports and people seeing the object descend]. At about 11:00 p.m., one of the lights went straight up. The captain had judged that the radar objects were naval vessels and the ascending light a helicopter; he had attached no significance to these observations until he had heard on the radio of the sightings; he then reported the foregoing observations.... However, since the position he reported for the objects was about 175 n. mi. from the original site, the two situations do no appear related.

No further investigation by the project was considered justifiable particularly in view of the immediate and thorough search [that had failed to find anything which would suggest that the Condon Committee should be interested in the case] that had been carried out by the RCMP and the Maritime Command.

Though I suppose I could argue that the point of the Condon Committee was to investigate UFOs and here was a case that had multiple witnesses, certainly more than just the teenagers that Levine mentioned, and there was a possibility of physical evidence, they declined to do it. Levine seemed to believe, or at the very least claimed he believed, that the sightings had been thoroughly investigated by others on the scene, that nothing of interest was found, and that the search had been called off.

I would suggest that here was an opportunity to review a case with possible physical evidence, but even if it was only witness testimony, an on-site investigation might have revealed something about UFO sightings and the people who make them. Add the possibility of physical evidence, and I see no reason not to head for Shag Harbour and begin a real, tough investigation.

The Condon Committee opted not to do that, and the case sort of fell through the cracks. No one was looking at it and no one seemed to care about it. Styles, on the other hand, wasn't as convinced as those scientists on the Condon committee.

*8.2. Shag harbor post office. Photo courtesy of Don Ledger.*

As Styles told the audience at the 1996 MUFON Symposium, "In the spring of 1993, I decided to reinvestigate the Shag Harbour crash...."

This interest was sparked, he said, by a rebroadcast of the *Unsolved Mysteries* segment about the Roswell UFO crash. He continued, telling the audience, "As compelling as the Roswell segment was, it was not long before my attention focused on a memory I had of a very different kind of UFO crash scenario."

One of the first things that Styles did was contact some of the divers from the *H C M S Granby* who had been involved in the search. He noted that some of them refused to talk but others did, on the condition they would not be identified. Of course, as Styles noted, there were only seven of them, and they were identified in some of the newspaper articles about the case. After his interviews with them, and after some success in locating documents, he was convinced that something important had happened in October 1967.

He wrote in his paper published in the MUFON Symposium proceedings, "At the time I didn't know what to make of such extraordinary testimony. I filed it away under 'interesting.' It wasn't long before 'the story' [as he thought of it] resurfaced."

Styles reported that information he obtained from the Canadian Forces Station Shelburne, which was North America's former coordination center for submarine detection in the Atlantic Ocean and sonar buoy drops from Argus Flights from the Canadian Forces Base Greenwood, led high-ranking military officers to speculate that a crippled UFO had hit the water, but had managed to get away. In other words, this seemed to confirm what witnesses on land had seen and to suggest that the object had traveled underwater to a position off Shelburne County's Government Point.

Styles, as he continued his search for more information, learned that several small boats sat over the submerged UFO for several days. There had been talk of some kind of retrieval attempt, but it was postponed when it was discovered there might be a second craft near the first.

After a week, a Soviet sub arrived, violating international law and Canadian territorial waters. Several of the surface vessels turned on an intercept course with the Soviet sub. As the maneuvering was being done on the surface, the two UFOs began to move, heading out to the Gulf of Maine. In open water they surfaced, leaped into the air, and then disappeared at a very high speed.

This fascinated Styles. He wanted to learn more about it. He later said that he heard what he thought of as The Story from a number of different witnesses, including admirals, colonels, pilots, and even cooks. With so many of them telling him the same thing, he believed that it must have some basis in fact.

As with any UFO story, verification is a necessity. Styles, checking the map, realized that those in the Cape Roseway lighthouse would have had an unobstructed view of any Naval operations that took place off Government Point, and wanted to see their logbooks. On October 25, 1993, he learned, in a letter to him and shared with me, "regretfully those records could not be located...further researching would be futile." The letter, according to Styles, was from the office of the Regional Superintendent for the Canadian Coast Guard Service.

But paper trails often have various forks, so Styles checked with Isabel Campbell who, at the time, was a senior archivist at the Department of National Defence Directorate of History. Styles asked for the 1967 Annual Stroker's Report, which would note any major target detection made by Canadian Forces facilities. In other words, Styles was now attacking the problem from another angle.

Within 10 minutes, Campbell called him back to tell him that the 1967 Stroker's Report was missing. This, according to Campbell, was strange, because it had to be signed out and only members of the staff were allowed to do that. It seemed odd that another of the documents Styles had wanted was now missing. Those with a conspiratorial turn of the mind might believe that someone was attempting to hide information about the UFO.

Two months later, when Styles tried again, he learned that the report had been found, but that it contained no mention of any target detections or Rescue Coordination Center inquiries. Styles thought that this was strange because, according to him in his MUFON Symposium presentation, "As late as one month after the Shag Harbour crash C.F.S. Barrington's Administration Officer ran appeals in the Nova Scotian newspapers that read, 'Military Wants U.F.O.'s Reported.'"

Continuing his research, Styles petitioned and received permission to review papers of the late Jesuit priest Father Michael Burke-Gaffney, who was a noted astronomer, professor, and UFO investigator for Canada's National Research Council. In those papers, Styles found 10 documents related to UFOs. One of them was an RCMP filed of another UFO incident on October 4, 1967—that is, the date of the Shag Harbour crash. This was also part of the Condon Committee report mentioned earlier.

The last sentence of the report, according to Styles, said, "I had never seen anything like it before but it sounds like the thing they are looking for down off Shelburne Barrington Passage." Styles thought his meant that the men were aware of the search effort off Government Point. He was able to locate Captain Leo Mersey, the master of the fishing vessel mentioned, who confirmed Styles's suspicions.

*8.3. The sound looking toward Bon Portage Island. Photo courtesy of Don Ledger.*

Styles found, this time with the help of UFO researcher Jan Aldrich, who had been studying the files of John Brent Musgrave, more important documents. Among those papers was an article from the June 1968 edition of the *Atlantic Advocate* that rehashed the events the previous October, but also named one of the RCMP sources: Corporal Werbicki. To that point, Styles had been unable to learn the names of the Mounties who were involved. Then, with the help of the MUFON Provincial Director for Nova Scotia, Steven MacLean, Styles found Ron Pond. In 1995, Pond went officially on the record saying that he believed that what he had seen in 1967 was the crash of an unidentified flying object. Werbicki later said much the same thing, corroborating Pond's statements.

Another was the report that had been sent on to APRO and Jim Lorenzen by Musgrave. Normally, such a document, though interesting, might not be of particular significance. However, this report, which gave the names, ranks, and office phone numbers of various members of the Maritime Command, also made a reference to USAF activity at Shag Harbour hours after the events of October 4. It also mentions the name of a Canadian scientific consultant who was put on standby to receive artifacts. That all suggested that someone believed that a real object had fallen into the harbor.

What makes the report particularly interesting is the reference to the U.S. Air Force. Here, according to the document created in 1967, was a suggestion of Air Force interest in a possible UFO crash. We know from other documents available in the United States through the Freedom of Information Act that Project Moon Dust provided the authorization for Air Force personnel to travel outside of the United States on missions surrounding the recovery of space debris of foreign manufacture or of unknown origin. The Shag Harbour incident fit into one of those categories. It would be seem that Moon Dust might have been the American end of the Shag Harbour UFO crash investigation.

The report sent to APRO suggested there was a scientist standing by to receive any physical evidence recovered. According to Styles, the Granby's divers checked the bottom of the sound with handheld lights. Although a low-tech way of searching when compared with today's methods, there were rumors that they did recover some kind of debris. A Shag Harbour fisherman, Donnie Nicerson, said that he watched divers bring up pieces of twisted aluminum-like metal. This could have been practically anything and not related to the crash. It has to be noted, as Styles was careful to do, that the official records claimed there were no results from the search efforts.

In May 1994, Styles interviewed Lawrence Smith, who was on the *Cape Islander,* the first boat to reach the last known position of the UFO before it submerged. He told Styles that he had personally seen the yellow foam that so many others had reported.

Not everything in 1994 broke Styles's way. In what he called his "Third Report.... Shag Harbour Investigation," he detailed the run around he faced trying to retrieve documents from the Canadian National Archives.

According to his report, he had prepared the way, attempting to locate documents that he might want to review and obtaining the necessary passes, and completed the necessary paperwork so that he might examine the relevant military files. But the moment he asked for the specific files, he told me he was told by the staff that "I may not be allowed access to that file group."

Styles responded with the documentation that said he would be allowed to see it, which resulted in a hurried staff conference and telephone calls to a higher authority. Even with a new permission, he was told it would take 24 hours for the records to be available because they were stored 90 miles away.

The next morning, he learned the records had arrived, but it would take another 24 hours before he would be able to review them. Styles spent the day studying the microfilms that were available in a self-service section of the archives.

The next day, he was told the records were still being held for review. Styles tried to hurry the process and was told that the documents covering the attempted recovery would probably never be sent to the National Archives. Styles wrote in the MUFON Symposium Proceedings, "They [those specific records] would be in that most important category. The one that is above top secret. It is impossible to fight for that that does not officially exist. The many clauses and subsections of Canada's access to information act say little on this simple evasive ploy."

The review was finally completed, and Styles hurried back to the National Archives main building. He found not the stack of information he had expected, but a small file with about two dozen documents in it.

He wrote:

None of the paperwork had anything to do with Target Detections or Flying Saucers. In the bottom of the "temporary box" as it was marked was a yellow slip of paper stating that this file group had been reviewed and suffered significant removals in July of 1994. None of the very significant documents that I received and sent as samples during my application were in there.

I suppose it could be argued that the information deleted had nothing to do with the Shag Harbour UFO, but had more to do with military controls and procedures initiated when the Soviet submarine attempted to penetrate Canadian coastal waters. The censorship here might have very little to do with the crash, but the outcome was the same: Documents that Styles needed were unavailable to him, for whatever reason.

Styles did met with a "former Brigadier [general] who served with the DOPS section of Canadian Forces H.Q.... He...was somewhat upset with my having located him through some document records that dealt with U.F.O. policy."

Styles then wrote:

The story told to me in Ottawa by the Brigadier contained all the verifiable bits and earlier partial stories of ships sitting over a submerged U.F.O off C.F.S. Shelburne's government point. The Brigadier's source was [sic] men who were loyal to him that were commandeered by NORAD and the navy to play the role of identification team if they found something physical. Apparently they did and according to the Brigadier the men claim that "There was no doubt." It was not a conventional aircraft or spacejunk [sic] originating from either 1967 superpower. They told their regular Canadian C.O. that "There was activity down there." In fact incredibly they say that there was a second craft. In the Brigadier's own lingo, "It was standing nines for the damaged saucer." The basic outline of the story ends when a russian [sic] sub enters the then 12 mile offshore international limit. The small flotilla sails toward the intruder to offer challenge. This is after a weeks [sic] observation by sonar and T.V. remote over the U.F.O.'s resting place. It is at this point that both U.F.O.'s [sic] begin moving under the water back towards the Shag Harbour area. Once they clear open water in the Gulf of Maine they surface and fly away. The Brigadier closed our meeting by stating that he doubts I will find any paperwork on this operation in Canada.

This is somewhat reminiscent of things that I have been told by high-ranking officers as I cased the Roswell UFO crash. Records were altered, files moved and destroyed, and the paper trail covered. Although the officers didn't know that in the future there would be open access to files that were once buried under high classification, they didn't want anyone tripping over the information. I was told this by both general officers and by colonels who had once been on the inside. Styles had just found a similar source who told him the same thing. It makes you wonder about what would be so important that such extraordinary efforts would be made to keep it buried.

This also suggests that many governments do classify their UFO information. Styles ran into the same sorts of road blocks in Canada that I have run into in the United States. Records unavailable. Records missing. Records incomplete or records so heavily redacted that only one word in 25 or 50 is visible.

What Styles had discovered, as well as Don Ledger, was something very interesting. They, through the documentation and eyewitness testimony, proved that something unusual happened on the night of October 4, 1967. All of this establishes the reality of the situation. That same documentation seems to suggest participation by the United States Air Force in the search efforts, which makes you wonder about the Condon Committee's lack of interest in the sighting. It would seem that they would have wanted to learn as much as they could before deciding that it was of no interest to their investigation, rather than making a couple of telephone calls.

None of this proves that this sighting was of an extraterrestrial craft, but it does provoke a few interesting questions. As with the Roswell case of 1947, what could the government, either Canadian or American, have been testing that would remain a secret today? Even the stealth technology that was the big secret of the 1980s is well known to everyone today. There is certainly no reason to keep this case buried if it was a secret craft flown by human pilots. Even catastrophic events from the past are published. Certainly no experiment conducted thenwould remain classified today.

We know that something that had been in the air fell, dove, or crashed into the water. We have three governments interested, if we accept the Soviet sub as having been on the scene. And, we have denials;

8.4. *Shag harbor UFO sign. Photo courtesy of Don Ledger.*

no one remembers a thing. Styles underscores this with an interview he conducted with Major Victor Eldridge, who, in 1993, denied any knowledge or involvement in the events at Shag Harbour, even though, according to the available documentation, he was serving at one of the facilities involved in the search and he was quoted in newspaper articles asking for help in reporting UFO sightings.

Styles wraps up his report in the MUFON Symposium Proceedings by writing:

> If one examines all the evidence on The Shag Harbour Incident, one must conclude that "something" extraterrestrial in origin was responsible for the strange events.... Even though the "nil results" were claimed as the final result to search efforts of agencies such as the RCMP, RCAF, Royal Canadian Navy, and NORAD, none of the aforementioned would drop their conviction that "something" described as "no known object" had indeed hovered, then crashed into the ocean. At this point in time, and until further explanation is forthcoming, The Shag Harbour Incident remains the only UFO crash scenario that is supported in that interpretation by available and unrestricted government documentation that is without controversy as to its origin.

## February 12, 1968

### OROCUE, COLOMBIA

Residents of the area reported that they heard three loud explosions where a disk-shaped, metallic-looking object had been only a few moments before. They began a search of an area where they believed they had seen debris falling. They found a large, lightweight, and very hard piece of metal that was about 10 feet in diameter, was about 18 feet long, and weighed 125 pounds. I suppose the suggestion of lightweight meant for the size of the object recovered. It was shaped like a mud guard on a car.

The metal was smooth, except for some tiny grooves that might have been caused by the explosion. There were green and orange hues in the metal and, when struck with a hammer, it seemed to magnify the sound. Attempts to cut it for transport failed, so it was shipped intact to Bogota. One air attache suggested that the metal was extraterrestrial in origin, but didn't explain what his expertise was or even who he was.

The American Air Attache claimed that the metal was from a spacecraft of some kind, but didn't say if he believed it to be alien. Later statements by U.S. officials claimed that the debris came from the reentry of an American satellite.

## March 25, 1968

### NEPAL

Four objects fell in Nepal and were recovered, with some of the debris being sent to the U.S. embassy in Kathmandu. Three of the objects were sent on to the United States for analysis, but the fourth, a "nose cone" remained in Nepal. It was suggested that the technical team should not report unless it was believed that visual examination of the fourth object was considered essential.

## October 7, 1970

### 0924N 1618E (MAP COORDINATES; NO NEARBY LANDMARKS)

An object was reported to have fallen with three loud explosions and then to have burned for five days. The recovered object looked like a pressurized fuel tank and could therefore by of terrestrial manufacture. This report came from Project Moon Dust.

## Summer 1971

### NEAR EDWARDS AIR FORCE BASE, CALIFORNIA

Debby Clayton reported that she heard a loud roaring sound and then a loud crash. Outside, she could see a cloud of dust several blocks away. She walked over to the crash site, and while other civilians were studying the craft, the military arrived, weapons drawn. One of the civilians named Dalton was taking pictures. An Air Force officer ripped the camera from his hands and smashed it, but didn't try to remove the film.

The craft had no markings, but seemed to be scratched. There were no windows or seams, and it appeared to be molded in one piece. It was a dark grayish color with greenish highlights. The texture was smooth.

The military told the witnesses to leave or be arrested. The military covered the craft with a large canvas and lifted it with cables attached to the canvas. Once it was loaded onto a military truck brought in for that purpose, the military left. There was no mention of the incident in the local newspapers.

## March 18, 1972

### St. Geniez, France

According to Len Stringfield in his *Status Reports,* Olivier Rieffel reported that an "unidentified aerial object" crashed onto the rocky slopes of a mountain near St. Geniez. One of the witnesses described it as a "red ball of fire." Another said that it was a "red-orange" object "shaped like a disk." The crash set a brush fire that burned 40 acres.

Jean Sider said, "The facts of the case remain classified in the files of the military and the Nationale Gendarmerie Archives. Confirming all the main details was a member of an intelligence agency who stated that 'something' was received by the Gendarmerie and shipped in a truck to a location near Paris."

The description given by the witnesses suggest that this was meteoric in origin.

## April 7, 1972

### New Zealand

The Space Defense Center reported that they had witnessed two objects "de-orbit" and that they objects fell to the ground in New Zealand. At least one of the objects was recovered and turned over to the police department in Christ Church, New Zealand. Captain D.W. Boucher from the U.S. tracking station at Mt. John, South Canterbury, said that he thought it was part of a pressure tank.

The ball was 48 inches in circumference and had a blue-green sheen to it. It left a 6-inch indentation in the ground when it hit. Two other balls were also discovered. All were made of titanium, which caused a New Zealand UFO expert, Captain Bruce Cathie to suggest it wasn't part of a prank. Titanium was too difficult to obtain for someone to use it as part of a joke. He had no real answer for what the balls were.

Officials in the Soviet legation in Wellington denied that the objects belonged to them.

The most likely answer here is that the objects are some type of terrestrially manufactured objects used in space flight.

## May 17, 1974

### CHILI, NEW MEXICO

An object 60 feet in diameter was discovered and taken to Kirtland Air Force Base in Albuquerque. An Air Force team recovered the metallic object. No other information has ever become available, and the source of the report is shaky at best. This is a hoax.

## July 15, 1974

### SPAIN

Although it was claimed that the source for this case was the *APRO Bulletin,* a comprehensive search of the back issues has failed to produce the report. The only information available suggests that Spanish military experts and scientists had recovered the wreckage of a disk-shaped craft. With the failure to locate the original source, and with no additional information available, a conclusion of hoax is almost required.

## August 25, 1974

### CHIHUAHUA, MEXICO

In a case that is reminiscent of the MARCEN 1948 "Tomato Man" photo report, the Del Rio UFO crash of 1950, and the Willingham story from the mid-1950s, we have another crash, just across the border in Mexico. According to the information in my files, the object was spotted on U.S. Defense Radar just after 11 p.m. (2207 hrs) heading toward the United States from over the Gulf of Mexico.

The object was at 75,000 feet, or just above 14 miles, on a course toward Corpus Christi, Texas. During the flight, the object made a series of stepped descents until it was at 20,000 feet. At some point, it disappeared from the radar, which suggested it had dropped below the radar coverage, but then it never popped up again.

Just after midnight on August 26th, there were reports that an airliner had crashed. The aircraft had left El Paso for Mexico City, or rather that is what had been reported. Search for the missing aircraft didn't begin until daylight, or several hours later.

About 10:30 the next morning, wreckage was spotted and, a few minutes later, there were reports of a second crash site. After the second site was reported, the Mexican military stopped all radio communication concerning all these events.

Even with the communications blackout, word of the crash reached the highest levels of the U.S. government, including the CIA. A recovery team was assembled and began staging out of Fort Bliss, near El Paso, Texas. Before they took off, there were a number of high-altitude reconnaissance flights over the crash site. They discovered that the Mexican Army had loaded everything onto trucks, but all the trucks and other vehicles had been stopped. The reconnaissance photos revealed there were a couple bodies lying outside the trucks. It was decided to launch the recovery team immediately. They boarded helicopters and headed south toward the crash sites.

The recovery team, in four helicopters, apparently three Hueys and one larger aircraft, flew to the site of the stopped convoy that was carrying the recovered material. This included, according to the various sources, a disk-shaped craft that was little more than 16 feet in diameter. All members of the convoy were dead, most inside their trucks.

The U.S. team, in their chemical suits (MOPP Gear), prepared the craft to be airlifted out by helicopter. That done, they gathered everything else of earthly manufacture together and destroyed it. According to the reports, this included parts of a civilian aircraft that was apparently involved in a mid-air collision.

The U.S. recovery team then contacted a truck convoy on the road between Van Horne and Kent, Texas, which is a very big stretch of highway. The craft and other material were transferred to the trucks, and they headed out, using the back roads to reach Atlanta, Georgia. The aircraft returned to their original bases for decontamination.

The craft was described as being convex on both the top and bottom, and there were no doors, hatches, windows, or portholes in it. It was made of a material that resembled polished steel, and there were no navigation lights and no obvious means of propulsion. There was some damage that was only about 2 feet wide, where it had been struck by the smaller, light aircraft. The whole thing weight only about three-quarters of a ton, or about 1,500 pounds.

There are no named sources with this case. It seems to be another version of a couple of stories. The lack of other detail and names to go with it are suggestive of hoax.

## November 9, 1974

### CARBONDALE, PENNSYLVANIA

Sometimes a case that has a solid solution, provided by a competent researcher, is dragged back into the public eye by those with ulterior motives. This seems to be one of those cases and, because of that, demands another look at the evidence so that the facts can be brought forward. I have found that even in the face of evidence, there will be those who refuse to understand that this case has a solution.

The story begins with several teenaged boys watching a fiery object cross the sky right around dusk, or maybe a little later. They thought that the light, the object, might have come down close to Russell Park and ran from the street corner where they were standing into the park a couple of blocks away. In a pond—though from the descriptions of it, I would think a small lake might be a better choice of words—they saw a strange light coming from under the water about 20 feet from shore. They thought they heard a slight sizzling sound, but that quickly faded. They hadn't seen anything hit the water; they just assumed it. They left the area about 7 p.m. to call the police, and, when they returned, they believed that the light had moved.

The light, according to them, was yellowish-orange or maybe yellowish-white, depending on who was describing it. The light at the water's surface seemed to be about 5 feet in diameter.

Matt Graeber, a researcher living in Pennsylvania, said that he first heard of the case while working on a project at home and listening to the radio. Graeber wrote on Bruce Hutchinson's *www.roswellfiles.com*:

I was working quite late on the night of 10 November 1974 (on a design project) and had sketches and blueprints scattered about on the dining room table and floor. It was a little after midnight, (actually 11 November) and I had been listening to a local radio talk show when the programme's host suddenly announced that his programme director had just handed him a note about an unidentified flying object which had apparently crashed at Carbondale, Pennsylvania. Since I had appeared on WWDB's Bernie Herman show several times discussing the UFO phenomenon, I phoned the station without hesitation and asked if the matter was legitimate or simply a prank. Both the show's host and his engineer assured me that the report was indeed "authentic" for they had just taken it directly from an Associated Press release.

I then contacted the Carbondale police department about the situation and spoke to a desk officer who told me that an airborne object had been observed by a group of five teens (but only three of the youngsters actually participated in our inquiry of the sighting), and that the UFO apparently plummeted into a pond and sank. The youngsters agreed that a fiery object had fallen to earth in a shower of sparks and splashed down into a large coal breaker pit or 'silt pond', as it was called by locals.

The police had cordoned off the area in an attempt to keep curiosity seekers from possibly getting injured at the site, as two areas of the bank of the pond were rather steep and slippery. The acting police chief, Sgt Francis X. Dottle, confided that he didn't know what the object in the water was, but that he and a couple of his men had observed it glowing while submerged on the night of 9 November.

Graeber had a number of ideas about the crash and asked if it might have been a small aircraft, but was told by the police that the object had been moving too fast and there was no wreckage floating on the surface. He also thought about "space junk" and was afraid that something from orbit might have fallen into the pond that could contaminate it. Graeber wrote:

This seemed to be highly improbable, but, then again, there was that strange light beneath the pond's surface, a light which appeared to pulsate with diminishing intensity and at one point suddenly rushed towards a small boat which police had launched to further investigate the matter. But, unknown to me at that time, Sgt Dottle (the Acting Police Chief) had already been in contact with Dr J. Allen Hynek's Center for UFO Studies in Evanston, Illinois about the situation. Dr Hynek advised Sgt Dottle that a meteor or a meteor fragment could not be the source of the light in the pond because burning meteors are immediately extinguished when they strike bodies of water. Sgt Dottle was further advised to obtain a Geiger counter to see if any radioactivity was present at the crash site, perhaps as a result of a faulty spacecraft or satellite re-entry. Obviously, Dr. Hynek also feared that a snap unit had survived the re-entry and may have been leaking its contents into the pond.

Graeber arrived there around 5 in the morning on November 11 and went directly to the police station. After talking to the police, including the acting chief, Sergeant Francis Dottle, Graeber was taken to the "crash" site. He found the area cordoned by Carbondale police officers and a group of Civil Air Patrol cadets, but no armed soldiers or military representatives of any kind. The CAP cadets would have been wearing their Air Force uniforms, with the proper insignia on them identifying them as CAP, rather than Air Force.

The scene started to get out of hand as the sun came up. Gaeber, describing the events, wrote:

By first light, several press people and scores of the general public were permitted to visit the site, as various attempts to locate the object were made and radiological surveys were performed. As the morning wore on, the news media people were clamouring for a conclusion to the drama as news story deadlines were rapidly approaching and the crowds which were estimated at between 1500 to 3000 people were becoming larger and larger. I later learned that perhaps as many as 10,000 people had jammed the roads leading into the city in an attempt to see what was going on. Chief Dottle even had neighbouring community police departments assist with the control of the increased traffic into the area. It looked just like a scene from a science fiction movie and fears grew that emergency vehicles could not have got through if they were needed. To make matters worse, although we hadn't a ghost of an idea of what was actually in the water, rumours were spreading like a brush-fire and a few very vocal UFO enthusiasts who were milling about at the site were questioning the effectiveness of the police, fire companies and UFO researchers' retrieval efforts.

Sgt. Dottle began to fear that some minor incident involving the control of the crowds might spark a riot (or a panic) that his small police force couldn't possibly handle. Sgt Dottle found himself caught in the rather unenviable position of being damned if he did and damned, still, if he didn't do what everyone expected of him. He wanted to ensure the safety of the public, his men and the volunteers at the pond, while the media and the saucer buffs in the crowd were chomping at the bit for a quick and spectacular climax to the story. The pressure and anticipation were building with each passing hour, and while Mr Dains and I shared Chief Dottle's concerns about safety, we were also concerned that the mysterious object in the water be spared from loss or damage by our recovery efforts.

Although the reporters attempted to find "experts" to interview, and although a TV station's helicopter circled the area, everyone was guessing about what had fallen into the pond. They could rule out many things and, though it was possible the boys had seen a meteor, Hynek's representative, as well as other astronomers, ruled that out. The list of possibilities was slowly shrinking until Graeber and the researchers were left with but a few ideas. Graeber, in fact, noted that his inspection of the site revealed nothing to suggest a plane, a large piece of space junk or a meteor had fallen.

In the end, based on what was seen, and what was recovered by a diver, the best answer seems to be that a battery-powered lantern had fallen into the pond and that was what the boys, and the others, had seen. No one was sure how the lantern had gotten in there.

Kurt Sutherly, another Pennsylvania researcher, also traveled to Carbondale and talked to Dottle. By the time he arrived, according to what he wrote in *Strange Encounters,* "the entire episode had been branded a hoax."

His reception at the police station was a little less than warm. When he introduced himself to Dottle, the acting chief said, "Not another one," meaning another reporter.

According to Sutherly in *Strange Encounters,* "A silence followed as I tried to decide how best to deal with the man. Dottle himself broke the silence as he reached behind his desk and waved a silvery object in my face. 'This is your UFO!' he declared. It was an electric railroad lantern."

Sutherly talked to some of the townspeople who thought something strange had fallen. There were hints of something large removed on a flatbed truck, but no one had seen anything like that. He just heard from others that it had happened. Sutherly thought there might be something more to the story, but he didn't find anything substantial.

Gareber would eventually write on the Roswell Files Website a number of articles about the Carbondale UFO crash, most of them in an attempt to correct faulty information. The most important revelation was:

> Despite the case being officially closed (By Dr. J. Allen Hynek), and deemed a probable hoax in 1974—along with the later confession of one of the individuals who perpetrated the hoax— there has been an "aggressive" attempt by [some] to resuscitate the long dead matter and "turn" the hoax into a genuine UFO incident....

## Spring 1975

### Near Ohio—Michigan Border

Bette Shilling reported to Len Stringfield that a friend, an Air Force officer, had told her that he'd seen a coded message telling of a flying saucer crash. According to that information, two of the aliens were dead and a third was still alive. The message was directed from a communications station in Detroit and sent to the commanding officer of a base somewhere in Ohio.

## Spring 1977

### Southwestern Ohio

Len Stringfield reported that he had received information that a disabled craft had crashed, or landed, southwest of Xenia, Ohio. A military detachment arrived on the scene and engaged in a gun fight with the aliens, resulting in 11 American casualties and an unknown number of alien casualties.

After Stringfield had presented the limited information in his first crash/retrieval paper, a source from Cincinnati called, claiming to have seen stretchers holding bodies delivered to Wright-Patterson Air Force Base. They were taken to a secure area.

The problem with the report is that it involved a secondhand source but no eyewitness testimony. Repeated attempts to locate the primary witness have failed.

## May 6, 1978

### TARIJA, BOLIVIA

Three engineers with the Banco Minero Boliviano along with a number of native Indians watched as an elongated object about 4 meters in diameter passed overhead. It crashed into the side of Cerro Taire with a tremendous explosion.

The area was sealed off when word of the crash reached authorities. A news release claimed that the government was afraid that sightseers would be injured if the object contained any radioactive material, suspecting that it might have been similar to the Soviet satellite that had crashed in Canada a few weeks earlier.

A secret telegram that was apparently sent by the U.S. Department of State said: "[The case] has been checked with the appropriate government agencies. No direct correlation with known space objects that may have reentered the earth's atmosphere near May 6 can be made. However, we are continuing to examine any possibilities." State Department officers referred to the "State Airgram A 6343 of July 26, 1973," which provides background information and guidance for dealing with "space objects that had been found."

The message concluded: "In particular any information pertaining to the preimpact observations, direction or trajectory, number of objects observed, time of impact and a detailed description including any markings would be helpful."

This clearly was part of the Project Moon Dust system but, without an identification of the object, it could be something of extraterrestrial origin, though the routine nature of the traffic suggests something more mundane.

# Chapter 9

## February 12, 1979 ─────────────────

### POCONO MOUNTAINS, PENNSYLVANIA

Len Stringfield was awakened by Larry Moyers, who said that he'd just spoken to a man named Ron Johnson who had hit a humanoid creature with his car. Unsure what to do, Johnson had called Moyers, the state director of the Mutual UFO Network (MUFON). Johnson said that he had loaded the injured creature into his car. When he checked it about three hours later, he found that it had died.

Johnson said the alien was about 3 feet tall, without a nose, and with a single ear (the other apparently ripped off in the accident). He said that it was covered with fuzz and that the hands had only three fingers with webbing between them.

Stringfield suggested an idea that included alerting medical experts and local authorities. Stringfield planned to make the arrangements for a press conference, if that was indicated by the evidence, though he suspected that this was a hoax.

The next morning, Stringfield and Moyers couldn't find Johnson. Neighbors at the address he had given didn't

Pre-1947

1947
Pre-Roswell

July 1947

October
1947–1948

1949–1952

1953–1964

1965

1966–1978

1979–1999

2000–2009

know anyone by the name of Johnson and the phone had been disconnected at the customer's request. Additional attempts to find Johnson failed to produce results.

## July 27, 1979

### OREGON—IDAHO BORDER

In this case, the witness came upon the scene after the retrieval had begun. Sitting on the back of a flatbed truck, under a tarp, seemed to be a circular craft with a dome on the top. There were some ruts carved into the ground, and some trees had been damaged.

The witness, a military man, was brought in to help load crates on the truck. He also claimed to have seen some metallic material on the ground. This was dull gray-brown and looked as if it had been heated at some point. Once the crates were loaded, he helped guard the site. Soon after this, the man was transferred to another assignment.

## November 25, 1979

### ELK RIVER, WASHINGTON

James Clarkson, who appeared at the 6th Annual UFO Crash Retrieval Conference in Las Vegas in 2008, hosted by Ryan Wood, made a good case for adding another UFO crash to the long list. According to Clarkson, on November 25, 1979, a number of people saw something fiery in the night sky and more than one of them thought of it as a craft without power. I use the term *craft,* though some of them described an airplane-like configuration with lighted windows and fire on one side.

Mrs. Ralph Case was riding in a car driven by her husband along State Route 12 in Washington and about 4 miles east of Aberdeen when she saw what she said was a plane with one side on fire. She reported this to the air traffic control tower at Bowerman Airfield, also near Aberdeen, at about 10 minutes to 11.

Ernest Hayes, driving along the same highway as Case, said that he had seen a very bright green flash overhead. He called the county sheriff at about 11 that same night, or some 10 minutes after Case had reported her sighting.

Estella Krussel, who Clarkson interviewed about eight years after the event, said that she'd seen an "unknown aircraft" fly over and thought of a passenger jet because of the illuminated windows. She thought it had a cigar shape, was narrower in front than the rear, and had an intense blue-white light shining from each of the windows. She was one of those who had the impression that it was out of power.

Things got stranger, according to Clarkson. He interviewed a number of witnesses who had driven out into the rough country, a crazy pattern of logging roads and paved highways, some of them in search of the object that others had seen.

Eight years after the crash, Clarkson interviewed Gordon Graham. Graham had heard about the crash from Donald Betts, and tried to drive out to find it. He was turned away by a military checkpoint.

Clarkson, who spoke at the 2008 UFO Crash Conference in Las Vegas, quoted Graham as saying, "I saw four military weapons carriers. There were at least ten soldiers there. They have the road blocked. They told us to get out of there. They didn't say it very politely either."

Here we run into a problem, and one that I should have mentioned to Clarkson. *Posse Comitatus* is a federal law that does not allow the use of active-duty soldiers in a law-enforcement function except in a very narrow range of situations. These soldiers, if active-duty, had no authority to block the roads. If they were members of the National Guard on "maneuvers" in the area, they would probably have been in what is known as Title 10 or Title 32 status and would have been in violation of the law when manning these roadblocks. This means that, had Graham driven on, the soldiers had no authority to stop or arrest him.

I know that National Guard soldiers, except in very limited cases, such as when called to State Active Duty, can then be used for law enforcement. If these soldiers were from Georgia, as Clarkson suggests, based on his investigation and the interviews he conducted, then they probably weren't on State Active Duty and they had no authority to enforce the roadblock. Of course, if they are standing there with loaded weapons, you might not want to challenge that authority.

I point this out only because it suggests something about the legality of the roadblocks and it might be something to investigate. Under normal circumstances, soldiers in this sort of duty would be paired with a sworn law-enforcement officer who would have the authority to arrest those who refused to obey the instructions.

Maybe this point is a little esoteric, but it seems to me that we all need to know about the limits of authority. Challenging them might not be the smartest thing to do, but then, they have no real authority to order civilians away from an area and they have no arrest powers except in limited cases, such as drug enforcement and by presidential direction.

This is not to say that those reporting this are inventing their tales, only that the soldiers, whoever they were, probably had no authority to stop civilians from using the public roads. If this had been an aircraft accident, then the checkpoints and access control would have belonged to law enforcement and not the military.

Clarkson reported in his published paper presented at the Crash Conference that Henry Harnden was another of the local residents who said he was threatened and chased from the area by troops. Harnden was the one who suggested they were from a "special division from Georgia."

An Elma, Washington police officer, Fred Bradshaw, told Clarkson that two or three days after the crash, he saw an Army "low-boy truck with a boom...[and two] deuce and half [trucks]" and a couple of jeeps. The Army certainly has the authority to use the public roads to move stuff, whatever that stuff might be, so there is no problem here.

Clarkson tells us that there were a number of witnesses to the "arrival of a fiery object" on November 25, 1979. He tells us that it hit the ground and might have exploded in the Elk River Drainage Area in a fairly inaccessible location that contains mud flats, marshes, or a nearby thick forest.

The official explanation of "helicopter exhaust glow," offered later, is ridiculous. Even a quick look at the descriptions by the witnesses shows this to be untrue. I've flown in a lot of helicopter formations at night, and the glow from the turbine just isn't all that bright.

Clarkson never really says that the craft was extraterrestrial, though I take that as his meaning. He suggests the possibility that what fell might have been something lost by the military, specifically some sort of missile test that failed. He does note that no one lost an aircraft on that night. There were no reports of either a military or civilian crash, and no reports of a missile gone astray.

As I say, there seem to be too many failures of alien craft. Some lists now top 200, and a couple are closing in on 300. But still, there are some very intriguing UFO crash cases, many of which have no solid explanation...yet. This is another to add to the file. Until someone tells us what crashed, with the appropriate documentation, this is another well-documented UFO crash.

## August 22, 1981

### ARGENTINA

Several witnesses claimed they saw a stricken, disk-shaped object as it plunged to Earth. It halted the descent, but then exploded, the debris raining down. Military jets were seen in the area shortly after the explosion. A search of the area revealed metal fragments and several unidentifiable large pieces of equipment. Military authorities moved in quickly, surrounding the area and barring the curious. There were reports that two badly burned bodies were recovered.

## February 19, 1984

### PUERTO RICO

There were many witnesses to the crash of a UFO in the heart of the El Yunque Rain Forest, according to Len Stringfield in his *Status Report*. It was said to be circular, white, and flying erratically before it crashed. Jorge Martin, a UFO researcher, said that there was a story that the object had been a meteor, but that was a "diversionary tactic." Martin said that people he interviewed said they had seen a large number of military personnel in the area, hinted at some kind of NASA presence, and some even said that pieces of debris had been retrieved. They didn't know who those people were, what they found, or where they sent it once it was sealed in wooden crates.

## January 29, 1986

### DALNEGORSK, SIBERIA

Eyewitnesses saw an object approaching from the southwest before it fell onto a hill. The witnesses reported that it tried to lift off six times, falling back each time. Finally it exploded and began to burn.

Valeir Dvushilny led a team of experts to the site five days later. They found damage to trees and debris including lead, iron, fine mesh, and glass.

About a week later, two yellow globes appeared from the north, circled the crash site several times, and then disappeared. Eighteen months later, there was a second display made by 33 UFOs.

## March 1987

### WESTERN KENTUCKY

Once again, Len Stringfield is the source for this report. According to what he wrote in *UFO Crash/Retrievals: Is the Cover-up Lid Lifting, Status Report V,* he learned that a rancher, to whom he spoke personally, found the skeletal remains of "two humanoid entities" and what he described as a "burned-out circle, about four feet in diameter, in an open grassy field."

According to Stringfield, the man was a retired physician, and he described the bodies as having large skulls, cat-like jaws, and a "barrel-like" rib cage. The arms were long and ended in three fingers. According to the story, he called local law enforcement and the next day Air Force officers visited him.

A colonel (and why is it always a colonel, never a captain or a major?) told the rancher that they were there to clean up the area. The rancher was taken to a military base where he was questioned about the find and shown pictures of other dead aliens.

The rancher said he was interested in Stringfield's work, but Stringfield never heard from him again.

## December 26, 1988

### NEAR DAYTON, OHIO

The assistant chief of police of Liberty, Ohio, saw a gigantic ball, lime green changing to orange, plunge through the clouds. It came straight down and slammed into the ground. Officials at Wright-Patterson Air Force Base were alerted and conducted a search. Nothing about the case—the search or the crash—appeared in the local newspapers.

## May 7, 1989

### KALAHARI DESERT, BOTSWANA

A series of documents appeared from South Africa in the late 1980s that suggested a spaceship had crashed there and that 500 pages of classified reports, memos, letters, and files could be had for a small investment by American and European UFO researchers. The man who had taken the papers, or at least who had obtained them from official sources, was James H. van Greunen, a former officer in the South African military, who, if he didn't get out of that country quickly, would be tried for treason.

The story originally surfaced at a UFO conference hosted by Michael Hesemann in Frankfurt, Germany, about 10 years ago. Tony Dodd, of England, in his lecture, said that he had received information there had been a flying saucer crash in South Africa on May 7, 1989. He based his information on that given to him and some of the classified documents that were being quietly circulated by van Greunen.

One of those documents, labeled as "Top Secret" and coming from the South African Air Force (SAAF), reported that on May 7, 1989, two Mirage jet fighters chased a UFO and shot it down with something called an experimental "aircraft mounted thor 2 laser cannon."

The document said:

The object entered South African air space at 13M52 GMT [1:52 p.m.]. Radio contact was attempted with object, but all communications to object proved futile. Valhalla Air Force Base was notified and two armed Mirage fighters were scrambled. The object suddenly changed course at great speed which would be impossible for military aircraft to duplicate.

Squadron leader Goosen reported that several blinding flashes eminated [sic] from the object. The object started wavering whilst still heading in a northerly direction. At 14M02 it was reported that the object was decreasing altitude at a rate of 3000 feet per minute. Then at great speed it dived at an angle of 25 degrees and impacted the desert terrain 80 km north of South African border with Botswana, identified as the Central Kalahari Desert. Squadron leader, Goosen, was instructed to circle the area until a retrieval of the object was complete. A team of air force intelligence officers, together with medical and technical staff, were promptly taken to area of impact for investigations of retrieval.

The findings were as follows:

1. A crater of 150 metres in diameter and 12 metres in depth.

2. A silver colored disc shaped object 45 degrees embedded inside the crater.

3. Around object sand and rocks were fused together by the intense heat.

4. An intense magnetic and radioactive environment around the object resulted in electronic failure in air force equipment.

5. It was suggested by team leader that object be moved to a classified air force base for further investigation and this was done.

The terrain of impact was filled with sand and rubble to disguise all evidence of this event having ever taken place.

Len Stringfield, in his *UFO Crash/Retrievals: The Inner Sanctum Status Report VI,* reported that Dr. John Kasher, a physics professor at the University of Nebraska, had been at the German UFO conference and, when he returned to the United States, he alerted MUFON Headquarters about the event, and the revelation of the UFO crash. The international director of MUFON at the time was Walt Andrus, and he sent a copy of Kasher's report on to Stringfield in Ohio.

Stringfield learned that Tom Adams and Christa Tilton were also working on the case, having learned of it from other sources who had been at the convention. Stringfield communicated with them, and in a couple of days they all, including Kasher, decided to work together to learn more about the crash. With the help of Adams and Tilton, Stringfield was able to get in touch with van Greunen in South Africa.

Stringfield reported in his *Inner Sanctum Status Report* that his first conversation with van Greunen was "reassuring." Stringfield was concerned, however, that the descriptions of the aliens were "strikingly similar to those described by my two medical specialists which I had published in [my] status report...in 1980." This meant that Stringfield wondered if van Greunen's story might not have been inspired by something that Stringfield had written some 10 years earlier.

Stringfield was only somewhat impressed with van Greunen, who promised to share more than 500 pages of documents with Stringfield and his team. Just as soon as van Greunen could get his family out of South Africa, the documents would be forwarded to the United States. The problem was that van Greunen needed money to get himself out of Africa and once clear, then they would work out the rest of the details for the surrender of the documents to Stringfield.

Van Greunen, to apply pressure in his quest for money, eventually called Kasher and told him that, if there was no money for his plane fare to Germany in two days, the whole deal was off. He would then destroy the documents. Kasher immediately talked to Andrus, and Andrus arranged for the money to be sent so that van Greunen could go to Germany and, somewhat surprisingly, for his family to fly to England.

Once van Greunen finally arrived in Germany, he met with Hesemann, as had been arranged, and he reported the documents were now safe. Van Greunen told Hesemann and each of the American team members that the documents were in a safe deposit box in Switzerland. He thanked everyone for their financial help and their understanding, and then basically dropped out of sight.

Before he disappeared, he had promised copies of some of the documents would be sent to the various researchers who had helped him, but never sent them. Stringfield asked that some be faxed, but they never arrived. Van Greunen always had some excuse. He complained that he had the flu. He had been frightened by the German police. Some suspected him of being a spy.

Hesemann tried to get copies, but failed. Instead Hesemann learned that van Greunen was dating a German girl he had met in the past and they had traveled to Italy. It began to seem that van Greunen had created the tale of the crash as a way of getting money to move his family to England and himself to Germany where, it was now obvious, he had a girlfriend.

At this point, when they learned that van Greunen had taken off for Italy, Stringfield wrote in his *Inner Sanctum Status Report* that he and his associates, "all agreed that James van Greunen was a con man and a hoaxer...."

But Stringfield wasn't ready to give up completely. He wondered, "Or, was the hoax actually a 'fix' to hide the real story of a crashed and retrieved UFO?"

Stringfield couldn't help but point out, "Some of VG's tricks pulled on a few of his contacts were so obviously fraudulent, that it seemed highly irregular for a person, hoping to appear genuine, to go such ludicrous extremes.... But, personally, I think that James Van Greunen was a womanizing con man, out for money."

It could be argued here that Stringfield, running his investigation from Ohio by using the telephone and fax, might not have been fully cognizant of all the important details developing in Europe and South Africa. Yes, he had spoken on the telephone with van Greunen, but he had not met him in person. That sometimes makes a world of difference in an investigation. This wasn't, of course, Stringfield's fault. He simply didn't have the resources to drop everything and head to Europe to chase down van Greunen.

And it wasn't as if some documents didn't exist. Stringfield had, according to what he wrote in 1991, "...seen several versions of the so-called five-page document with the code names either deleted or changed." He noted that he (Stringfield) had retyped the documents for clarity. In comparing Stringfield's version with the poor-quality originals, it was obvious that misspellings had been removed. For example, in one place *dessert* had been changed to *desert*. These few alternations would later become important when attempts to understand the value of the documents were made.

Michael Hesemann did meet van Greunen when he came to Germany. Hesemann tried to keep track of the man, but had a tough time doing it. One of Hesemann's German friends, Baron of Buttlar, was contacted by van Greunen a number of times looking for money. That certainly didn't bode well for the validity of van Greunen's credibility. He was asking everyone for money, suggesting that he would withhold or destroy the documents if he didn't get what he wanted. Hesemann soon had enough of van Greunen.

Eventually van Greunen, upon repeated requests by various investigators, provided the names of a number of other South African officers who were somehow involved. In Stringfield's 1991 report, he wrote:

> The "real" important thing in this document was something else, a "requested" list of all officers involved, including "J.H. Van Greunen, Captain, Counter Intelligence". Some of the other names sound quite suspect, like "Major Fielding" (the late husband of lady-contactee Elisabth Klarer), "Capt. Spaulding" (head of GSW [the defunct Ground Saucer Watch], AZ), "D.B. Labuschagne" (a friend of James living in Sedona/AZ) and "Capt. Forbes" (Ann Forbes is a UFO book-shopkeeper in S.A. and a good friend of JvG). Furthermore, more than 16 spelling-mistakes on two pages made us even more suspicious, as well as the mentioning of Dr. Henry Azahedel as a "'possible security leak in Europe".

Hesemann, according to Stringfield in his *Inner Sanctum Status Report,* then added his voice to those suspecting that this was all a hoax. Later he wrote, "In the meantime, I found that the entire document [one that was eventually given to UFO researchers] is a fabrication, that James used a seal from his passport and the head and stamp of his birth certificate to do a 'cut and paste' job."

Some of the most important information about the crash and about van Greunen came from Cynthia Hind, the late UFO investigator and researcher who lived in Harare, Zimbabwe. Alerted to the case by her daughter, she soon heard from van Greunen herself. He didn't seem interested, at first, in talking about the alleged crash, but instead wanted to know if she (Hind) would be willing to speak to his UFO group. She agreed.

Stringfield reported in his *Inner Sanctum Status Report* that Hind said:

> I heard from my source in Johannesburg, that apparently my talk would be given on December 29. I was surprised that Van Greunen

had not contacted me...within a few days, Van Greunen phoned again, confirming the date and mentioning the name of the hotel in Johannesburg.... When I arrived in Johannesburg...there were no messages waiting for me...I phoned Van Greunen and there was no reply.... Subsequently, on the 13th of January, 1990, Prier Wintle learned of Van Geunen's NURORIN magazine in which he had announced that I would be speaking at the Johannesburg Hotel.... I have since learned...that...people turned up that night and were furious at being dupe[d].

This is important, not because Hind didn't speak, but because the engagement apparently was just a ruse to put a little extra money into van Greunan's pocket. It gives us a glimpse at the mental processes of the man and reveals that he is just a con man at heart, willing to take advantage of anyone, even when the profit, for him, is quite small.

In fact, before Hind left for Johannesburg, she had received a mysterious telephone call that suggested that van Greunen was a South African intelligence agent and that she would be in serious trouble if she allowed him into her house. Hind had apparently offered van Greunen a place to stay if he made it to Zimbabwe. Stringfield noted in his *Inner Sanctum Status Report* that she was told by the unidentified caller that van Greunen was "a crook, a liar, and a disgrace to South Africa."

She said the caller also warned her that if she attempted to investigate "an incident on the Botswana border [that is, the alleged UFO crash]," she would be in worse trouble. She said that the line then went dead, suggesting that the caller had been cut off—or had simply hung up.

Hind, like the others, believed the case to be a hoax, not because she thought it impossible, but because of other problems with it. She noted in her report to Stringfield, and it published in his *Inner Sanctum Status Report,* that the official government documents were not in English but in Afrikaans, which is the "official" language of South Africa (or was in 1989). She noted that the spelling errors were "rampant," and that the SAAF would "never pass anything like this." The document "tells of Squadron Leader.... There is no such rank in the SAAF."

So Hind, who was on the scene in South Africa, and who had talked to van Greunen on the telephone, said, "I can only say that, in my opinion, the story is one big 'con.'" In that, she agreed with Stringfield and the international team that he had put together to investigate the case.

In fairness, there are those, or were those, who believed the story might be true. Although English researcher Timothy Good, who had written a number of UFO books, believed the story bogus, others in England, including Harry Harris, believed the story to be true. Harris claimed that he had gotten other documents, from another source, that confirmed the crash, but Harris was not going to reveal them or his source to Stringfield or others because "Ufologists had exploited him."

Tony Dodd, who originally mentioned the case to the public, and Dr. Henry Azahedel, who is also known as Dr. Armen Victorian, believe the case authentic. According to them, van Greunen was a con man who got a single, original document from Captain Henry Greer of South African Air Force intelligence. They claimed to have confirmation of that.

And there was, of course, the claim that the whole episode was just disinformation. For some reason the South African government was interested in creating the illusion that something from outer space had crashed in their country. Disinformation usually has a purpose, but this seemed to have none. Of course, the claim of disinformation is a way of suggesting that there was some legitimate event and that the government is now hiding it. This was not disinformation because there is no evidence to support the idea.

What is interesting here is that, like the MJ-12 papers, the documents can be traced to a dubious source and no farther. They certainly can't be linked directly into the South African government, and there is no reason to believe them to be authentic, other than the claims of the man who released them, and a few Ufologists who would like to believe them authentic.

Like MJ-12, the documents contain flaws that most researchers believe destroy them. In citing the reasons to reject these South African documents, the multiple spelling errors and the incorrect use of English is given. For the researchers, these were good reasons to eliminate them. With MJ-12, similar flaws are ignored with the suggestion that all government documents have misspellings in them.

This is what strikes me as odd. Those who endorse MJ-12 as real— who refuse to acknowledge that the multiple flaws are indicative of it being a hoax—are quick to reject the South African crash documents for those very same reasons. They realize that the lack of provenance for these documents tends to sink them immediately, but when the same argument is presented against MJ-12, they begin to make excuses about how the lack of provenance is, in reality, an argument for their authenticity.

To understand these sorts of things—that is, how government documents "leak," how they come into private hands, and how we establish the authenticity of them—it is sometimes illustrative to examine parallel cases. In this case, the researchers looked at the evidence, compared the documents to real ones, looked at the background of the man who had the documents, and searched for corroboration. When they found all the problems, the documents, and the man's tale, were rejected.

With MJ-12, they said the comparisons with authentic documents made no difference and the backgrounds of those promoting the documents were irrelevant. When the corroboration for much of the information failed to be found, it was then claimed it was because everything was so highly classified. In the South African case of questioned documents, everyone seems to have understood the problems and reacted to them with intelligence. In the case of MJ-12, the proponents began making excuses, rather than investigating these red flags. It seems that in Ufology, we just never learn our lesson.

## November 4, 1989

### CARP, ONTARIO, CANADA

The Canadian Defence Department reported that radar had picked up an object traveling at high speed near Carp. It stopped suddenly and dropped to the ground.

After the crash site was located in a swamp, three helicopters appeared. Two AH-64 Apaches fired all their missiles, carrying a neuroactive gas that kills on contact but breaks down rapidly in the atmosphere. After they finished firing the missiles, they headed back toward the American border. The last helicopter, a UH-60, landed, and a recovery team emerged. They entered the craft and found three bodies.

The craft, according to sources in Canada, was taken apart and transported to a secret facility in Kanata, Ontario. No one explained how the technicians took it apart, or even how they knew the process to do it. There were no rivets, bolts, or welds, and, when it was reconstructed, there were no seams. The source also mentioned that the craft had been heavily armed and armored.

The creatures were packed in ice and sent to the University of Ottawa. CIA physiologists performed the autopsies. There is no explanation for that, and it doesn't make sense. Why would the United States be involved at all? Aren't there competent pathologists in Canada?

Stringfield, in his *Crash/Retrievals Status Report* said that the creatures were reptilian "fetus-headed beings," which must mean that the heads were disproportionally large. They "were listed as CLASS I NTE's (Non-Terrestrial Entities)." This, I suppose, is an attempt to invent a term like EBE (extraterrestrial biological entity), which appeared in the MJ-12 papers.

On board the craft were a large number of nuclear weapons of Soviet manufacture. Apparently, these had been stolen. It is not explained why a race that could construct an interstellar craft would have to steal atomic weapons from the Soviets.

A videotape of part of the crash, or part of the attack, or part of the event, did surface and land in the hands of UFO researchers. The consensus was that the tape, which showed a bright light and something that looked like the spinning rotor mast of a helicopter, was a fake. Detail was difficult to make out, adding to the confusion.

Len Stringfield told me he believes this to be a hoax designed to take advantage of the confusion inside the UFO community as researchers tried to understand the South African crash. There is so much about this case that fails to make sense that it is doubtful that anyone, with few exceptions, actually believed the report.

At the other end of the spectrum are some researchers who believe there is more to this case. Bob Oeschler found an eyewitness who confirmed some of what was on the tape, saying that she had seen the object herself. Bruce Macabbee reviewed the tape carefully, along with the evidence that Oeschler found during his visits to Canada, and wasn't convinced that the case should be dismissed out of hand.

The consensus, however, is that this was a hoax.

## September 2, 1990

### MEGAS PLATANOS, GREECE

George Pantonulas reported that shepherds and some villagers saw a small group of UFOs at about three in the morning on September 2nd. They seemed to be escorting one that was having difficulty. The damaged UFO suddenly lost altitude and crashed about 550 yards from where a shepherd identified as Trantos Karatranjos was watching. He heard no noise, but did see a fire begin to spread.

Two of the other objects landed, and in a few minutes, the fire was out. Pantonulas and the others then began to transport unidentified material from the crash site to the craft that remained overhead. Around dawn the operation ended and all the UFOs disappeared.

The shepherds and villagers examined the crash site, and saw a burned oval on the ground and damage to a pine tree in the center of it. There were some small pieces of metal, which the people recovered.

Some hours later, according to Pantonulas's report, a team from the Hellenic Air Force (Greek Air Force) arrived and told the villagers that the crash was nothing serious. It was a Soviet satellite, or maybe a small aircraft that had crashed. They took some of the pieces of the metal when they left.

According to Pantonulas, Argyris Alevantas sent a piece of the metal to the Space Research Institute in Brussels for analysis. According to him, they replied that the metal was from space, but that doesn't tell us if it had just been in space or if there was something about the composition of the material that suggested it was of extraterrestrial origin. And, of course, we were not treated to copies of the research report for verification.

## December 14, 1992

### ARIZONA

According to some reports, Air Force fighters intercepted a UFO over Arizona and forced it down at one of the bases in the state. It was suggested that the UFO had some sort of trouble that allowed the jets to catch it. Both sides, meaning the Air Force and the aliens, fired at one another, but the aliens missed. Some have suggested that the aliens could have shot down the fighters but for some reason decided to land rather than fight.

There are reports that the craft and the crew were recovered and are being held. The aliens are described as being about 4 feet tall and having smooth heads and large eyes.

This reads as if it was part of the plot for *Independence Day,* and there are no names associated with it.

## November 24, 1992

### Southaven Park, Long Island, New York

John Ford mentioned that a number of people traveling on the Sunrise Highway told him they thought that an airplane had crashed at about 7 p.m. There was a fire that seemed to be related and reports that a road around the park had been barricaded by police. The park was closed in the days that followed.

Records seem to corroborate that the park was closed, and there are some residents nearby who reported power surges. Ford said that he and members of his Long Island UFO Network found a burned-out area and some trees that had been damaged. There was a section that looked as if it had been plowed by heavy machinery, and Ford and his colleagues had found radiation readings that seemed to exceed normal background levels.

Ford did receive a videotape, a copy of which was given to the South Shore Press, that showed, according to their news story,

> people examining a bright reddish, metallic-type object about four-square feet that appears to be emitting a white, cloudy gas, and a hissing sound can be heard—a sight and sound that resembles dry ice that has been exposed to warmer temperatures. The next shot shows what appears to be a person trying to life up a body near a tree, but the poor quality of the film makes positive identification impossible.

Ford believes that what fell was an extraterrestrial craft. He believes that there were alien pilots and that it crashed into the park.

## October 31, 1994

### COTSWOLDS, ENGLAND

Witnesses in several small communities around Cotswolds, England, said they had seen a barrel-like object descend or fall into a field at Hepton Hill. There were reports that the military quickly sealed off the area and prevented civilians from getting close to the crash site.

The military, most likely the Royal Navy, loaded some unidentified object on a truck, which left the area quickly. Inquiries to both the Army and the Navy were met with strong denials that they had been to Hepton Hill or that they had recovered anything there.

Paul Brooke, identified as one of the witnesses, said that the object was like a 40-gallon drum and that there were fire engines and police in the area, stopping people from getting too close. He said that the object was taken away on a Royal Navy truck with a police escort.

## December 7, 1999

### GUYRA, NEW SOUTH WALES, AUSTRALIA

Reports to radio stations suggested that something had crashed into the reservoir near Guyra. It had skipped across the surface of the lake and left a gouge of flattened reeds and mud that was about 50 feet by 24 feet. The first person to see the evidence of the crash was a maintenance worker.

Though they could find no evidence that anything terrestrial had fallen into the reservoir, water restrictions were put into place and divers were sent in. When they determined there was nothing toxic in the lake, they lifted the ban.

Speculation about the object ran from the natural to the mundane, including returning space junk. There was a report that divers had found a meteorite lodged in a cave, but that doesn't mean that what fell was a meteor.

# Chapter 10

## April 27, 2000 ———————————————————————

### Worcester, West Cape, South Africa

This seems to be more a case of something falling out of the sky rather than a UFO crash, but some have listed it as such. According to the best information, a sphere, weighing about 70 pounds, which some suggested had been on fire, fell into a vineyard some 40 miles from Capetown.

One of the witnesses said that he had seen it fall into the vineyard and that it was too hot to touch for some 30 minutes. The object was solid iron, and had some bolts on one section of it. A police official said that he didn't know what it might be.

There was a second event not long after this in which a heavy object, weighing more than 200 pounds, fell in Durbanville. Witnesses there said that there had been a double explosion before the object—whatever it was—crashed to the ground.

Supposedly both were taken to Pretoria for analysis and the South African government had asked NASA for assistance in determining what these things were. I will

Pre-1947

1947
Pre-Roswell

July 1947

October
1947–1948

1949–1952

1953–1964

1965

1966–1978

1979–1999

2000–2009

note here that both would have been covered under the rules for Project Moon Dust (or whatever name was assigned to the project when Moon Dust was compromised), which was to recover and attempt to analyze objects of foreign manufacture that fell. I'll also suggest that I doubt either of these cases had anything to do with the extraterrestrial.

## May 15, 2004

### Puerto Ordaz, Venezuela

Scott Corrales, a researcher who follows UFO events in Central and South America, reported that an unidentified object had crashed near the Raul Leoni Hydroelectric Station (now known as the Simon Bolivar Hydroelectric Station) about 90 miles from the mouth of the Orinoco River. The object was seen by the workers of the dam and, according to Corrales, security was tightened immediately as members of the National Guard (meaning here the Venezuela National Guard or Guardia Nacional) cordoned the area. The residents of Puerto Ordaz reported they saw a number of low-flying black helicopters, which may or may not have anything to do with this report. Interestingly, a number of Americans (or, for those who understand these things, Norte Americanos) were seen, which, according to Corrales, is quite common in UFO crash reports.

Corrales noted that a seismography unit at the university in Caracas did register some sort of event at that time the crash was reported. He also said that there were no reports of an alien presence, but that access to the crash site had been complicated due to torrential rains in the area. He did say that accredited personnel from Proyecto Orion (Project Orion) were on the site gathering information that he expected to be released in the near future.

Although this event happened a number of years ago, I was unable to find anything more about it after the initial reports. I am bothered by the suggestion of Americans on the crash site, but only because of the hostility of Hugo Chavez to the American government and especially to George Bush, who was president at the time.

## May 20, 2006

### PORT SHEPSTONE, SOUTH AFRICA

According to reports at *News24.com*, a South African online news service, there were many eyewitnesses in the Port Shepstone area to something falling into the ocean beyond the breaker-line off the beach. The witnesses, which included teachers, pupils at a high school sporting event, fishermen, and others, thought they had seen an aircraft, or what others said was an "unidentified object," crash into the sea in an explosion of water. Some said they had seen flames, and others reported smoke.

The police responded, as did the National Sea Rescue Institute (NSRI). A spokesman for the NSRI, Craig Lambinon, said that a search that had covered some 12 square nautical miles had found no debris or other signs of a crash. He said, "Witnesses said they thought they saw an unidentified object, possibly an aircraft crash into the sea, but absolutely nothing has been found."

There was a suggestion by the NSRI Shelley Beach station commander, Eddie Noyons, that what was seen was some kind of weather activity that gave them the impression that something had crashed. Some suggested it might have been a water spout that had made it seem that something had crashed into the ocean.

There seems to be nothing new in this case, other than News24 mentioned that after they posted the original story their Website registered 30,000 hits, which I suppose means that they normally don't get that many. UFO sightings do generate a great deal of interest.

## December 1, 2006

### KRASNOYARSK, SIBERIA

According to various news services, local villagers had seen something crash into the forests between the towns of Yeniseisk and Lesosibirsk that started a forest fire. Various government agencies said that there had been no aircraft accidents and that no "air vessels" were missing. The news service called the object a "flying apparatus" that hit the ground at about 10 in the morning.

Paul Stonehill, a UFO researcher, said that the case was a hoax, and I have no reason to doubt this assessment. He told reporters that nothing had been found and, in the opinion of various law enforcement agencies in the area, the whole thing was someone's idea of a joke. According to Stonehill, the person who made the report is being sought and the police apparently have his telephone number.

## January 1, 2007

### LEPHALALE, SOUTH AFRICA

News24 in South Africa reported that Leonie Ras was lying in bed when she heard a noise that she described as the sound of a jet revving up. At her bedroom window, she saw a bright object that fell from the clouds at a terrific speed and slammed into the ground with a loud explosion. The object, according to her report, was round in front and had an orange-red tail that she said reminded her of Halley's Comet.

Police in Lephalale said that they had received many similar reports but said the area was so large that they didn't know where to begin their search. Some thought the object might have landed, or crashed, in Botswana, about 40 miles away.

Police said that they had many questions, but few answers. There is nothing new on this case.

## May 14, 2008

### NEEDLES, CALIFORNIA

I first learned about this case while at the 6th Annual UFO Crash Retrieval in Las Vegas while walking through one of the restaurants in the hotel. I had heard nothing about it, but within 24 hours, I learned everything I needed to know. George Knapp, an investigative reporter for a Las Vegas TV station, told me about the UFO crash along the Colorado River near Needles, California. Make no mistake here. There was a UFO crash, but also remember that UFO doesn't necessarily translate into extraterrestrial.

Knapp told me personally and also told the audience during his keynote address at the conference that he had investigated the case from the beginning, talked to the witnesses, and learned that five helicopters had flown into the area within minutes of the crash. Something real had happened, and there were many witnesses.

According to some of those witnesses, at around three in the morning, a cylinder-shaped object with a turquoise glow fell out of the sky and crashed west of the Colorado River. A witness, known as Bob on the River (because he lives on a houseboat and they "bob" in the water as they float, and he didn't want any more of his identity exposed) and who lives in Topock, Arizona, said that he had seen

10.1. George Knapp, Needles crash. Author's photo.

the object as it flew over. He thought it was on fire. He didn't see it hit the ground, given the terrain, but he did hear it. He told Knapp that it smacked into the sand.

Bob tried to call for help, but his satellite phone wouldn't work. Not long after the crash, however, he heard the pulsating beat of rotor blades and saw five helicopters in a loose formation heading toward the crash site. One of them broke off to circle his houseboat and then rejoined the others. These might have been Huey's, though it seems that's a name applied to many helicopters. I suspect that they were Black Hawks, but no matter.

The helicopters located the wreck and, according to Bob on the River, the fifth helicopter, known as a Sky Crane, retrieved the object. Although unseen by any of the witnesses, some of the helicopters had to land so that the object, whatever it was, could be rigged for lifting.

Bob said that the object, still glowing, was airlifted from the site, and carried away. All the helicopters went with it.

Had Bob on the River been the lone witness, we might have been able to dismiss his story as the musings of a loner who lived on a houseboat. This is not to mention that not long after this happened, Bob disappeared.

Frank Costigan, once the chief of airport security at the Los Angeles airport and a retired police chief, and a man who would seem to be more credible than Bob, said that he had seen the object when he got up at three to let out his cat. He said that he knew the object was not a meteorite because it seemed to change speed. According to Costigan, it was bright enough to have illuminated the ground. It disappeared behind some hills and didn't reappear. Clearly it was down.

In a bizarre incident, David Hayes, the owner of KTOX radio in Needles, said that on his way to work he saw a strange assortment of odd vehicles getting off the highway. He produced a rough drawing that he showed to George Knapp. This seemed to be a "Men in Black" sighting.

There were all sorts of other, seemingly related events. According to what Knapp told me in 2008:

*Out of the blue the station got a call from a friend in Laughlin [also on the Colorado River] who said the Laughlin Airport had been inundated on the night of the crash with so-called Janet planes. That's the airline that flies workers to top secret Area 51. Costigan says the airport could not confirm this because no one is on duty after 6 p.m... not even the tower.*

Knapp continued, "The black vehicles have left Needles. Bob the houseboat guy can't be found either.... The point is, something definitely happened."

Knapp, of course, continued the investigation. He learned that the vehicles, sometimes black, were often seen in the Needles area and he, along with his camera crew, were able to spot and photograph them. Knapp said that he joined in the formation as it drove down the road. One of the vehicles eventually pulled over, and Knapp did the same thing.

There was an encounter with the crew, who were armed and who suggested they were federal agents. One of them flashed an ID at Knapp, who said that he hadn't gotten a good look at it and was shown it again.

Eventually the confrontation, if that's what it was, ended, and everyone went on their own way. Later, Knapp received a call from a friend with the Department of Energy who told Knapp he was lucky that the confrontation ended as peacefully as it did.

Knapp would learn that these agents, black vehicles and all, had nothing to do with the UFO crash, if that's what it was, but with a very real and security-wrapped federal mission. Knapp would be the first reporter allowed to see the training of the agents. These dark vehicles, often on the roads around Needles, had nothing to do with the object's crash.

So, one mystery solved, but what happened to Bob on the River? Knapp eventually found him and talked to him at length about what he had seen. Bob on the River couldn't add much to the descriptions that others had—or rather, he had given to others. The object struck with a thud, like something smacking into sand.

Knapp said at the Crash Retrieval Conference that he knew Bob's real name and even showed us video of the interviews that hadn't aired on Las Vegas television. Bob told a solid story, and his somewhat unorthodox lifestyle didn't play into it. Bob on the River had seen something fall out of the sky.

Knapp, in his presentation, made it clear the helicopters had been on the scene in less than 20 minutes, and that meant that someone, somewhere, had been monitoring the progress of the object. Someone, somewhere knew what it was. Knapp gave the impression that he didn't believe it to be of extraterrestrial origin.

The next day (meaning the next day after Knapp's presentation, not the next day after the crash), I had a chance to talk to Knapp about this. He told me that he believed, based on what he had seen and learned, that the object was an experimental craft that had failed. The helicopters got there too fast for anything else.

In the end, there are two solutions to this. One is the extraterrestrial, but that seems to be the least likely. The other is that this was an experimental object, probably some sort of advanced unmanned aerial vehicle (UAV) belonging to the U.S. government. They retrieved it before anyone in Needles or Topock got a good look at it. At the moment, that is the explanation that I prefer.

## June 20, 2009

### Gin-Gin Queensland, Australia

Although this has been added to some UFO crash lists, witnesses described the object as a fireball that set nearby trees on fire. A search of the area failed to find any debris or what might have started the fire.

Most of those investigating, both officially and unofficially, thought that the object might have been returning space junk or a small meteorite. If it was space junk, it might have fallen under the auspices of the organization that replaced Moon Dust. There is nothing in the reports to suggest any attempts by U.S. officials to learn more about the object.

A local (meaning Australian) UFO researcher suggested this might have been some kind of "unmanned" (unoccupied) probe sent by an alien civilization to monitor the Earth. The suggestion here was that it had run out of energy or simply failed and fell to the ground.

The most likely explanation, however, is more mundane. Meteorites rarely cause fires, but space junk sometimes does. There was no reason to suggest this was alien or extraterrestrial, other than the wild speculations of the media and some UFO researchers.

## July 27, 2009

### OTTAWA, ONTARIO, CANADA

According to the newspaper account that appeared in *The Welland Tribune,* dozens of people in and around Ottawa saw something flash across the sky and smash into the river. They heard an explosion that was described as thunderous.

Witnesses said that the object appeared to change course a number of times and that there were lights on it rather than it glowing. Some thought it might have been a small aircraft in trouble, and, because of that, emergency search and rescue crews began to probe the river with sonar and underwater cameras.

A doctor, Dirk Keenan, who was out sailing with friends, said that the object was a very bright light in the east, close to Quebec. He thought it was like the headlight of a car that was descending rapidly, leveled off, and then disappeared.

On the next afternoon, at about 1:30 p.m. the rescue workers located an object about 30 feet below the surface. The current prevented divers from entering the water. A police spokesman told reporters that the size and shape suggested it had not come from an aircraft and that it could be a rock or logs stuck together. No one had come forward with any sort of photograph or video of it, though there might be a reason for that: Some claim that the video footage had been confiscated by authorities.

To this point, it isn't known if the object found under water is the same as that people reported or something that has been there for a long time. No aircraft were reported missing, and it doesn't seem that this was a piece of terrestrially launched space debris. In other words, this is the classic unknown.

It turns out that one of the newspaper stories mentioned Chris Rutkowski, a UFO researcher in Canada that I know, so I asked him what he knew about the case. He e-mailed me: "I can tell you what I know about the Ottawa 'crash,' although I'm not convinced anything really crashed!"

10.2. Chris Rutkowski, Ottawa crash. Author's photo.

He said that he had called the MUFON representative in the area, but she hadn't interviewed any of the witnesses. He said that some people had seen the police searching the area stop the search after the mass was located, and some of them thought a cover-up was now in place because there was no new information reported. There was speculation that the United States—here meaning the CIA—was now somehow involved, though Rutkowski didn't subscribe to those ideas.

He wrote to me:

From piecing together what info I have, here's what I think happened: Lights were seen in the sky and loud booms were heard along the Ottawa River. I spoke with a reporter, and he said that it was his impression that the lights were seen "towards" the other side of the river from where the witnesses were located. (It's a very wide river at that point.) I do not think anyone saw anything "crash" or (more likely) "splash" into the water. It was assumed that falling lights must have been on a falling object and that since the river was in that direction, whatever was falling must have fallen into the river.

Rutkowski did learn that some people had been setting off fireworks that might well account for the booming because sound carries well over water. He didn't know what the object that had been detected was, writing, "Who knows? A car? Jimmy Hoffa? The Ottawa River is like the one that flows through my city, and they're always pulling things out of it."

Rutkowski said that the key would be to find the two witnesses who might have seen the lights smashing into the water: "Until then, we have no convincing evidence that a UFO crashed in Ottawa on July 27th."

# EPILOGUE

So now we've looked at some of the best and some of the worst of the UFO crash reports. We've seen that mundane objects, meteorites, returning space debris, and pieces of aircraft can account for some of these reports. There have been hoaxes, and we have found liars. There are unintentional mistakes and obvious misinterpretations and, in all that, we've only looked at a little more than 100 of the nearly 300 UFO crash reports. What about all those others?

Well, frankly, some of them don't deserve more scrutiny. More than one case was from a single witness, and parts of the story seemed to be unverified fiction. It might not have been conscious invention, but it was a story that didn't seem to be based in reality. The Santa Rosa story by a medical technician who told of an emergency call that took her and an ambulance driver some 18 miles from town is a case in point.

She told researchers that when they reached two police cars blocking the road, she and the driver got out of the ambulance to talk to one of the State Troopers. They saw three small bodies on the ground. The nurse thought immediately of children and asked about parents, but was told there weren't any parents. She did see some wreckage, enough to suggest two cars might have collided, but she couldn't identify the type of the cars of the wreckage.

The little bodies were only 3 to 3 1/2 feet tall and had been burned. They were oozing a brownish fluid. One of the bodies had an arm that was broken or damaged in some way. She could find no vital signs, but they put them into the ambulance to return to town anyway.

At the hospital, she took x-rays of all three. About an hour after they reached the hospital, the Air Force arrived and she said an officer, who she thought was a colonel, ordered everything removed, including the x-rays and any notes she had. She also saw that the Air Force had a flatbed truck with something covered by a tarp. Once the Air Force had everything gathered up, they drove off.

According to Ryan Wood's *Majic Eyes Only,* she had never mentioned the crash because she had been warned that the government had "a long arm." She was never to speak of this. And she didn't talk about it until she saw pictures of hungry children in Somalia. She thought they looked like the little bodies that had been recovered, meaning the strangely shaped bodies and the overly large appearing heads looked something like the starving children.

So why leave this 1963 case out of the listings? Because I couldn't find anything more about it, it was single witness, and there was something about it that suggested to me that it wasn't grounded in reality. It simply did not belong on the list. This is, of course, a very subjective and personal opinion.

And you're thinking, "But you included other cases about which you could say much the same." With this case, there wasn't much about it on any of the other UFO listings. It is sort of out there, but in a limited fashion, and maybe that is the difference here. You might say that it's a tough call, but you now do have some additional data about it.

Cliff Stone told of his involvement in a recovery at Indiantown Gap in Pennsylvania in 1969, which was handled by the 95th Civil Affairs Group. Stone said that he was there as part of a secret unit that had the mission of retrieval of crashed alien craft. He said that there were three bodies and an object that, when he approached, he realized was extraterrestrial rather than some wrecked aircraft.

So why leave this case out? Again, it was single-witness and again it isn't on many of the crash lists. But for me, the problem is the source. I find him to be unreliable, though there are many others who have a much higher opinion. What it boils down to here is that, without independent corroboration of this case, I don't believe it should be on these lists. A footnote maybe, but it just shouldn't occupy a real spot.

And again, I know what you're thinking. We could say the same thing about the Willingham case of the UFO crash just over the border in Mexico. The difference is that the Willingham case, in its several different guises, has made all the lists and is well publicized in many different arenas. To fully investigate UFO crashes, it is necessary to look at the Willingham case in some detail, even if the evidence suggests that it is not grounded in reality.

Another reason to ignore some crash cases is because they stand very little chance of corroboration. The very nature of them prevents any sort of corroboration, though others have some corroboration available to them. I think here of the Fort Polk case, where we have only the initials of the man who reported it to Len Stringfield. We have a vague date and nothing much else to go on. Unless another witness can be found, or Len's files surface to give us a name, this case is dead.

I suppose you could say much the same thing about the Cape Girardeau case, which is, essentially, single-witness, but with great potential. We have names of people involved, and there are a couple of others who have mentioned a secondhand knowledge of the case. We have the potential for many additional witnesses, though, given the time frame, that is becoming less likely almost daily. This does, however, demonstrate the difference between the Fort Polk case and the Cape Girardeau case.

The real answer, I suppose, is that the reports included on my listing are the ones that I find the most interesting or the ones that have the greatest potential for additional information, or the ones that I'm sure have a valid solution to them. It is clear to me, if not to others, what fell. That ranges from an alien ship to an extraterrestrial bit of metal called a meteorite. Many times the debris is of foreign manufacture, but not of alien creation.

I had thought of creating a listing of all the crash reports that I hadn't included here, but that would be a very time-consuming task that probably wouldn't be worth the effort. Maybe the best thing to do is point out that, if I haven't included a specific case, then there is a major problem with it. That problem might be the source, the location, or contradictory information. And yes, I have included those kinds of reports repeatedly.

In the end, I had to limit the listing and the selection method was purely subjective. If I had additional information, if I could add something important, if I could make a case one way or the other, then I tried to incorporate it here. If there was little information about it, or I had nothing to say about it, then it might not have made the cut.

You might say that the Ghost Rockets or the Great Airship stories, with few exceptions, fit into that description. The difference in here is that there are multiple reports. It's not a single airship, but a group of sightings clustered around a specific date that relate to one another. The airship is something more than just the Aurora, Texas, crash and, by looking at all the reports together, we begin to understand something about what was happening in the spring of 1897. The total gives us a clue about the individual.

And the same can be said about the Ghost Rockets, a group of sightings clustered around Scandinavia in the summer of 1946 that suggest something about the whole. The Ghost Rockets are something more than just one report that is rather vague and unimportant, and it leads into the summer of 1947.

I think I got all the really important cases, such as Roswell, Kecksburg, and Shag Harbour. I hit the high points on many of the others such as Ubatuba. And I changed my opinion on the validity of others such as Kingman, based on our new ability to find many things on the Internet and in databases that didn't exist even five years ago.

I'm tempted to say that if I didn't include it, then it's probably not worth a lot of time to research, but that suggests an ability that I simply don't possess. I have tried to hit the important ones, cases that reflect UFO crashes, and left out those that are probably more akin to landings than crashes, or obvious hoaxes when the case has received little publicity. I have tried to provide a few answers where they are deserved, and moved onto other things when they were not.

The bottom line is this: In the last four or five years, I have worked to update the crash material I have in my files. These were the cases that I could do something with. The others are out there, and I have nothing new about them at this time. If and when that changes, I'll update the case on my blog at *www.KevinRandle@blogspot.com*. I have recently learned of another witness to the Roswell crash and have a witness who might have been involved with the autopsies, and I have been told that Robert Willingham has found 50 documents to confirm his military service, but I have yet to see them. What this means is that the research is ongoing and often quite complex. It requires that I keep reevaluating what I have written.

There are indices out there that list hundreds of crashes, and it is obvious that some just do not belong there. I've seen several crashes from various parts of Russia and the old Soviet empire, but those are difficult to investigate. It's always some obscure village with witnesses and scientists who somehow can't be located. There is always some way to prevent any verification of the information.

And maybe that is another problem. The old tabloid newspapers used that trick: Proof of something, UFOs, bigfoot, extreme old age, was out there because someone in a remote part of the world had the evidence. Names were often named, but that person or those witnesses couldn't be found easily and, in the pre-Internet days, most forms of research wouldn't help. You needed to travel into that part of the world if you wanted to learn the truth.

Today, we can do much better with nearly everything put on the Internet. You have an obscure village? Google Earth will point you there, down to the houses lining the streets.

You have something quoted from a rare or old newspaper or magazine? A search engine will find it for you, and then you can learn if the passage had been misrepresented.

Someone claims military service as part of his resume and to prove he is reliable? E-mail a query to military organizations and learn the truth in a matter of hours. You can even file FOIA requests online and receive a response in a day or two.

Research that used to take years now takes days. I can find answers to most questions quickly. And with those answers, I was able to eliminate many crash reports from the database created here. Sometimes the information was included because I had a new perspective. Sometimes because I solved the case and thought it should be reported. But sometimes, I hit another wall and by publishing this information, hope to learn something in the future.

So, yes, the selection of cases was subjective. Yes, some of those I report on are very limited in scope. Yes, some of those I have left out probably deserve a closer scrutiny. And yes, some of those I do include probably could have been left out. But the point is this: I had the information, and I believe it to be the best and most current. It might answer some questions, but I know that it will generate others.

The real point here is that I have attempted to thin the field with some solid research. I have attempted to bring to the front those cases that deserve another look because, to my mind, some of it leads directly to the extraterrestrial and to the eventual answer about life on other worlds. And that, finally, is the real point here.

# BIBLIOGRAPHY

Air Defense Command Briefing, January 1953, Project Blue Book Files.

Alberts, Don E., and Allan E. Putnam. *A History of Kirtland Air Force Base 1928–1982.* Albuquerque, N.M.: 1606th Air Base Wing, 1985.

Allan, Christopher D. "Dubious Truth about the Roswell Crash," *International UFO Reporter 19, 3* (May/June 1994): 12–14.

Anderson, Michele. "BIOSPEX: Biological Space Experiments," *NASA Technical Memorandum 58217,* NASA, Washington, D.C., 1979.

Anderson, Ted. Alleged diary for July 1947.

Asimov, Issac. *Is Anyone There?* New York: Ace Books, 1967.

"Army Ordnance Department Guided Missile Program," Tech Bulletin, January 1948.

"ATIC UFO Briefing," Project Blue Book Files, April 1952.

"The Aurora, Texas Case," *The APRO Bulletin* (May/June 1973): 1, 3–4.

Baker, Raymond D. *Historical Highlights of Andrews AFB 1942–1989.* Andrews AFB, Maryland: 1776th Air Base Wing, 1990.

Barker, Gray. "America's Captured Flying Saucers—The Cover-up of the Century," *UFO Report 4, 1* (May 1977): 32–35, 64, 66–73.

——. "Archives Reveal More Crashed Saucers." *Gray Barker's Newsletter* (March 14, 1982): 5–6.

——. "Chasing Flying Saucers." *Gray Barker's Newsletter 17* (December 1960): 22–28.

——. "Von Poppen Update." *Gray Barker's Newsletter* (December 1982): 8.

Barnett, Ruth. Personal Diary, 1947.

Baxter, John, and Thomas Atkins. *The Fire Came By.* Garden City, N.Y.: Doubleday, 1976.

Beckley, Timothy Green. *MJ-12 and the Riddle of Hangar 18.* New Brunswick, N.J.: Inner Light, 1989.

Berlitz, Charles, and William L. Moore. *The Roswell Incident.* New York: Berkley, 1988.

"Big Fire in the Sky: A Burning Meteor," *New York Herald Tribune,* December 10, 1965.

Binder, Otto. *What We Really Know About Flying Saucers.* Greenwich, Conn.: Fawcett Gold Medal, 1967.

——. *Flying Saucers Are Watching Us.* New York: Tower, 1968.

——. "The Secret Warehouse of UFO Proof," *UFO Report, 2, 2* (Winter 1974): 16–19, 50, 52.

Bloecher, Ted. *Report on the UFO Wave of 1947.* Washington, D.C.: Author, 1967.

Blum, Howard. *Out There: The Government's Secret Quest for Extraterrestials.* New York: Simon and Schuster, 1991.

Blum, Ralph, with Judy Blum. *Beyond Earth: Man's Contact with UFOs.* New York: Bantam Books, 1974.

Bontempto, Pat. "Incident at Heligoland." *UFO Universe 5* (Spring 1989): 18–22.

——. "The Helgoland Crash: A Dissection of a Hoax." Author, 1994.

Bowen, Charles (ed). *The Humanoids.* Chicago: Henry Regency, 1969.

Bourdais, Gildas. *Roswell.* Agnieres, France: JMG Editions, 2004.

Braenne, Ole Jonny. "Legend of the Spitzbergen Saucer." *International UFO Reporter 17, 6* (November/December 1992): 14–20.

Brew, John Otis, and Edward B. Danson. "The 1947 Reconnaissance and the Proposed Upper Gila Expedition of the Peabody Museum of Harvard University." *El Palacio* (July 1948): 211–22.

"Brilliant Red Explosion Flares in Las Vegas Sky," *Las Vegas Sun,* April 19, 1962, p. 1.

Britton, Jack, and George Washington, Jr. *Military Shoulder Patches of the United States Armed Forces.* Tulsa, Okla.: MCN Press, 1985.

Brown, Eunice H. *White Sands History.* White Sands, N.M.: Public Affairs Office, 1959.

Buckle, Eileen. "Aurora Spaceman—R.I.P.?" *Flying Saucer Review* (July/August 1973): 7–9.

Buskirk, Winfred. *The Western Apache: Living in the Land Before 1950.* Norman, Okla.: University of Oklahoma, 1986.

Cahn, J.P. "The Flying Saucers and the Mysterious Little Men," *True* (September 1952): 17–19, 102–12.

——. "Flying Saucer Swindlers," *True* (August 1956): 36–37, 69–72.

Cameron, Grant, and Scott T. Crain. *UFOs, MJ-12 and the Government.* Seguin, Tex.: MUFON, 1991.

Candeo, Anne. *UFO's The Fact or Fiction Files.* New York: Walker 1990.

Cannon, Martin. "The Amazing Story of John Lear," *UFO Universe* (March 1990): 8.

Carey, Thomas J. "The Search for the Archaeologists," *International UFO Reporter* (November/December 1991): 4–9, 21.

Carpenter, John S. "Gerald Anderson: Truth vs. Fiction." *The MUFON UFO Journal, No. 281* (September 1991): 3–7, 12.

——. "Gerald Anderson: Disturbing Revelations." *The MUFON UFO Journal, No. 299* (March 1993): 6–9.

Cassidy, Jadyn. "Australia UFO crash: Meteor of extraterrestrial craft?" All News Web Website. *www.allnewsweb.com/page646948.php.* June 20, 2009.

Catoe, Lynn E. *UFOs and Related Subjects: An Annotated Bibliography.* Washington, D.C.: Government Printing Office, 1969.

"A Celestial Visitor," *Nebraska State Journal,* June 8, 1884.

Chaikin, Andrew. "Target: Tunguska." *Sky & Telescope* (January 1984): 18–21.

Chamberlain, Von Del, and David J. Krause. "The Fireball of December 9 1965—Part I." *Royal Astronomical Society of Canada Journal, 61, No. 4.*

Chariton, Wallace O. *The Great Texas Airship Mystery.* Plano, Tex.: Wordware, 1991.

Chavarria, Hector. "El Caso Puebla," *OVNI*: 10–14.

Citizens Against UFO Secrecy. "MJ-12: Myth or Reality?" *Just Cause* (December 1985).

——. "Confirmation of MJ-12?" *Just Cause* (June 1987).

——. "The MJ-12 Fiasco." *Just Cause* (September 1987).

——. "More On MJ-12." *Just Cause* (March 1989).

——. "MJ-12 Update." *Just Cause* (June 1989).

——. "Conversation with Dr. Sarbacher." *Just Cause* (September 1985).

Clark, Jerome. "The Great Unidentified Airship Scare." *Official UFO* (November 1976).

——. "The Great Crashed Saucer Debate." *UFO Report* (October 1980): 16–19, 74, 76.

——. "Crashed Saucers—Another View." *Saga's UFO Annual 1981* (1981): 44–47, 66.

——. *UFO's in the 1980s.* Detroit, Mich.: Apogee, 1990.

——. "The Great Crashed Saucer Debate," *UFO Report 8, 5* (February 1980): 16–19, 74, 76.

——. "Crash Landings." *Omni* (December 1990): 91–92.

——. "UFO Reporters. (MJ-12)," *Fate* (December 1990).

——. "Airships: Part I," *International UFO Reporter* (January/February 1991): 4–23.

——. "Airships: Part II," *International UFO Reporter* (March/April 1991): 20–23.

——. "A Catalog of Early Crash Claims," *International UFO Reporter* (July/August 1993): 7–14.

——. *The UFO Encyclopedia.* Detroit, Mich.: Omnigraphics, 1998.

Clarkson, James. "The Wesport UFO Crash Retrieval Event." In *6th Annual UFO Crash Retrieval Conference.* Broomfield, Colo.: Wood and Wood Enterprises, 2008.

Committee on Science and Astronautics report, 1961.

Cohen, Daniel. *Encyclopedia of the Strange*. New York: Avon, 1987.

——. *The Great Airship Mystery: A UFO of the 1890s*. New York: Dodd, Mead, 1981.

——. *UFOs—The Third Wave*. New York: Evans, 1988.

Cooper, Milton William. *Behold a Pale Horse*. Sedona, Ariz.: Light Technology, 1991.

Cooper, Vicki. "Crashed Saucer Stories," *UFO 6, 1* (1991): 15.

——. "The Roswell Case Revived: Was It An Alien Saucer," *UFO* (January/February 1991): 25–29.

Corso, Philip J., and William J. Birnes. *The Day After Roswell*. New York: Pocket Books, 1997.

"Could the Scully Story Be True?" *The Saucerian Bulletin 1, 2* (May 1956): 1.

Crary, Dr. Albert. Personal Diary, June–July 1947.

Creighton, Gordon. "Close Encounters of an Unthinkable and Inadmissible Kind," *Flying Saucer Review* (July/August 1979).

——. "Further Evidence of 'Retrievals.'" *Flying Saucer Review* (January 1980).

——. "Continuing Evidence of Retrievals of the Third Kind," *Flying Saucer Review* (January/February 1982).

——. "Top U.S. Scientist Admits Crashed UFOs," *Flying Saucer Review* (October 1985).

Davies, John K. *Cosmic Impact*. New York: St. Martin's, 1986.

Davis, Richard. "Results of a Search for Records Concerning the 1947 Crash Near Roswell, New Mexico." Washington, D.C.: GAO, 1995.

Davison, Leon, ed. *Flying Saucers: An Analysis of Air Force Project Blue Book Special Report No. 14*. Clarksburg, Va.: Saucerian Press, 1971.

Dawson, William F. "UFO Down off Shag Harbor," *Fate 21, 2* (February 1962): 48–53.

"The Day a UFO Crashed Inside Russia," *UFO Universe* (March 1990): 48–49, 62.

Dennett, Preston. "Project Redlight: Are We Flying The Saucers Too?" *UFO Universe* (May 1990): 39.

"Did a UFO Blast a Hole in Russia?" *The New UFO Magazine, 13, 4* (November/December 1994): 8–9, 46–49.

Dobbs, D.L. "Crashed Saucers—The Mystery Continues." *UFO Report* (September 1979): 28–31, 60–61.

"DoD News Releases and Fact Sheets," 1952–1968.

Dolan, Richard M. *UFOs and the National Security State*. Charlottesville, Va.: Hampton Roads Publishing Company, 2000.

Douglas, J.V., and Henry Lee. "The Fireball of December 9, 1965—Part II." *Royal Astronomical Society of Canada Journal 62, no. 41*.

Earley, George W. "Crashed Saucers and Pickled Aliens, Part I," *Fate 34, 3* (March 1981): 42–48.

——. "Crashed Saucers and Pickled Aliens, Part II," *Fate 34, 4* (April 1981): 84–89.

Eberhart, George. *The Roswell Report: A Historical Perspective.* Chicago: CUFOS, 1991.

Ecker, Don. "MJ-12 'Suspected Forgery,' Air Force Says," *UFO 8, 3* (1993): 5.

Edwards, Frank. *Flying Saucers—Here and Now!* New York: Bantam,1968.

——. *Flying Saucers—Serious Business.* New York: Bantam, 1966.

——. *Strange World.* New York: Bantam, 1964.

"Effect of the Tungussk Meteorite Explosion on the Goemagnetic Field," Office of Technical Services U.S. Department of Commerce, December 21, 1961.

Eighth Air Force Staff Directory. Texas, June 1947.

Endres, Terry, and Pat Packard. "The Pflock Report in Perspective." *UFO Update Newsletter, 1,5* (Fall 1994): 1–6.

Estes, Russ (producer). *Quality of the Messenger.* Crystal Sky Productions, 1993.

"Experts Say a Meteor Caused Flash of Fire," *Deseret News,* April 19, 1962, p. 1.

"Facts about UFOs." Library of Congress Legislative Reference Service, May 1966.

Fawcett, Lawrence, and Barry J. Greenwood. *Clear Intent: The Government Cover-up of the UFO Experience.* Englewood Cliffs, N.J.: Prentice-Hall, 1984.

Friedman, Stanton. "MJ-12—Secret Document Proves Govt. Has Crashed Saucers and Alien Beings." *UFO Universe 1, 2* (September 1988): 8–12, 68.

——. *Top Secret/Majic.* New York: Marlowe and Company, 1996.

——. "Roswell and the MJ-12 Documents in the New Millennium." In *MUFON Symposium Proceedings* (2000): 193–220.

Finney, Ben R., and Eric M. Jones. *Interstellar Migration and the Human Experience.* Calif.: University of California Press, 1985.

"Fireball Explodes in Utah," *Nevada State Journal,* April 19, 1962, p. 1.

"Fireball Fame Comes to Lapeer," December 10, 1965.

"First Status Report, Project STORK" (Preliminary to Special Report No. 14), April 1952.

"Flying Saucers." *Look (1966).*

"Flying Saucers Again," *Newsweek,* April 17, 1950: 29.

"Flying Saucers Are Real." *Flying Saucer Review* (January/February 1956): 2–5.

Foster, Tad. Unpublished articles for Condon Committee Casebook. 1969.

Fowler, Raymond E. *Casebook of a UFO Investigator.* Englewood Cliffs, N.J.: Prentice-Hall, 1981.

——. "What about Crashed UFOs?" *Official UFO 1, 7* (April 1976): 55–57.

Genesce County (Michigan) telephone directories, 1945–1950.

Gevaerd, A.J. "Flying Saucer or Distillation Machine?" *Brazilian UFO Magazine,* November 2006.

Gillmor, Daniel S., ed. *Scientific Study of Unidentified Flying Objects.* New York: Bantam Books, 1969.

Goldsmith, Donald. *Nemesis.* New York: Berkley Books, 1985.

——. *The Quest for Extraterrestrial Life.* Mill Valley, Calif.: University Science Books, 1980.

Good, Timothy. *Above Top Secret.* New York: Morrow, 1988.

——. *The UFO Report.* New York: Avon Books, 1989.

——. *Alien Contact.* New York: Morrow, 1993.

Gordon, Stan, and Vicki Cooper. "The Kecksburg Incident,"
*UFO, 6, 1* (1991): 16–19.

Gordon, Stan. "After 25 Years, New Facts on the Kecksburg, Pa. UFO Retrieval
are Revealed." *PASU Data Exchange #15* (December 1990): 1.

——. "Kecksburg Crash Update," *MUFON UFO Journal* (September 1989).

——. "Kecksburg Crash Update," *MUFON UFO Journal* (October 1989): 3–5, 9.

——. "The Military UFO Retrieval at Kecksburg, Pennsylvania," *Pursuit, 20,*
*No. 4* (1987): 174–79.

"Great Lakes Fireball," *Sky & Telescope* (February 1966): 78, 79, 80.

Graeber, Matt. "Carbondale UFO Crash Chronicles No. 10—Case Closed."
*www.roswellfiles.com/AARE/Carbondale.htm,* 2009.

——. "The Reality, the Hoaxes and the Legend." Author, 2009.

Greenwell, J. Richard. "UFO Crash/Retrievals: A Critque." *MUFON UFO*
*Journal 153* (November 1980): 16–19.

Grenfell, E.W. "First Report on a Captured Flying Saucer," *Sir!,* 1954.

Gribben, John. "Cosmic Disaster Shock," *New Scientist* (March 6, 1980): 750–2.

"Grudge—Blue Book, Nos. 1–12." Status reports.

"Guidance for Dealing with Space Objects Which Have Returned to Earth,"
Department of State Airgram, July 26, 1973.

Hall, Richard. "Crashed Discs——Maybe," *International UFO Reporter, 10, 4*
(July/August 1985).

——. *Uninvited Guests.* Santa Fe, N.M.: Aurora Press, 1988.

——, ed. *The UFO Evidence.* Washington, D.C.: NICAP, 1964. *UFO* (January/
February 1991): 30–32.

Hanrahan, James Stephen. *History of Research in Space Biology and Biodynamics*
*at the Air Force Missile Development Center 1946–1958.* Alamogordo, N.M.:
Office of Information Services, 1959.

——. *Contributions of Balloon Operations to Research and Development at the Air*
*Force Missile Development Center 1947–1958.* Alamogordo, N.M.: Office of
Information Services, 1959.

Hastings, Robert. *UFOs and Nukes.* Bloomington, Ind.: Author House, 2008.

Haugland, Vern. "AF Denies Recovering Portions of 'Saucers.'" *Albuquerque*
*New Mexican,* March 23, 1954.

Hazard, Catherine. "Did the Air Force Hush Up a Flying Saucer Crash?"
*Woman's World* (February 27, 1990): 10.

Hegt, William H. Noordhoek. "News of Spitzbergen UFO Revealed." *APRG*
*Reporter* (February 1957): 6.

Henry, James P., and John D. Mosely. "Results of the Project Mercury
Ballistic and Orbital Chimpanzee Flights," *NASA SP-39,* NASA, 1963.

Hessmann, Michael, and Philip Mantle. *Beyond Roswell: The Alien Autopsy*
*Film, Area 51 and the U.S. Government Cover-up of UFOs.* New York, N.Y.:
Marlowe and Company, 1991.

Hippler, Robert H. "Letter to Edward U. Condon," January 16, 1967.

"History of the Eighth Air Force, Fort Worth, Texas" (Microfilm). Air Force Archives, Maxwell Air Force Base, Alabama.

"History of the 509th Bomb Group, Roswell, New Mexico" (Microfilm). Air Force Archives, Maxwell Air Force Base, Alabama.

Hogg, Ivan U., and J.B. King. *German and Allied Secret Weapons of World War II.* London: Chartwell, 1974.

Hughes, Jim. "Light, Boom a Mystery. *Denver Post,* January 12, 1998.

Huneeus, J. Antonio. "Soviet Scientist Bares Evidence of 2 Objects at Tunguska Blast," *New York City Tribune,* November 30, 1989, p. 11.

——. "Great Soviet UFO Flap of 1989 Centers on Dalnegorsk Crash," *New York City Tribune,* June 14, 1990.

——. "Spacecraft Shot out of South African Sky—Alien Survives." *UFO Universe* (July 1990): 38–45, 64–66.

——. "Roswell UFO Crash Update," *UFO Universe* (Winter 1991): 8–13, 52, 57.

——. "A Full Report on the 1978 UFO Crash in Bolivia," *UFO Universe* (Winter 1993).

Hurt, Wesley R., and Daniel McKnight. "Archaeology of the San Augustine Plains: A Preliminary Report," *American Antiquity* (January 1949): 172–94.

Hynek, J. Allen. *The UFO Experience: A Scientific Inquiry.* Chicago: Henry Regency, 1975.

Hynek, J. Allen, and Jacques Vallee. *The Edge of Reality.* Chicago: Henry Regency, 1972.

"Ike and Aliens? A Few Facts about a Persistent Rumor," *Focus 1, 2* (April 30, 1985): 1, 3–4.

"International Reports: Tale of Captured UFO," *UFO 8, 3* (1993): 10–11.

Jacobs, David M. *The UFO Controversy in America.* New York: Signet, 1975.

Johnson, J. Bond. "'Disk-overy' Near Roswell Identified As Weather Balloon by FWAAF Officer," *Fort Worth Star-Telegram,* July 9, 1947.

Jones, William E., and Rebecca D. Minshall. "Aztec, New Mexico—A Crash Story Reexamined," *International UFO Reporter 16, 5* (September/October 1991): 11.

Jung, Carl G. *Flying Saucers: A Modern Myth of Things Seen in the Sky.* New York: Harcourt, Brace, 1959.

Kean, Leslie. "Forty Years of Secrecy: NASA, the Military, and the 1965 Kecksburg Crash," *International UFO Reporter, 30, 1:* 3–9, 28–31.

Keel, John. "Now It's No Secret: The Japanese 'Fugo Balloon,'" *UFO* (January/February 1991): 33–35.

——. *UFOs: Operation Trojan Horse.* New York: G.P. Putnam's Sons, 1970.

——. *Strange Creatures from Space and Time.* New York: Fawcett, 1970.

Kennedy, George P. "Mercury Primates," American Institute of Aeronautics and Astronautics (1989).

Keyhoe, Donald E. *Flying Saucers from Outer Space.* New York: Henry Holt and Company, 1953.

——. *Aliens From Space.* New York: Signet, 1974.

Klass, Philip J. *UFOs Explained.* New York: Random House, 1974.

——. "Crash of the Crashed Saucer Claim," *Skeptical Inquirer 10, 3* (1986).

——. *The Public Deceived.* Buffalo, N.Y.: Prometheus Books, 1983.

——. "Roswell UFO: Coverups and Credulity," *Skeptical Inquirer 16, 1* (Fall 1991).

——. *The Real Roswell Crashed-Saucer Coverup.* Amherst, N.Y.: Prometheus, 1997.

Knaack, Marcelle. *Encyclopedia of U.S. Air Force Aircraft and Missile Systems.* Washington, D.C.: Office of Air Force History, 1988.

LaPaz, Lincoln, and Albert Rosenfeld. "Japan's Balloon Invasion of America," *Collier's* (January 17, 1953): 9.

Lasco, Jack. "Has the US Air Force Captured a Flying Saucer?" *Saga* (April 1967): 18–19, 67–68, 70–74.

Lester, Dave. "Kecksburg's UFO Mystery Unsolved," *Greenburg Tribune-Review,* December 8, 1985, p. A10.

"Little Frozen Aliens," *The APRO Bulletin* (January/February 1975): 5–6.

Lore, Gordon, and Harold H. Deneault. *Mysteries of the Skies: UFOs in Perspective.* Englewood Cliff, N.J.: Prentice-Hall, 1968.

Lorenzen, Coral, and Jim Lorenzen. *Flying Saucers: The Startling Evidence of the Invasion from Outer Space.* New York: Signet, 1966.

——. *Flying Saucer Occupants.* New York: Signet, 1967.

——. *Encounters with UFO Occupants.* New York: Berkley Medallion Books, 1976.

Low, Robert J. Letter to Lt. Col. Robert Hippler, January 27, 1967.

Maccabee, Bruce. "Hiding the Hardware," *International UFO Reporter* (September/October 1991): 4.

——. "What the Admiral Knew," *International UFO Reporter* (November/December 1986).

"The Magical Meteor," *Nebraska State Journal,* June 10, 1884.

Marcel, Jesse, and Linda Marcel. *The Roswell Legacy.* Franklin Lakes, N.J.: New Page Books, 2009.

Matthews, Mark. "Armageddon at Tunguska!" *Official UFO* May 1979: 28–30, 58, 60.

McAndrews, James. *The Roswell Report: Case Closed.* Washington, D.C.: Government Printing Office, 1997.

McCall, G.J.H. *Meteorites and their Origins.* New York: Wiley & Sons, 1973.

McClellan, Mike. "The Flying Saucer Crash of 1948 is a Hoax," *Official UFO 1, 3* (October 1975): 36–37, 60, 62–64.

"McClellan Sub-Committee Hearings," March 1958.

"McCormack Sub-Committee Briefing," August 1958.

McDonald, Bill. "Comparing Descriptions, An Illustrated Roswell," *UFO 8, 3* (1993): 31–36.

McDonough, Thomas R. *The Search for Extraterrestrial Intelligence.* New York: Wiley & Sons, 1987.

Menzel, Donald H., and Lyle G. Boyd. *The World of Flying Saucers.* Garden City, N.Y.: Doubleday, 1963.

Menzel, Donald H. Ernest Taves. *The UFO Enigma.* Garden City, N.Y.: Doubleday, 1977.

"Meteor Explodes in the City," *Dublin Press,* June 20, 1891.

"Meteor Lands in Utah, Lights Western Sky," *Los Angeles Times,* April 19, 1962.

Meteorological Balloons (Army Technical Manual). War Department. Washington, D.C.: Government Printing Office, 1944.

Michel, Aime. *The Truth about Flying Saucers.* New York: Pyramid 1967.

"Monkeynaut Baker Is Memorialized," Press release, Space and Rocket Center, Huntsville, Alabama, December 4, 1984.

Moore, Charles B. "The New York University Balloon Flights During Early June, 1947," Author, 1995.

Moore, Charles B., Benson Saler, and Charles A. Ziegler. *UFO Crash at Roswell: Genesis of a Modern Myth.* Washington, D.C.: Smithsonian Institute Press, 1997.

Moore, William L., and Jaime H. Shandera. *The MJ-12 Documents: An Analytical Report.* Burbank, Calif: Fair Witness Project, 1991.

Moseley, James W., and Karl T. Pflock. *Shockingly Close to the Truth.* Amherst, N.Y.: Prometheus Books, 2002.

Mueller, Robert. *Air Force Bases: Volume 1, Active Air Force Bases within the United States of American on 17 September 1982.* Washington, D.C.: Office of Air Force History, 1989.

Murphy, John. "Object in the Woods," WHJB Radio broadcast, December 1965.

Neilson, James. "Secret U.S./UFO Structure," *UFO, 4,1* (1989): 4–6.

"New explanation for 1908 Siberian blast," *Cedar Rapids Gazette,* January 25, 1993.

NICAP, *The UFO Evidence.* Washington, D.C.: NICAP, 1964.

Nickell, Joe. "The Hangar 18 Tales," *Common Ground* (June 1984).

Nickell, Joe, and John F. Fischer. "The Crashed-Saucer Forgeries," *International UFO Reporter 15, No. 2* (March/April 1990): 4–12.

——. "Further Deception: Moore and Shandera." Unpublished paper, 1993.

"No Reputable Dope on Disks," *Midland (Texas) Reporter Telegram,* July 1, 1947.

Northrup, Stuart A. *Minerals of New Mexico.* Albuquerque, N.M.: University of New Mexico, 1959.

"No Sign of 'UFO,'" *NSRI.* News24, May 5, 2006.

Nukegingrich. "UFO Crash still a mystery." News24, January 3, 2007.

Oberg, James. "UFO Update: UFO Buffs May Be Unwitting Pawns in an Elaborate Government Charade," *Omni 15, No. 11* (September 1993): 75.

O'Brien, Mike. "New Witness to San Agustin Crash," *MUFON Journal No. 275* (March 1991): 3–9.

"Office of Naval Research 1952 Greenland Cosmic Ray Scientific Expedition," Fact sheet, October 16, 1952.

Oldham, Chuck, and Vicky Oldham. *The Report on the Crash at Farmington.* Lansdowne, Penna.: Authors, 1991.

Olive, Dick. "Most UFO's Explainable, Says Scientist," *Elmira (NY) Star-Gazette,* January 26, 1967, p. 19.

"Operation Majestic 12." Briefing document, November 18, 1952.

Packard, Pat, and Terry Endres. "Riding the Roswell-go-round." *A.S.K. UFO Report 2* (1992): 1, 1–8.

Papagiannis, Michael D., ed. *The Search for Extraterrestrial Life: Recent Developments.* Boston: 1985.

Peebles, Curtis. *The Moby Dick Project.* Washington, D.C.: Smithsonian Institution Press, 1991.

——. *Watch the Skies!* New York: Berkley Books, 1995.

Pegues, Etta. *Aurora, Texas: The Town that Might Have Been.* Newark, Tex.: Author, 1975.

Pflock, Karl. *Roswell in Perspective.* Mt. Rainier, Md.: FUFOR, 1994.

——. "In Defense of Roswell Reality," *HUFON Report* (February 1995): 5–7.

——. "Roswell, A Cautionary Tale: Facts and Fantasies, Lessons and Legacies." In Walter H. Andrus, Jr., ed. *MUFON 1995 International UFO Symposium Proceedings.* Seguin, Tex.: MUFON, 1990: 154–68.

——. "Roswell, The Air Force, and Us," *International UFO Reporter* (November/December 1994): 3–5, 24.

——. *Roswell: Inconvenient Facts and the Will to Believe.* Amherst, N.Y.: Prometheus Books, 2001.

Plekhanov, G.F., A.F. Kovalevsky, V.K. Zhuravlev, and N.V. Vasilyev. "The Effect of the Tungussk Meteorite Explosion on the Geomagnetic Field," *U.S. Joint Publications Research Service,* December 21, 1961.

Presidential documents. National Security Agency. Washington, D.C. Executive Order 12356, 1982.

"Press Conference, General Samford," Project Blue Book Files, 1952.

"Project Blue Book" (microfilm). National Archives, Washington, D.C.

"Project Twinkle," Final Report. Project Blue Book Files, November 1951.

Prytz, John M. "UFO Crashes," *Flying Saucers* (October 1969): 24–25.

"RAAF Base Phone Book," Roswell, New Mexico, August 1947.

"RAAF Yearbook," Roswell, New Mexico, 1947.

Randle, Kevin D. "Mysterious Clues Left Behind by UFOs," *Saga's UFO Annual* (Summer 1972).

——. "The Pentagon's Secret Air War Against UFOs," *Saga* (March 1976).

——. "The Flight of the Great Airship," *True's Flying Saucers and UFOs Quarterly* (Spring 1977).

——. *The October Scenario.* Iowa City, Iowa: Middle Coast Publishing, 1988.

——. *The UFO Casebook.* New York: Warner, 1989.

——. *A History of UFO Crashes.* New York: Avon, 1995.

——. *Conspiracy of Silence.* New York: Avon, 1997.

——. *Project Moon Dust.* New York: Avon, 1998.

——. *Scientific Ufology.* New York: Avon, 1999.

——. *Roswell Encyclopedia.* New York: Avon, 2000.

——. *Roswell Revisited.* Lakeville, Minn.: Galde Press, 2007.

Randle, Kevin D., and Robert Charles Cornett. "Project Blue Book Cover-up: Pentagon Suppressed UFO Data," *UFO Report 2, No. 5* (Fall 1975).

——. "Siberian Explosion, Comet or Spacecraft?" *Quest UFO, 1, 1 (1977)*: 10–15.

Randle, Kevin D., and Donald R. Schmitt. *UFO Crash at Roswell.* New York, N.Y.: Avon, 1991.

——. *The Truth about the UFO Crash at Roswell.* New York: M. Evans and Company, 1994.

Randles, Jenny. *The UFO Conspiracy.* New York: Javelin, 1987.

Redfern, Nick. "Tunguska: 100 Years Latter (sic)." In *6th Annual UFO Crash Retrieval Conference.* Broomfield, Colo.: Wood and Wood Enterprises, 2008.

"Report of Air Force Research Regarding the 'Roswell Incident'," July 1994.

"Rocket and Missile Firings," White Sands Proving Grounds, January–July 1947.

Rodeghier, Mark. "Roswell, 1989," *International UFO Reporter* (September/ October 1989): 4.

Rodeghier, Mark, and Mark Chesney. "The Air Force Report on Roswell: An Absence of Evidence," *International UFO Reporter* September/October 1994).

Rosignoli, Guido. *The Illustrated Encyclopedia of Military Insignia of the 20th Century.* Secaucus, N.J.: Chartwell, 1986.

Ruppelt, Edward J. *The Report on Unidentified Flying Objects.* New York: Ace, 1956.

Russell, Eric. "Phantom Balloons Over North America," *Modern Aviation* (February 1953).

Rux, Bruce. *Hollywood Vs. the Aliens.* Berkeley: Frog, Ltd., 1997.

Sagan, Carl, and Thornton Page, eds. *UFO's: Scientific Debate.* New York: Norton, 1974.

Sanderson, Ivan T. "Meteorite-like Object Made a Turn in Cleveland, O. Area," *Omaha World-Herald,* December 15, 1965.

——. "Something Landed in Pennsylvania," *Fate 19, 3* (March 1966).

——. *Uninvited Visitors.* New York: Cowles, 1967.

——. *Invisible Residents.* New York: World Publishing, 1970.

Saunders, David, and R. Roger Harkins. *UFOs? Yes!* New York: New American Library, 1968.

Schaffner, Ron. "Roswell: A Federal Case?" *UFO Brigantia* (Summer 1989).

Schmitt, Donald R. "New Revelations from Roswell." In Walter H. Andrus, Jr., ed. *MUFON 1990 International UFO Symposium Proceedings.* Seguin, Tex.: MUFON, 1990: 154–68.

Schmitt, Donald R., and Kevin D. Randle. "Second Thoughts on the Barney
   Barnett Story," *International UFO Reporter (May/June 1992)*: 4–5, 22.
Scully, Frank. "Scully's Scrapbook," *Variety* (October 12, 1949): 61.
——. *Behind the Flying Saucers*. New York: Henry Holt, 1950.
Shandera, Jaime. "New Revelation about the Roswell Wreckage: A General
   Speaks Up," *MUFON Journal* (January 1991): 4–8.
Sheaffer, Robert. *The UFO Verdict*. Buffalo, N.Y.: Prometheus, 1981.
Simmons, H.M. "Once Upon A Time in the West," *Magonia* (August 1985).
Slate, B. Ann. "The Case of the Crippled Flying Saucer," *Saga*
   (April 1972): 22–25, 64, 66–68, 71, 72.
Smith, Scott. "Q & A: Len Stringfield," *UFO 6,1* (1991): 20–24.
Smith, Willy. "The Curious Case of the Argentine Crashed Saucer,"
   *International UFO Reporter 11, 1* (January/February 1986): 18–19.
"The Space Men at Wright-Patterson," *UFO Update*.
"Special Report No. 14," Project Blue Book, 1955.
Spencer, John. *The UFO Encyclopedia*. New York: Avon, 1993.
Spencer, John, and Hilary Evans. *Phenomenon*. New York: Avon, 1988.
Stanyukovich, K.P., and V.A. Bronshten. "Velocity and Energy of the Tungusk
   Meteorite," National Aeronautics and Space Administration,
   December 1962.
Steiger, Brad. *Strangers from the Skies*. New York: Award, 1966.
——. *Project Blue Book*. New York: Ballantine, 1976.
——. *UFO Missionaries Extraordinary*. New York: Pocket Books, 1976.
——. *The Fellowship*. New York: Dolphin Books, 1988.
Steiger, Brad, and Sherry Hanson Steiger. *The Rainbow Conspiracy*. New York:
   Pinnacle, 1994.
Steinman, William S., and Wendelle C. Stevens. *UFO Crash at Aztec*. Boulder,
   Colo.: Authors, 1986.
Stone, Clifford E. *UFO's: Let the Evidence Speak for Itself*. California:
   Author, 1991.
——. "The U.S. Air Force's Real, Official Investigation of UFO's." Private
   report. Author, 1993.
Stonehill, Paul. "Former Pilot Tells of Captured UFO." *UFO 8,2*
   (March/April 1993): 10–11.
——. "Russia: False Siberian UFO Crash." December 7, 2006.
Story, Ronald D. *The Encyclopedia of UFOs*. Garden City, N.Y.:
   Doubleday, 1980.
——. *The Encyclopedia of Extraterrestrial Encounters*. New York: New American
   Library, 2001.
Stringfield, Leonard H. *Situation Red: The UFO Siege!* Garden City, N.Y.:
   Doubleday, 1977.
——. *UFO Crash/Retrieval Syndrome: Status Report II*. Seguin, Tex.:
   MUFON, 1980.

——. *UFO Crash/Retrieval: Amassing the Evidence: Status Report III.* Cincinnati, Ohio: Author, 1982.

——. *UFO Crash/Retrievals: The Inner Sanctum Status Report VI.* Cincinnati, Ohio: Author, 1991.

——. "Retrievals of the Third Kind." In *MUFON Symposium Proceedings* (1978): 77–105.

——. "Roswell & the X-15: UFO Basics," *MUFON UFO Journal No. 259* (November 1989): 3–7.

Sturrock, P.A. "UFOs—A Scientific Debate," *Science 180* (1973): 593.

Styles, Chris. "Sag Harbor in Perspective." In *MUFON Symposium Proceedings* (1996): 26–52.

Sullivan, Walter. *We Are Not Alone.* New York: Signet, 1966.

Summer, Donald A. "Skyhook Churchill 1966," *Naval Reserve Reviews* (January 1967): 29.

Sutherly, Curt. "Inside Story of the New Hampshire UFO Crash," *UFO Report* (July 1977): 22, 60–61, 63–64.

Swords, Michael D., ed. *Journal of UFO Studies, New Series, Vol. 4.* Chicago: CUFOS, 1993.

Tafur, Max. "UFO Crashes in Argentina." *INFO Journal 75* (Summer 1996): 35–36.

"Target: Tunguska," *Sky & Telescope* (January 1984): 18–21.

Templeton, David. "The Uninvited," *Pittsburgh Press,* May 19, 1991, pp. 10–15.

Thompson, Tina D., ed. *TRW Space Log.* Redondo Beach, Calif.: TRW 1991.

Todd, Robert G. "MJ-12 Rebuttal," *MUFON Journal* (January 1990): 17.

Todd, Robert G., Mark Rodeghier, Barry Greenwood, and Bruce Maccabee. "A Forum on MJ-12," *International UFO Reporter* (May/June 1990): 15.

Torres, Noe, and Ruben Uriarte. *The Other Roswell.* Roswell Books, 2008.

Trainor, Joseph. "UFO Crashes into Dam in New South Wales," *UFO Roundup 4, 34* (December 16, 1999).

"Tunguska and the Making of Pseudo-scientific Myths," *New Scientist* (March 6, 1980): 750–51.

"UFOs and Lights: 12 Aliens on Ice in Ohio?" *The News 10* (June 1975): 14–15.

"Unidentified Aerial Objects, Project SIGN." Technical report, February 1949.

"Unidentified Flying Objects, Project GRUDGE," Technical report, August 1949.

U.S. Congress, House Committee on Armed Forces. Unidentified Flying Objects. Hearings, 89th Congress, 2nd Session. April 5, 1966. Washington D.C.: U.S. Government Printing Office, 1968.

U.S. Congress Committee on Science and Astronautics. Symposium on Unidentified Flying Objects. Hearings, July 29, 1968. Washington, D.C.: U.S. Government Printing Office, 1968.

Vallee, Jacques. *Anatomy of a Phenomenon.* New York: Ace, 1966.

——. *Challenge to Science.* New York: Ace, 1966.

——. *Dimensions*. New York: Ballantine, 1989.

——. *Revelations*. New York: Ballantine, 1991.

"Visitors From Venus," *Time* (January 9, 1950): 49.

Webber, Bert. *Retaliation: Japanese Attacks and Allied Countermeasures on the Pacific Coast in World War II*. Corvallis, Ore.: Oregon State University Press, 1975.

Weaver, Richard L. and James McAndrew. *The Roswell Report: Fact vs Fiction in the New Mexico Desert*. Washington, D.C.: Government Printing Office, 1995.

Webb, Walter N. "An Anecdotal Report of a UFO Crash/Retrieval in 1941, Part I," *International UFO Reporter 21, 4* (Winter 1996): 20–28.

——. "An Anecdotal Report of a UFO Crash/Retrieval in 1941, Part II," *International UFO Reporter 22, 1* (Spring 1997): 28–32.

Wenz, John. "Nebraska May Have Its Own Roswell in 1884," *The Daily Nebraskan*, March 19, 2007.

Whiting, Fred. *The Roswell Events*. Mt. Rainier, Md.: FUFOR, 1993.

"It Whizzed Through the Air; Livonia Boys Find Fireball Clues," *Livonian Observer & City Post*, December 16, 1965.

Wilcox, Inez. Personal writings, 1947–1952.

Wilkins, Harold T. *Flying Saucers on the Attack*. New York: Citadel, 1954.

——. *Flying Saucers Uncensored*. New York: Pyramid, 1967.

Wise, David, and Thomas B. Ross. *The Invisible Government*. New York: 1964.

Wood, Robert M. "Forensic Linguistics and the Majestic Documents." In *6th Annual UFO Crash Retrieval Conference*. Broomfield, Colo.: Wood and Wood Enterprises, 2008: 98–116.

——. "Validating the New Majestic Documents. In *MUFON Symposium Proceedings* (2000): 163–92.

Wood, Ryan. *Majic Eyes Only*. Broomfield, Colo.: Wood Enterprises, 2005.

"World Round-up: South Africa: Search for Crashed UFO," *Flying Saucer Review 8, 2* (March/April 1962): 24.

Young, Kenny. "A UFO Crash in 1941?" Author, May 1, 2000.

Young, Robert. "Old-Solved Mysteries: What Really Happened at Kecksburg, PA, on December 9, 1965," *Skeptical Inquirer 15, 3* (1991).

Zabawski, Walter. "UFO: The Tungus Riddle," *Official UFO* (May 1977): 31–33, 59–62.

Zeidman, Jennie. "I Remember Blue Book," *International UFO Reporter* (March/April 1991): 7.

Zigel, F. Yu. "Nuclear Explosion over the Taiga (Study of the Tunguska Meteorite)." U.S. Department of Commerce, Office of Technical Services, Joint Publications Research Service (September 8, 1964).

# INDEX

# T

# U

# V

# W

# Y

# Z

# ABOUT THE AUTHOR

KEVIN D. RANDLE has, for more than 35 years, studied the UFO phenomena in all its various incarnations. Training by the Army as a helicopter pilot, intelligence officer and military policeman, and by the Air Force as both an intelligence officer and a public affairs officer, provided Randle with a keen insight into the operations and protocols of the military, into their investigations into UFOs, and into a phenomenon that has puzzled people for more than a century.

Randle's educational background is a diverse as his military experience. As an undergraduate at the University of Iowa, he studied anthropology. Graduate work included journalism, psychology, and military science at the University of Iowa, California Coast University, and the American Military University. He has both a master's and doctoral degree in psychology, and a second master's degree in the Art of Military Science.

During his investigations, Randle has traveled the United States to interview hundreds of witnesses who were involved in everything from the Roswell, New Mexico, crash of 1947, to the repeated radar sightings of UFOs over Washington, D.C., in 1952, to the latest of the abduction cases. Randle was among the first writers to review the declassified Project Blue Book files, among the first to report on animal mutilations, and among the first to report on alien abductions.

He was the first to report the alien home invasions and among the first to suggest humans working with aliens.

Randle has written extensively on UFOs, beginning in 1973 with articles in various national magazines. He has published many books about UFOs, starting with *The UFO Casebook* in 1989 and continuing to *Roswell Revisited* in 2007.

Randle was away from his UFO studies when recalled to active duty with the Army that included a tour in Iraq from 2003 to 2004. He recently retired from the Iowa National Guard as a lieutenant colonel.

He hosts a blog that can be found at *www.KevinRandle.blogspot. com.* His mailing address is PO Box 10934, Cedar Rapids, IA 52410, and his e-mail address is *Krandle993@aol.com.*